D1165771

The Modern Self in the Labyrinth

The Modern Self in the Labyrinth

POLITICS AND THE
ENTRAPMENT IMAGINATION

EYAL CHOWERS

HARVARD UNIVERSITY PRESS
Cambridge, Massachusetts
London, England 2004

The quotation in the epigraph is reprinted from "Covered Mirrors," from *Collected Fictions* by Jorge Luis Borges, translated by Andrew Hurley, copyright ©1998 by Maria Kodama; translation copyright © 1998 by Penguin Putnam Inc. Used by permission of Viking Penguin, a division of Penguin Group (USA) Inc.

Cataloging-in-publication data is available from the Library of Congress

ISBN: 0-674-01330-1

Contents

Acknowledgments

This work has taken many years to complete. While there are numerous disadvantages to this pace of writing, it allowed me to benefit from the insights and comments of many friends and colleagues. I would like to thank, in particular, Iddo Landau, Natalie Oman, José Brunner, Yaron Ezrahi, Miriam Reich, Leora Bilsky, Michael Kochin, Azar Gat, Sharon Bergner, Tracy Strong, Tsipi Kuper-Blau, Nancy Schwartz, and Eva Illuz. Shoshana Liessmann helped me with some of the research for this project, particularly in the French and German languages. To Janet Benton I would like to offer special thanks for her many comments on the style and content of this text, and for teaching me an unforgettable lesson in clarity.

This work would have been greatly diminished without the support and inspiration of Charles Taylor and James Tully. Beyond contributing directly to my Ph.D. dissertation—the early version of this work—they also provided me with an understanding of modernity that made this project possible in the first place. While they did not necessarily agree, each for his own reasons, with some of the main tenets of this project, they greatly helped me to improve it.

A grant from the Austrian ministry of education allowed me to stay in Vienna during part of my research, and the Max Bell Open Fellowship provided more financial assistance. I thank both for their support. Professors Abraham Ben-Zvi, Michael Keren, Yossi Shain, and Azar Gat, my colleagues from Tel-Aviv University, were kind enough during their tenure as Chairs of the Political Science Department to ensure that I will have the proper conditions to conclude this work. The Van-Leer Jerusalem Institute allowed me to use its library for many years, and in general offered a very welcoming and intellectually stimulating environment.

I would like to thank the APSA for granting me the Leo Strauss Award for my dissertation. Paradoxically perhaps, this award convinced me that it might be worth while to invest considerably more work in this project, rewrite it, and do justice to the original ideas that inspired it.

I would also like to thank my students, first at McGill University and in recent years at Tel-Aviv University. Their probing questions and insightful suggestions greatly contributed to the clarity and consistency of the arguments advanced below.

Finally, I would like to thank my daughter Ya'ar for demanding my presence, thus motivating me to complete this project, and to Eppie Kreitner, for her continuous support and for being my most trusted reader. I dedicate this work to the memory of my father, Israel Chowers (1923–1989), a master physician with the soul of a philosopher.

On judgment day, Islam professes, everyone who had ever made a portrait of an animated being will be brought back to life. Then he will be ordered to infuse his creations with life, and, after he shall ultimately fail, he will be thrown together with his artifacts into a purifying fire. Ever since my childhood, I have experienced this fear from the doubling or onerous visual repetition of reality, especially in face of the great mirrors. The endless, smooth operation of these mirrors, their surveillance of my actions, their cosmic mimicking—all these had something supernatural about them, especially when night settled in. One of my most passionate prayers to God or my guardian angel was to grant me sleep without dreaming of mirrors. As I now recall it, mirrors were a source of anxiety for me: sometimes I feared that they would begin to veer off from reality; other times, that I would see my face in them disfigured by strange misfortunes. I have learned that this horror is monstrously abroad in the world again.

—Jorge Luis Borges, *Covered Mirrors*

~ Introduction

T HE PROSPECT OF HUMAN CLONING from somatic cells has received attention that has been denied to other inventions and experiments of contemporary medical research. While heart transplants from baboons to human babies, or the production of transgenic mammals (such as cows, pigs, mice, etc.) in order to generate human protein go almost unnoticed, human cloning through nuclear transfer engenders intensified public debate. This may seem odd: as far as we know at this point, no human being has been cloned and the prospect of success is unclear.[1] Moreover, even the medical benefits from cloning are debatable, since the main reasons for cloning, such as overcoming male infertility problems or the production of stem cells for organ regeneration, could reasonably be resolved by other means.[2] Cloning, it seems, attracts our attention not because it promises a medical payoff more significant than other medical breakthroughs, but because it resonates with profound dilemmas of modern culture—such as what constitutes the fabric of our selfhood and its befitting boundaries.

Human cloning presents two main threats to the self: these could be termed "sameness" and "doubleness"—the lack of distinguishing inborn characteristics when genetic material is identical, and the lack of a clear circumference in a mirroring world wherein the clone could be seen as an extension of oneself in time and space. Human cloning may undermine the notion of a distinct human identity and the claim to dignity that springs from this distinctiveness:[3] it threatens the view of the individual as an irreplaceable event—whose birth contains a particular promise and whose passing away is an irrevocable loss. It is doubtful that there will be mass production of the same type of clone, as prophesized by Aldous Huxley in *Brave New World*, or as is currently being attempted with cattle. What is crucial, however, is the essence of cloning technology (as Heidegger would say), the idea and truth that it discloses.[4] And the truth revealed by this technology is that human beings are essentially replicable creatures, that they harbor a biological potential for radical sameness, and that they *could* be harnessed into a production line in which they are both the means and the ends.

The cloning of human beings, however, also brings to a head the notion of doubleness that has been intrinsic to the modern imagination for a number of centuries. "For man," writes Marx, "duplicates *(verdoppelt)* himself not only intellectually, as in consciousness, but also actively, in reality, and therefore contemplates himself in a world that he has created."[5] Cloning is perhaps the ultimate expression of this modern urge for duplication, and provides the supreme opportunity for contemplating our humanness through self-objectification. From a Marxian perspective, cloning underscores the "cloned social space" we inhabit, where objects, norms, and even social institutions are perceived as fabricated by and reflective of human beings; it epitomizes the Promethean vision of moderns. With human cloning, the creator and created become one, and moderns demonstrate their ability to create even the creator. Cloning, then, embodies the tautological quality of the modern imagination: through it human beings confirm that they have overcome any inexplicable force (whether transcendental or natural) at work in the social world, and could in principle encounter only endless repetitions of themselves. However, this procedure establishes a paradox, since precisely when moderns celebrate their Promethean omnipotence through self-duplication, they are also exposed in their utmost pitifulness as harboring sameness in the very nucleus of their being.

This book examines a modern dilemma I call "entrapment," which foreshadowed our obsession with cloning. By entrapment I mean the dehumanizing sameness that springs from the duplication of the social—the menace of homogenized existence in a world conceived of as self-made. Entrapment refers to the predicament wherein social institutions, which are perceived as overpowering and inescapable, sap moderns of their distinct identities. The origins of entrapment thinking can already be found in the late eighteenth century, where the self is first depicted as engaged in a conflictual relation with the social, political, and economic domains that have grown estranged from and hostile to it; a conceptual and existential rift opens up between the self and these necessary domains of collective life. This rift leads the self to experience itself as under threat of subjection—not to any specific person or transcendental entity—but to collective institutions, the self's "great double." Moreover (and as manifested in the debate about cloning), entrapment involves a sense that the source of dehumanization is human inventiveness itself, particularly when engaged in efforts to improve various aspects of the human predicament—from intensifying production and improving social organization to advancing human communication and synchronization. In fact, the irony of entrapment thinking is that it first emerged precisely when individuals were beginning to celebrate their capacity for progressive rational conduct and for general authorship over the world; in this sense, entrapment signifies for moderns their failure to set bounds, to contain their own deeds, and to fathom their inner forces. It is the notion that human action is not answerable to nor harnessed by any natural or divine scheme that haunts the modern imagination: entrapment occurs in a world experienced as self-fabricated; the difficulty of coming to terms with this world is exacerbated because its ills are seen as self-inflicted and devoid of deterministic necessity.

This lack of determinism has generated great optimism in some critics of modernity, since it allows one to envision radical changes. Entrapment thinking, in contrast, is characterized by a spirit of realism, suggesting that social institutions are too powerful, complex, pervasive, and fragmented for any collective action to successfully transform them—and hence this mode of thinking does not offer a clear, overarching strategy enabling the self to transcend its dehumanizing circumstances. Furthermore, entrapment refers to the *modernity* of civilization, to phenomena that have emerged in the last few centuries or that have taken a radically different shape during this era: mass-organizations such as bureaucracies and corporations, the nuclear family with its bourgeois mores, human and social sciences and the institutions supported by them, and so forth. These modern phenomena, according to entrapment theories, ingrain destructive patterns of thinking and acting that were absent in other epochs. I believe that this mode of entrapment thought reached full development in the twentieth century. Among its paradigmatic representatives are Weber, Freud, and Foucault, the main authors to be studied in this work.

In contrast to central debates in political philosophy during the last decades, particularly the one between liberals and communitarians, these entrapment writers develop a contextualized reading of the self.[6] The self, according to entrapment writers, is not to be analyzed ontologically and ahistorically, but as a concrete being that bears the imprints of particular life-orders. The self is rather elastic; political philosophy must therefore spoor specific contours. On the one hand, this reading brings out the limited usefulness of individual rights in guarding the formation of the self: the physical, emotional, and mental attributes of a person are shaped through family interactions, occupational activities, linguistic interaction, and the like—where juridical bulwarks are, for the most part, irrelevant. The liberal faith in the human capacity for an autonomous choice of the good life and for rational deliberation in matter of values is a mere promise; whether it is fulfilled or not hinges on our experiences in a specific reality, which may encompass everything from the instrumental rationality permeating the offices we inhabit during the day to our tendency to equate truth with the statistical findings we find in the evening newspaper. On the other hand, the entrapment perspective also reveals the limited prospects for harmonious communal life and for a constitutive role of the cultural tradition in forming the self. In the modern eidos, tradition is not the humanizing force opposing the anonymity of social institutions and the subjection ingrained by them; rather, the two meet in a desire for normalization whose aims may differ, but whose effect upon the de-assertion of the self is similar. The experience of distance, of trying to keep society at arm's length, characterizes the modern self in its relation to social institutions as well as to its tradition—and the two types of distance enhance one another. These and other implications of entrapment writings for liberalism and communitarianism are examined in the third and fourth chapters of this study, where I argue that any study of the modern self must be rooted in a methodology that is centered on the historically given, not the universally valid.

As previously noted, in exploring the theme of entrapment I examine the works of Weber, Freud, and Foucault. This unconventional choice of authors springs from the fact that entrapment is central to their thought, and from the prominent place these authors hold in our culture in general and in our social and political theory in particular. Not only do these three authors presuppose a gulf and a battle between the self and social institutions, but they also betray a shared historical consciousness in other respects. In contrast to writers such as Marx and Nietzsche (who could be termed "proto-entrapment" writers) Weber, Freud, and Foucault are skeptical about the possibility of defeating the malaise of modernity through revolutionary action or through personal transformation. Entrapment writers replace a politics aimed at transcending historical circumstances with one aimed at teaching us how to cope with dignity while enmeshed within these circumstances; instead of the human omnipotence characterizing their nineteenth-century predecessors, entrapment writers betray a sober recognition of our limited ability to shape or escape the present. Indeed, one of the central purposes of this inquiry is to highlight the shared presuppositions and beliefs underlying the writings of Weber, Freud, and Foucault, and to argue that they articulate a new view of the self's place in history in general and in modernity in particular. A comparative study of these thinkers may expose a mode of thought central to the twentieth century, one that has been neglected thus far because these three writers have hardly been examined systematically in relation to one another and because only now do we possess the small, yet necessary, temporal distance that enables us to perceive this essential aspect of the past century.[7]

Conversely, a study of the shared historical consciousness of Weber, Freud, and Foucault calls for a reexamination of each individual author. As in any hermeneutical circle, a reconstruction of the whole alters our understanding of the parts, and this study aspires to demonstrate that the consciousness of entrapment shaped the very core of these theorists' work. In addition to its overarching goal, then, this study aims at contributing to the existing scholarship on each of these writers and to do so precisely by virtue of developing a comprehensive view of a particular historical problematic. However, this approach does not imply that one should highlight only the similarities between entrapment theorists; in fact, they were selected for this study partly because of their differences. Weber, Freud, and Foucault each present a distinct idea about the nature of the present malaise. These include: the evaporation and impoverishment of meaning in a world dominated by mass-organizations (Weber); overinhibited instincts, psychic and social homelessness, and subjection to the social through intimate family interactions (Freud); and the imposition of confining scientific language, as well as normalized modes of being through reformative *dispositifs* (Foucault). While sharing an interpretive grid, these writers differ in their perception of the snare and where it lies. Hence, despite a certain amount of overlap, Weber, Freud, and Foucault inquire into different aspects of modernity: the sociology of religion, bureaucracy, and capitalism; psychosexual development, psychic constitution, and cultural mores; language, human and social sciences, and the micro-operations of power. This heterogeneity of perspectives allows us to see entrapment as a pervasive problematic which is not confined to one aspect of contemporary life.

Finally, it should be emphasized that the study of entrapment is an investigation of the modern self as a social being. That is, I will examine the self as it works and produces within institutions, as it forms intimate and formal relations based on existing cultural patterns, as it becomes part of a collective entity that is subject to statistical studies and predictions of individual behavior, and more. But to fathom entrapment means also to study the self as both a temporal being and a biological one. The modern self is a temporal being because the substance of its identity is often explicated in historical terms. In modernity, atemporal truths about human nature increasingly give way to depictions of human beings whose cognition of the phenomenological world, inner motivations, external deportment, core values, and psychological makeup are all shaped by their era. Since the late eighteenth century, observes Koselleck "time is no longer simply the medium in which all histories take place; it gains a historical quality. Consequently, history no longer occurs in, but through time. Time becomes a dynamic and historical force in its own right."[8] The entrapment writers studied in this work accept this view of the self as profoundly stamped by its times, and they assay to illuminate the present conditions influencing the self through selective comparisons with past epochs. However, they also tend to embrace a tragic view of historical time, which they depict as permeated through and through by chance. The challenge of entrapment writers, then, is to recover and affirm the self without relying on inevitable historical progress and increasing liberation on the one hand, or on any essentialist buried truths about humans on the other.

But the study of entrapment demands an awareness of the self as a biological being as well: Although historical time no longer ensures a consummated selfhood in the distant future, the body is no longer the bastion of naturally given individuality. The origins of this skepticism are in the theory and practice of medicine during the seventeenth century. Beginning with the discovery of the circulation by William Harvey, this medicine eliminated the Greek and Roman notion of a distinct and pregiven physiological character, one based on a singular combination of humours (*crasis*) and present throughout life; instead, it suggested a human physiology grounded in constant movement and applicable to all human beings. The individualized treatments of the sanguine and phlegmatic, melancholic and choleric (and of the endless character types springing from their various combinations) disappeared and gave way to the production of medicines considered suitable for an indistinguishable mass of bodies and their similar illnesses. It is beyond the scope of this book to trace the influences of this medical philosophy on the social field, but the latter gradually presented corresponding developments of depersonalization of the body. A well-known example would be the emerging view that individuals are capable of working a given number of hours a day, of producing a certain quantity of work in that day, of performing useful movements and functions with their trained bodies, and of having certain predictable needs required to preserve their vitality. The body (as Marx, Weber, Foucault, and others students of discipline have noted), became in modernity a great resource demanding calculative management that is indifferent to its individual characteristics. This leveling of the individual body is echoed and magnified by the modern notion of a social body—composed of a gigantic race or a nation—in which singular bodies lose their identity and standing. The threat of entrapment could thus be seen as the menace of sameness that springs from dense social and institutional life, without either history or nature, time or body, offering a check to or a limit on this sameness.

The structure of this book is as follows. Before examining the entrapment imagination and the individual authors who embody it, we must understand the emergence of this imagination and the legacy of Post-Enlightenment social and political theory. Chapter 1 thus probes into the origins of entrapment theories in the late eighteenth and early nineteenth centuries. The first section of this chapter examines those distinctively modern institutions that are perceived as constituting the cardinal threat to the identity and character of the individual by imposing demands for what could be termed "hyper-order." The second section of the first chapter inquires into the Kantian origins of the notion that a gulf exists between self (noumenal) and civilization (phenomenal reality). For Kant, the supreme role of practical reason is to overcome this gulf; I later juxtapose this position to that of *Frankenstein*, where the Romantic skepticism regarding the organizing function of reason is symbolically and forcefully expressed, and where the gulf between humans and their double is presented as insurmountable. In the second chapter, I construct two ideal types that capture the main strategies espoused by nineteenth-century writers in their attempts to confront the danger springing from a civilization apparently out of human control: (1) cultivation of individual, authentic difference, and (2) communal remolding of the social; I take Nietzsche to represent the first strategy and Marx the second. In the second section of that chapter,

I demonstrate the failure of these strategies by examining Weber's critique of Marx and Nietzsche, a critique that signifies the transition from proto-entrapment to entrapment writers.

In the subsequent chapters (3–5), I turn to systematic studies of entrapment in the works of Weber, Freud, and Foucault. My overarching purpose in these chapters is to demonstrate how these authors helped, each in his own way, to radically redefine the political imagination of the modern self; indeed, I believe that despite the vast literature about the modern self, its essential political mode of being as it is expressed by these writers has not been explored. The imagination of this self, I shall argue, is essentially tragic: on the one hand, it presents human beings as elastic creatures who are capable of being fabricated by social institutions, as having no ontological "ground" on the basis of which they could resist the normalization that inheres in daily work, in the family, or in language itself. On the other hand, the main option left for the self in resisting this predicament is one of coping, of an individualistic-agnostic response that does not aspire to devise an encompassing vision of emancipation. We have lost the faith in a guiding reason that would have the audacity to take history into its own hands: our politics (if it could be termed that) is less about finding the winning ideology and the right institutional structure, and more about enhancing our inner integration and authorship over the fabric of our own selfhood. Indeed, we have come to perceive the social world as too powerful, fragmented, and amorphous to permit profound transformation; increasingly, this world offers its inhabitants either the individual response of coping with its dehumanization, or destructive, violent eruptions in the form of riots and terror.

~ 1

Modernity: Hyper-Order and Doubleness

Modernity and the Imposition of Hyper-Order

With the collapse of natural law theories and Deism at the end of the eighteenth century and the beginning of the nineteenth, two contrasting pictures of social order emerged. On one hand, theorists like Kant and Condorcet believed that human beings could establish order and arrange their institutions to promote human happiness and well-being.[1] The self, according to this view, was finally awakening from its slumber, was gaining an inkling of hitherto dormant and powerful forces that were clouded because of tradition and dogmas, and would now be able to improve its condition by deliberate, calculated, and informed actions. But this optimistic and familiar world-view of Late Enlightenment theorists had another side: it is precisely this celebrated view of man's ingenuity that raises the disquieting notion that we may lack the necessary insight and means required to oversee the social world we have energetically brought about. We begin to recognize that the introduction of machines may chain us to a uniform and degrading existence, that the erection of elaborate state institutions may lead to our subjection, that the mushrooming spheres of arts, sciences, and public discussion may establish new domains of conformism. When the human world is no longer conceived of as circumscribed and naturally ordered, the effects of our unopposed actions can be limitless, and the possibility of reversing these effects always doubtful. To put it differently, political philosophy begins to grapple with two, interrelated problems: the emergence of normalization in new social institutions and a sense of rift that exists between the self and a civilization conceived of as self-made; indeed, the inability to control our offspring expresses itself primarily in our subjection to collective institutions that induce sameness. The two parts of this chapter discuss the problems of normalization and the self-civilization rift sequentially.

The etymology of the word "norm" already connotes an invented or artificial formation. Sophists such as Antiphon and Callicles saw in *nomos*—the written, city law—a mere convention that originates simply because of the functional need of society to maintain order. The notion of a normalized society takes this view to the extreme, because it sees the norm not in legal terms and as pertaining to questions of justice, but as a tool that allows a far more extensive systematization of the social universe. This concern with over-crystallized institutions and modes of life is rather recent, beginning with eighteenth-century writers and their critique of the uniformity and the dearth of autonomy that they saw evolving around them.[2] Three major sources were thought to have bred these developments: the division of labor associated with commercial society, the various bureaucratic agencies of the state, and urban culture with its public spaces. Each of these sources was perceived as distinctively modern, and hence traditional forms of expressing social criticism seemed to offer little guidance: neither a religious discourse about faith and the good nor a legalistic one about individual rights and just government seemed to address the new plight of moderns. In the middle of the eighteenth century, then, a new mode of reflection emerged, one that concerned the relation between the identity of the self and the nature of the evolving life-orders. The rationale of the latter is characterized by an urge for order and regularity that has gone wild and that demands an ever-narrower delineation of human conduct. We can see this type of reflection in the following three examples, each of which presents the dangers of homogenization and subjection in a different sphere.

In the first book of *The Wealth of Nations*, Adam Smith celebrates the division of labor inaugurated by capitalism. Not only, he avers, does this division increase the wealth of the community and better the circumstances of the poor, but it also has benign effects upon the *character* of those immersed within it (in other words, most members of society). The competition constitutive of the market galvanizes conduct, invigorates the spirit of invention, enhances the virtues of sobriety and punctuality, and even fosters independence and the capacity for reasoning. Thus, while acknowledging the dominance of self-love and of the hunger for self-esteem in bourgeois society, Smith suggests powerful *moral* reasons for extolling the new economic system. But in the fifth book of his work we find a different Smith. In words that echo those of his contemporaries (Millar, Wallace, and especially Ferguson), he voices apprehension and dismay in the face of the impact the division of labor has over the personality.

> In the progress of the division of labor, the employment of the far greater part of those who live by labor, that is, of the great body of the people, comes to be confined to a few very simple operations, frequently to one or two. *But the understandings of the greater part of men are necessarily formed by their employment.* The man whose life is spent in performing a few simple operations, of which the effects too are perhaps always the same . . . has no occasion to exert his understanding or to exercise his invention in finding out expedients for removing difficulties which never occur. He naturally loses, therefore, the habit of such exertion and generally becomes as stupid and ignorant as it is possible for a human creature to become.
>
> The uniformity of his stationary life naturally corrupts the courage of his mind, and makes him regard with abhorrence the irregular, uncertain, and adventurous life of the soldier.[3]

In commercial society, individuals may manage to achieve material well-being or even to secure their mere existence only by harnessing their energies and skills to a specialized task. Capitalism contains a strange paradox: while the system offers infinite possible occupations, each of these demands a strict and monotonous operation as a precondition of success; thus, while we may each have a singular vocation, uniformity is nevertheless entrenched in all of us. In precapitalist societies, according to Smith, individuals were adept at performing numerous, nonspecialized tasks. Not being tethered to an economic function, one could (at least in certain societies) expand one's experience and horizons by participating in the political and military life of the community. Persons moored to a specific vocation, in contrast, lack the leisure, the motivations, the knowledge, and the "courage of mind" necessary to engage in reflection upon matters that exceed the immediate occupation; they embody sameness, since they are devoid of the resources needed to develop their person. The colonialization of life by uniformity in the economic sphere has, in short, both a positive (forming) and a negative facet: first, the rhythm of the occupation itself ingrains homogeneity of conduct;[4] second, the system perpetuates the underdevelopment of the personality, the absence of distinctiveness. These two facets in conjunction forge an individual for whom predictability and orderliness are not evils to be endured, but rather an ethos to be embraced.

For some eighteenth-century writers, the modern state is the chief threat to the identity of the individual. This view is expressed, for example, by Herder, who witnessed the penetration of a growing number of state agencies into most spheres of social and economic life, at the time of Frederick the Great's extensive bureaucratic reforms (especially after the annexation of Silesia). State officials regulated internal and external trade, levels of production, construction and transportation projects, taxation, education and language use, health and hygiene, festivities and the calendar, and more.[5] This tightening of state control over the individual and society was combined with the establishment of a large army notorious for its strict discipline and hierarchy, an institution, incidentally, that Herder regarded with special dislike. Frederick saw the population, with its institutions and the things it produced, as a resource to be employed deliberately and precisely in order to magnify state power and status; in his proclamations at least, he collapsed the idea of politics into dutiful civil service, that of leadership into instrumental regulation. Frederick followed reason-of-state theorists in understanding the state as having objective needs that must be studied through new bodies of knowledge and that should be answered through the formulation of distinct codes of action that may be at odds with conventional morality; the state, in other words, is a synchronized and cohesive entity with its own singular rationale. Herder, who was the apostle of modern notions of authenticity, held this philosophy in contempt.

> Since we are told by the political scientist that every well constituted state must be a machine regulated only by the will of one, can there conceivably be any greater bliss than to serve in this machine as an unthinking component? What, indeed, can be more satisfying than to be whirled around all our lives on Ixion's wheel, contrary to our better knowledge and conscience, with no comfort other than that of being relieved of the exercise of our free and self-determining mind in order to find happiness in functioning as insensible cogs in a perfect machine?

The state can give us many ingenious contrivances; unfortu-
nately it can also deprive us of something far more essential: our
own selves.[6]

While Herder's theories of language and society present a holistic
view that eschews the contemplation of a presocial predicament, he
conceives of human beings as limbs only of "natural" units such as
families and tribes. The modern state, in contrast, is a mere artifact and
tool, its legitimacy always open to question according to whether or not
it benefits the lives of its *individual* citizens. But the state poses a
dilemma: in some ways it undeniably improves the well-being and
security of its citizens; this is achieved, however, only by expanding the
bureaucratic apparatus and its authority, by mobilizing this machine
according to a *modus operandi* that is rationalized and universal. The
spaces left open to personal judgment, untrammeled conduct, and the
cultivation of distinctiveness continually shrink in such a state because
of both unspoken expectations and overt regulation. The modern state
imposes uniform administration and ordinance upon groups that have
divergent geographic conditions, economic needs, social practices, and
cultural heritages; in its overseas colonies, the state is equally culturally
blind in its exploitation. (The nation-state may avoid this pitfall, but
Herder seems to have been ambivalent about even this type of state, his
contribution to nationalist thought notwithstanding.)

Yet it was Rousseau, of course, who advanced the most profound and
influential critique of the dearth of autonomy and the uniformity inherent in modern institutions and culture. "Civilized man is born and dies
a slave," he writes in *Emile*. "The infant is bound up in swaddling
clothes, the corpse is nailed down in his coffin. All his life long man is
imprisoned by our institutions."[7] Our multifaceted other-dependency
is the chief reason for this social imprisonment, Rousseau declares. On
the most immediate level, the advent of civilization involves the spawn-
ing of (artificial) needs, and these can be addressed only by a sophisticated division of labor. "The bonds of servitude are formed merely from
the mutual dependence of men and the reciprocal needs that unite
them; it is impossible to enslave a man without having first put him in
the position of being incapable of doing without another."[8] To gratify
our material needs, we must live together and establish lasting bonds,
sell our labor, obey our superiors, and maintain smooth relations as a
background to our economic transactions.

Rousseau, however, is more concerned with another facet of other-
dependency, one more tethering than shared material exigencies: in

modern culture, he argues, the individual is psychologically dependent upon others for securing his very sense of existence and selfhood. "The savage lives in himself; the man accustomed to the ways of society is always outside himself and knows how to live only in the opinions of others. And it is, as it were, from their judgment alone that he draws the sentiment of his own existence . . ."[9] The savage is motivated by internal and immediate wants, upon which others have little bearing; the modern individual acquires a consciousness of his being only through the recognition and approval of his fellows and is driven by an insatiable hunger for self-esteem. The other becomes both a necessary support (because without him our ego is weak and has no experience of itself) and a harsh competitor (since the search for recognition in society is a zero-sum game). With this ambivalence toward the other, the self becomes fractured, torn between outer affability and benevolence on the one hand and inward envy and contempt on the other.

Rousseau, as is well known, distinguishes sharply between the psychological makeup of the savage and that of the modern individual. The former experiences only *amour de soi-même*, that is to say, "a natural sentiment which leads every animal to be vigilant in its own preservation," or an unreflective love of self that does not involve reliance on or harm to others. The civilized individual, in contrast, knows only *amour propre*, that is, "a purely relative and factitious feeling, which arises in society, and leads each individual to make more of himself than any other, causes all the mutual damage men inflict on one another, and is the true source of the sense of honor."[10] As social beings, we can love and respect ourselves only through the affirming gaze of others and through comparison with them; bound to live on the surface, we are alienated from our inwardness (that which Rousseau sometimes calls "the voice of nature within"). In the "Discourse on the Sciences and the Arts," Rousseau notes the relation between the production of sameness in modern society and this self-alienation.

> Today, when the more subtle inquiries and a more refined taste have reduced the art of pleasing to established rules, a veil of deceitful uniformity reigns in our mores, and all minds seem to have been cast in the same mold. Without ceasing, politeness makes demands, propriety gives orders; without ceasing, common customs are followed, never one's own lights. One no longer dares to seem what one really is; and in this perpetual constraint, the men who make up this herd we call society will, if placed in the

same circumstances, do all the same things unless a stronger motive deters them.[11]

Civilization means the progressive withdrawal of self, its de-assertion. In order to win approval, we must espouse the prevalent cultural codes of decorum, which dictate similar ways of speaking, feeling, dressing—the imperceptible ways in which society imposes certain predictable modes of human interaction. But Rousseau is even more troubled by an intellectual homogenization that emerges in the (partly) new public spaces of the eighteenth century. We usually think of social institutions such as the court, the salon, the theater, the newspaper, or the bookstore as essential to the development of our contemporary culture, as establishing the context for the exchange of ideas and debate among distinct individuals. Rousseau does not deny this, yet he highlights the pressures constitutive of these spaces: they provide unprecedented room for the directive force of public opinion, a new and anonymous entity whose weight the individual finds hard to escape, and dangerous to ignore. In the arts, believes Rousseau, this phenomenon generates writings and other types of cultural production aimed at entertaining and pleasing the audience rather than at challenging it; conformity is the sacrifice that fame commands. Furthermore, in our moral practice we prefer to abide by what is expected by tradition and conventions—even if these expectations are foreign to our inner life and authentic existence, even if they may lead to our unhappiness and ruin. "When we do not live in ourselves but in others, it is their judgments which guide everything. Nothing appears good or desirable to individuals which the public has not judged to be such, and the only happiness which most men know is to be esteemed happy."[12]

Smith, Herder, and Rousseau articulate new apprehensions about the self: concerned with the economic, political, and social spheres, respectively, all three argue that the modern forms of these spheres mold individuals who are more similar and predictable, more disciplined and submissive. In the history of political thought, a Hobbesian, chaotic state (of nature, in Hobbes' case) was often perceived as the imminent danger; now, hyper-order emerges as the most pertinent threat. For these three critics of modernity, the crystallized patterns that govern human life were not a source of solace: they feared that there was something arbitrary about these patterns, something pathologically out of control. There seems to be no way to ground existing social configurations in the "nature of things," to depict them as ultimately beneficial and benevolent (although Herder and especially Smith also voice the opposite view). In short, the critiques of uniformity and subjection that we have examined reveal the breakdown of prevailing visions of order during the seventeenth and eighteenth centuries, visions exemplified by natural law and Deist theories.[13] A few words about these two schools are in order, then, although the relation between the human and natural orders during the seventeenth and eighteenth centuries is too complex to be examined here in depth.

Natural law theorists saw nature as offering rational, permanent organizing principles for human conduct and institutions. The foundations of this view were laid in the seventeenth century by diverse Protestant writers such as Grotius, Pufendorf, and Locke. They argued that human beings could attain normative guidance by extrapolating from nature their objective goods, ends, duties, rights, and more—without needing the aid of revelation and intuition, religious teachings and mediating authorities, or tradition and example. Locke, for example, professes that if we examine the reason imbued in nature, we shall discover that we have a right to life, health, freedom, and property—and that we must respect the right of others to the same, must assist the preservation of mankind and the enhancement of human sociability. For Locke, the law that posits these objective truths is inscribed everlastingly in the world regardless of cultural conditions or historical circumstances; it presupposes, moreover, a corresponding, unchanging human nature. There is a harmony not only between the structure of the world and human needs, but also between human reason and God's reason; this latter compatibility permits an epistemological transparency of humans in relation to the world and involves their ability to comprehend the justifications for its specific makeup. Most importantly, the reason and law governing the world (and humans as part of it) impose an order that, in broad outline, is immune to transformations and innovations regardless of anyone's volition. For Locke, as James Tully observes, God "made humans for certain purposes which can be discovered by rational reflection on his workmanship, and natural duties and rights can be derived from them. *These limit both human will and the will of the lawmaker* (or government)."[14] In regard to human will, the law of nature serves as a standard for criticizing any breach of the timeless, underlying order by positive law. The obligations of the law of nature, claims Locke, "cease not in Society. . . Thus the Law of Nature stands as an Eternal Rule to all Men, legislators as well as others."[15] By being sensible, noncontingent, and transparent to all, the law of nature introduces continuity and unity into human existence and history. Any social and political dilemma could—in principle at least—be resolved with confidence and consensus by referring to some pregiven order that always remains germane and binding. Locke further claims that each individual is not only fully capable of recognizing violations of natural law, but also bears the responsibility of restoring it; the force of this law is immense since each individual—rather than a few kings, priests, or experts—is a shepherd of the transcendent order that he or she has been entrusted with.

These convictions of natural law theorists received an even stronger endorsement from the natural theology of Deist authors such as Hutcheson, Collins, Shaftesbury, Tindal, and Fontenelle, among others. Deists believed that God is the omnipotent creator of the world, but that there is no divine intervention in the world after the act of creation; in other words, order is preordained and immutable, not actively maintained. Moreover, many Deists believed that with correct, free, and reasoned reflection, one could discover a providential arrangement in which things coexist in interlocking harmony (a state often typified by the image of a clock). Alexander Pope, whose poetry is a celebrated representation of this school, believed that things are already orchestrated for the best as they are, and that they operate in a machine-like fashion. Pope affirms reality and aspires to display the perfect agreement that exists not only between human beings and nature, but also among the purposes and occupations of members of society. These purposes and occupations naturally mesh, and when the principles of instrumental conduct and self-love are followed, the outcome is the greatest benefit for all. Pope recognizes the pivotal role of shifting passions and destructive pride in human motivations, the frustration and pain every person encounters during life, the evil that humans are capable of. Yet he calls upon human beings to transcend their particular state and moment by embracing an inclusive view of the universe.

One should look, according to Pope, at "that chain which links the immense design, joins heaven and earth, and moral and divine; sees that no being can any bliss can know, but touches some above, and some below." Pope suggests that this type of transcendental and overarching reflection will lead humans to see that "*whatever is, is right*; that *reason, passion*, answer one great aim." This divine aim combines narrow, egoistic passions, with long-term social interest, allowing us to grasp that while some evil is necessary, from an overarching view "the whole worlds of reason, life and sense" should be seen as "one close system of benevolence."[16] Just when the notion of a pregiven, benevolent order came under scrutiny by *philosophes* such as Diderot, Deism expressed the most ardent version of this belief in an essentially static, divine order and strove to address the existential and theological doubts of its contemporaries. "And who but wished to invert the laws *of order*, sins against the eternal cause."[17] To conclude, then, for writers such as Locke and Pope, human life could be pictured as a "jigsaw puzzle," to use Isaiah Berlin's term.[18] The nature of human beings, the objective goods they should strive to gain, the social norms that should govern their lives, the outlines of the best political regime, the limits of power, and the rights of the individual—all of these and other elements of social life were pieces of a single puzzle that fit together. In fact, many Enlightenment thinkers believed that these questions could be objectively resolved in the same way that Newton resolved the riddles of physics.

There is something reassuring about this world-view. Human endeavors are imagined to be carried out within a *contained* world: even if these endeavors are innovative and extreme, misguided and dangerous, there are nevertheless given boundaries to the transformations we may introduce—it is impossible, after all, to change the constitution of men and women, the goods that are fundamental to their being, or the makeup of nature itself. This vista further suggests that, however much we may have departed from what is natural and right, however much we may live in distortion, the possibility exists of uncovering the buried truths and recuperating from our present malaise. A restoration of harmony—between humans and nature and among humans—is always a possibility. The problem of order, then, hinges upon an epistemological challenge, not an ontological one: it may be difficult to fathom reality, but a given rational order has preceded us and will outlast us; it is independent of us, yet also within us.

The rapid pace of transformations in the economic, political, and social spheres helped render the initial natural order of things an increasingly irrelevant point of reference. Hence, when natural law theories and Deistic theologies lost their grip over the European imagination toward the end of the eighteenth century, those who lived in the subsequent period had to struggle with a new suspicion: that the task of political and moral theory may not be to discover a pregiven order and to organize society accordingly, but to recognize the absence of such an ontological order. This suggests that the universe may not be rationally orchestrated and was never meant to be. Indeed, the breakdown of the essential presupposition of order implied that we must not assume that things are structured and oriented toward increasing our well-being and happiness; what is "out there" may be entirely indifferent to our fate. Even more disturbing was the perception that, since there is no given frame to the world, we have the capacity to revolutionize with alacrity existing economic, political, and civic institutions—and could transform ourselves along the way—without encountering any limits. There is no available circumference, in theory or in practice, that would demarcate the range of possible changes in the character of the individual or the composition of the collective. Finally, the absence of a predetermined order invites the idea that our social arrangements and institutions are merely the fruition of chance. (Rousseau's account of the emergence of private property in the "Discourse on the Origin of Inequality" demonstrates the role of accidental events in decisively shaping human history.) In a world understood as devoid of a Great Chain of Being or of the organizing mind of God, hyper-order may be conceived of as a feat of chance—and as a movement in a hazardous direction advancing *ad infinitum*. Nothing necessarily steers us along this path; nothing would necessarily thwart it.

Late Enlightenment writers sought to fill the void established by the crisis of natural law theories and Deism by depicting a world in which human reason was the new organizing principle. The Deists conceived of a self attuned to a cosmic order, constantly striving to decipher the intentions of nature and God; the *Aufklärer* of a self marked by rational control and ingenuity, a creature imposing order where it was originally absent. Since then, modernity has been haunted by the question of whether order can be spawned and maintained by reason (in its various facets) or whether reason is precisely the force that drives us either to generate a dehumanizing order or to frustrate any possibility of order altogether.

Civilization as a Self-made Other: Doubleness in Kant and *Frankenstein*

The threat of a misguided, dehumanizing social order that preoccupied hyper-order theorists is intertwined with another idea concerning the relation between self and civilization that emerges toward the end of the eighteenth century. Kantian philosophy may be seen as the turning point in this respect, since it depicts an unbridgeable rift between the self and its social institutions. This *conceptual* rift is grounded in the duality of the self. Kant partitions the self into a phenomenal component that is the vehicle of history, and a noumenal-moral component that embodies our humanity. The world we inhabit is the fruition of actions driven by our empirical, deterministic nature, which therefore stands at a necessary distance from our rational and autonomous self. While depictions of the self as divided are nothing new, I would like to argue that *Kantian philosophy transforms a relation within the self into a relation between self and civilization:* the Otherness of the empirical within is projected outward and assigned to self-produced, social institutions. Or, conversely, one could say that an aspect of the self becomes an antagonist just because it is seen as the agent within of a hostile social matrix.

Now there are two contrasting ways to perceive this conceptual hiatus between the self and its other—civilization. First, in his philosophy of history, Kant strives to demonstrate that in praxis there is an incremental abatement of the gulf between the self (as practical reason) and its social institutions. Championing the Enlightenment idea of rationality as an organizing principle, Kant studies the modern forms of economy, politics, and society, and defends that which was criticized by Smith, Herder, and Rousseau. He avers that in each of these spheres, the conditions have become ripe for reason to manifest its independence and moral character: through an international division of labor and economic interdependence, peace among nations is enhanced; through a growing state apparatus and improved enforcement of positive law, liberal conduct compatible with morality is finally habituated; through new social spaces and opportunities for public debate, enlightenment is advanced and individuals are able to articulate themselves in ways unimaginable in the past. Kant does not see the increasingly orderly character of modern life as problematic; on the contrary, for the first time in human history, in his view, there is an opening for realizing the kernel of our humanity in a civilization rendered increasingly hospitable to this humanity.

Yet some of Kant's contemporaries envisioned a radically different relation between the self and its products, as exemplified by Mary Shelley. *Frankenstein* incarnates two of the Kantian presuppositions: that human beings are assigned a Promethean role and that a gulf exists between humans and their creations. But in contrast to Kant, Mary Shelley pictures a proliferation of otherness, a growing estrangement and friction between the self and its creations. The foreignness of the social world and our sense of homelessness within it grows, she argues with the English Romantics, as we valorize the dominance of disembodied rationality. If, for Kant, man is the proud founder of his orderly world—historically, morally, and epistemologically—for Mary Shelley, man is a misguided sovereign, haunted by his own monstrous and unpredictable artifacts. Reading these two writers, we see that the Enlightenment's confidence in human powers is mirrored by a consciousness of uncertainty and anxiety *in direct relation* to the perceived potency of these powers. If there are no limits to the cultivation of our skills, imagination, creativity, and energy—attributes that constantly disrupt existing circumstances—how can we hope for a stable social order? How can we be certain that we have the capacity to control ourselves, particularly in a culture that celebrates the overcoming of boundaries? If the human being is clouded—because it is a "thing-in-itself" or because it constantly evolves historically—how can we be sure that this creature is not swarming with destructive forces, even, and perhaps especially, in the faculty called reason? On one hand, then, theorists such as Kant tried to argue that order itself is a human creation, and that nature had willed that man "produce everything from himself *(alles aus sich selbst herausbringen)*. . . as if she aimed more at his rational self-esteem *(seine vernünftige Selbstschätzung)* than at his well-being."[19] On the other hand, others thought that self-esteem is absurd, since rationality introduces an addled environment, despite its declared intentions. Indeed, Frankenstein expresses precisely this trepidation in face of one's own world-transforming reason. "All my speculations and hopes are as nothing," he cries, "and like the arch-angel who aspired to omnipotence, I am chained in an eternal hell."[20]

In her critique of reason-based order, Mary Shelley exemplifies a profound affinity with hyper-order theorists. The latter, as we saw above, are troubled by a social world that is becoming too uniform, predictable, and confining; this world conceives of human beings as tools to be manipulated for the sake of efficiency, wealth, and the power of mass-organizations. Mary Shelley, on the other hand, is concerned that this world is becoming too chaotic, incomprehensible, and boundless. Nevertheless, there seem to be shared apprehensions underlying these visions: both argue that human agents act and invent within a social space unbridled by a pregiven format, that they lack the wisdom and dexterity required to master and amend the effects of their deeds, and that these deeds establish an overbearing reality inclined to wreck its founders—either their very physical existence or their dignity as individuals. Hyper-order and hyper-chaos, we shall see, are two facets of the very same historical imagination.

Kant and the Ebbing of Otherness

> I summon up all the material stuff of all worlds in a universal
> confusion and create out of this a perfect chaos. According to the
> established laws of attraction, I see matter developing, and it
> modifies its motion through repulsion. Without the assistance of
> arbitrary fictions, I enjoy the pleasure of seeing a well-ordered
> totality emerge under the influence of the established laws of
> motion, something which looks so similar to the same planetary
> system which we see in front of us, that I cannot prevent myself
> from believing that it is the same . . . The confidence increases
> with each step I take as I continue on, and my timidity disappears
> completely.
>
> ∽Immanuel Kant, Universal Natural History and Theory of Heaven (1755)

In his early works, Kant strove to explain how what begins as total chaos
in nature gradually turns into a harmonious arrangement. He believes
this transformation occurs without divine intervention and that nature
is self-sufficient; God is the initial creator of matter and the guarantor
of the Newtonian laws of motion that govern it, but not an active force
in the history of the cosmos. Rather, matter contains the principles of
its own motion; because these principles are applicable across sub-
stances and particles, the various composites of nature can affect each
other to produce an orderly "community" and thereby consummate
their telos as an intrinsic, coherent system.[21] The same urge for order
and its depiction as self-forming is displayed later in Kant's writings, in
his philosophy of history. Here, however, Kant is interested in the
human universe and provides an account of the mechanisms that
beguile and mobilize human beings into creating a culture *(Kultur)*;[22]
he believes that we have grounds to presuppose that a well-ordered
human world is being gradually created through the inclinations
and acquired skills of individuals. In contrast to the natural order,
however, the formation of a human, harmonious order faces an
immense obstacle, in Kant's view, since there is a rift between humans
and their civilization. This rift exists because the self has two points of
view from which it can understand itself and its own motivations.

The Kantian self is divided, both from an epistemological point of
view and from a moral one. According to Kant's transcendental idealism, the self constitutes its empirical facet by employing certain a priori
categories and concepts; although the very existence of "me" as a physical object is not a product of my mind, this mind is nevertheless the

epistemological "creator" of my body as an object.[23] This partition creates a clear hierarchy within the self. "That I am conscious of myself," explains Kant, "is a thought that already contains a twofold self, the I as subject and the I as object." However, continues Kant, "only the I that I think and intuit is a person; the I that belongs to the object that is intuited by me is, similarly to other objects outside me, a thing."[24] As a subject, man commands respect as an immutable shaper of the empirical world; as an object or a thing, his materiality is akin to the organic matter of things around him, and he obeys the same natural laws that are inescapable for other things. Man is both the legislator of these laws and the subject obeying them.

The Kantian epistemological dichotomy also means that human beings obey two different systems of law. Man "can consider himself *first*—so far as he belongs to the sensible world—to be under the laws of nature (heteronomy); and *secondly*—so far as he belongs to the intelligible world—to be under laws which, being independent of nature, are not empirical but have their ground in [practical] reason alone."[25] In accordance with the Cartesian-Hobbesian mechanistic tradition, Kant claims that the individual—as the phenomenal being that produces and shapes history—is propelled by brute desires and by complex, self-centered interests that also spring from the same bodily source. This mechanistic process is ongoing: accomplishing our desires and interests does not generate satisfaction, but rather establishes room for new wants. In fact, argues Kant, man is a hostage to his empirical aspect, since "it is not his nature to rest and be contented with the possession and enjoyment of anything whatever."[26] The individual then comes to view the material and social worlds as means to be intelligently utilized in abetting his fame and power, happiness and wealth. In contrast to this empirical self, however, Kant postulates a noumenal self characterized by its unconditioned freedom; this self (or "person," as Kant names it) is capable of wholly autonomous choices, since it is unfettered by causality. Detached from the narrow horizons of egoism and present-centered desires, the noumenal self is insulated from both external and internal circumstances. Kant thinks the self's humanity resides in this capacity to disengage—to embrace an objective point of view from which it can rationally deliberate about moral dilemmas. This deliberation leads the self to act according to formal imperatives that command absolute universality, as well as respect for the other and for oneself as ends in themselves.[27]

According to Kant, then, reason (as pure or understanding) constitutes a phenomenal, essentially mechanistic self. Since (as we shall see below) this latter self is the engine of history and culture, practical reason is *homeless*, encountering a human reality that is wholly foreign to its moral motivations and freedom of will. Moreover, the empirical, social world rebuffs the disposition of reason toward action based on principle: despite the rigid, natural laws of motion that govern their bodies, in social life individuals oscillate between inclinations and interests, passions and illusions in a manner that seems chaotic and unpredictable: "The movement of matter follows a certain determinate rule," writes Kant, "but those of men *[Menschen]* are without rule."[28] History (understood as a progression in which human beings change their social institutions as well as themselves) thus becomes vital for Kant: it is the theater where men and women gradually accept self-determined rules (both legal-positive and moral), and where the pragmatic and rational aspects of the self become more compatible—though never fully harmonized.

In explicating how civilization evolves, Kant suggests that nature employs at least three different strategies, ones that could be termed physiological, psychological, and existential. To begin with, he claims that our sense of existence depends on perpetual movement. "To feel alive, to enjoy ourselves, is the same as to feel ourselves constantly impelled to leave our present state." We have a need to experience gushing sensations in order to feel alive, since we are a kind of empty form that longs to be filled through engagement with the sensate world. Putting this even more strongly, Kant says that "nature has put *pain (Schmerz)* in man as the unavoidable spur to activity, so that he may constantly progress toward something better;"[29] forced to be on the move because of their bodies, individuals ceaselessly cultivate themselves, interact with others, work and produce. In addition to this physiological explanation for progress and social change, Kant suggests a psychological one: he believes that human beings are motivated by "self-love" *(Selbstliebe)*, which can be mollified only somewhat in the presence of others and only in a relative fashion. "Only in comparison with others," observes Kant, "does one judge oneself happy or unhappy. Out of this self-love originates the inclination to gain worth in the opinion of others."[30] In the beginning, Kant believes, self-love only requires equality of respect among people; gradually, however, insecurity as to the feasibility of this *status quo* of equality infiltrates their thoughts. Individuals then remain dependent on the recognition of others, but they also begin to see these others as potential rivals. Recognition is a zero-sum game, and our sense of worth hinges on others lacking it; we have to constantly improve our achievements and acquire public signs of success in order to bring others to value us rather than themselves. The third strategy Kant suggests for the emergence of civilization hinges on humans' inborn, existential desire to maintain empirical freedom and exercise their heteronomous will without being restricted by others. We realize that we could achieve these goals only by augmenting the stores of goods offered by social life (for example, wealth, power, and public esteem); even if we do not value these goods in themselves, we are driven to acquire them in order maintain the natural freedom we had prior to joining society.

On the basis of the second and third strategies, Kant suggests that human beings are both psychologically attracted to and existentially repelled by social life, mired in an eternal ambivalence that leads to their dependency on and antagonism toward each other—in short, to their "unsocial sociability" *[ungesellige Geselligkeit]*.[31] The combination of a hunger for the recognition of others on the one hand and a quest for freedom from them on the other, engenders cooperation and mutual dependency—but also spite and envy, aggressiveness and competitiveness. Kant claims, however, that this latter facet of social existence serves the species, since nature "wanted to use the idea of such competitiveness . . . only as an incentive to culture."[32] To achieve social goods, men and women must perfect their skills and achieve distinction in the arts and sciences;[33] the total accomplishments of civilization are the by-product of this ongoing effort and competition among individuals who are most often ignorant of the genuine and long-term value of their own actions. Only gradually do individuals realize that their contribution to culture has an intrinsic value, and Kant indeed claims that we have ["an imperfect"] duty to cultivate our talents.[34]

For Kant, then, civilization is a rather disorderly creation: physiology goads individuals to perpetual motion, and their thirst for power and riches, fame and influence, induces them to advance their own interests at the expense of social and international arrangements—to reject any rules that do not further their personal purposes. Moreover, civilization is the embodiment of incentives and deeds that oppose the human transcendence of both ego-centeredness and instrumentalism toward others; it involves exploitation and manipulation, oppression and destruction, stimulating rather than repressing the empirical facet of one's being. This is a rather formless and immoral tale, in the face of which practical reason can experience nothing but alienation. Now if Kant had stopped here, he would have had to admit that his moral theory was of little use, since it is consistently rebuffed by human reality. To avoid this pitfall, it is essential for him to demonstrate that, in the course of history, social institutions are rendered increasingly compatible with and allow the performance of the maxims of morality—despite the conscious intentions of the actors. Civilization must become less of an other; a seemingly chaotic social predicament must become an order agreeable to reason.

Kant argues that if we examine history carefully, we shall discern a teleological, invisible-hand-like plan of nature. (As he explains in the *Critique of Judgment*, we are permitted to contemplate this plan through the "reflective power of judgment" *[reflektierende Urteilskraft]* without, however, attributing to it an ontological status.) In pursuing its aim, nature uses the self-seeking inclinations of humans, whereby "one inclination is able to check or cancel the destructive tendencies of the others. The result for reason is the same as if neither sets of opposing inclinations existed, and so man, even though he is not morally good, is forced to be a good citizen." This means, according to Kant's well-known proclamation, that "even a people comprised of devils" could form a well-ordered and externally just society.[35] Humans are the autonomous generators of order, since their contingent and self-centered intentions produce, despite themselves, a rule-governed, social universe where their autonomy and equality is respected.

Kant seems to ground his argument by reinterpreting and introducing political and temporal dimensions into a familiar tradition of early modern thought.[36] According to this tradition, the stability of civil society and of the capitalist market are dependent upon a useful inner dynamic of human predispositions, whereby one set of inclinations called "passions" (envy, violence, revenge, sexual lust, craving for pleasure) is opposed to and checked by another set of inclinations called "interests" (gain, good name, status). Social harmony is a macrophenomenon that is morality-free: it emerges despite the conscious intentions of actors and presupposes their self-serving interests. Kant employs this argument (which was used by others mostly in the economic sphere and in a nonhistorical context) to explain the piecemeal formation of political institutions that embody the principles of right. He avers that, while individuals are predisposed to defy impediments to their private will, they are nevertheless obliged to check this tendency because they also wish to preserve their person, possessions, and status; moreover, with communal life only amplifying the available social goods, the incentive to preserve them is enhanced. Civilization has a built-in mechanism that promotes its security: the greater the opportunity to acquire wealth, honor, power, and the like, the greater the anxiety over losing them.

Mutual suspicion, then, convinces self-seeking individuals to establish a system of jurisprudence *(Rechtslehre)* and a civil society to protect their equal rights to life, property, privacy, freedom of action and belief, and the like. These liberal principles are best protected by a constitutional (preferably republican) regime that embodies universal principles of enforcement. Similarly, at the international level, states concerned with their economic power and the well-being of their citizens are led to recognize the destructiveness of war to their society and to common trade. Out of purely utilitarian considerations, these states are impelled to form a great "body politics" *(Staatskörper)*, by which Kant means that free states take part in a transnational league that promotes peace among them.[37] In this fashion, an external legal order is erected, which both curtails the turbulent implications of humans' animality and allows the full development of humans' skills and talents, since it creates a free and safe space for their play. More importantly for Kant, internal and external peace—and the burgeoning of civilization as a whole—institute the objective, receptive conditions for the assertion of practical reason. "As concerns the discipline of the inclinations," writes Kant, "there is manifest in respect of this . . . requirement for culture a purposeful striving of nature to a cultivation which makes us receptive of higher purposes than nature itself can supply."[38] Kant seems to affirm the tendency of modern life-orders to increase the self's control over its emotions, its habituation of conduct, its action according to rules, and its respect for social conventions. The discipline of the modern, which hyper-order theorists saw as an impediment to the assertion of individuality is, according to Kant, a precondition for asserting a higher kind of individuality—a moral personality.

The abatement of the otherness of civilization demands, however, more than can be delivered by the plan of nature alone. Practical reason should become an *active force in history*, a governing principle that imposes its form on reality and penetrates its otherness.[39] Kant calls for inducing compatibility between humans as an ethical community and the historical-political configuration in which humans pursue their natural ends of happiness. He calls this regulative, ideal state of compatibility the "highest good" *(summum bonum)*, and writes that it is founded upon two steps of conscious synchronization. First, humans should gradually establish a borderless ethical community in which they should regard each other as ends and moral personalities, abiding by the same moral law regardless of their differences: "(A) multitude of human beings united in that purpose [of being a political community] cannot yet be called the ethical community as such but only a particular society that strives toward complete uniformity and concordance of all human beings . . . in order to establish an absolute ethical whole."[40] This uniformity and unanimity at the ethical level paves the way for the harmonization of humans and their social institutions, since the latter can be made to reflect the moral essence of humanity, not of particular individuals. A "universal cosmopolitan condition" (ein allgemeiner, weltbürgerlicher Zustand),[41] for example, is the phenomenal counterpart of the kingdom of ends.[42] More generally, Kant believes that in order to strive towards the idea of the supreme [or highest] good, one may and should assume that the world is to harmonize with . . . the ultimate end of all things according to the law of freedom."[43] The highest or supreme good, then, pictures an architectonic and totalizing structure for human actions and ends in history: it is a condition of an all-engulfing harmony between duty and happiness, between a community of moral agents and their (multiple) political and social institutions—in short, between self and civilization.

The highest good conveys meaning and purpose not only for the human world, but for creation as a whole. "Man is the final purpose of creation, since without him the chain of mutually subordinated purposes would not be complete as regards its ground. Only in man, and only in him as subject of morality, do we meet with unconditional legislation in respect of purpose, which therefore alone renders him capable of being the final purpose, to which the whole of nature is teleologically subordinated."[44] The only being capable of salvaging the world from its purposelessness and its mechanistic mode of operation, holds Kant, is the self of practical reason. Inanimate material and the creatures of nature (including man as phenomenon) are helplessly fettered within a chain of causality; only the actions that spring from reason are not conditioned in their origins and have intrinsic value, independent of actual consequences. To be sure, the project of moral self-discovery and engagement in praxis is ongoing and unending. As Yirmiahu Yovel observes, in Kantian philosophy "man enjoys a central position not by virtue of what he is, but by virtue of what he *ought* to do and become. He must *make* himself the center of creation by using his practical reason to determine its end and by consciously acting to realize it."[45] The emergence of a moral and free self on the scene of history is an ideal to be approximated; but the comprehension of man's destiny at last confers a meaning upon the past—upon the isolated interactions of human beings with nature and each other. Moreover, this insight into man's destiny serves as a guide to future praxis: when moral considerations (both regarding particular instances and through the overarching duty to promote the highest good) begin to shape political and social action, the human world ceases to be extraneous to the self and becomes a manifestation of its essence. The world, rather than being an impediment to reason, becomes a reality that mirrors individuals, promoting their self-knowledge and confidence.

For Kant, man is not only the purpose of creation, but seems partly to replace the creator altogether. In striving to accomplish his moral, final goal, writes Kant, "man thinks of himself on an analogy with deity, which while subjectively needing no external (independently existing) thing, can nonetheless not be thought of as enclosed within itself, but rather as determined by the consciousness of its complete self-sufficiency to bring about the highest good outside itself."[46] Kant avers that we must presuppose the existence of God (otherwise, the highest good might seem like an empty idea, too distant from empirical reality), but he also indicates the creator's redundancy. Reason takes on God's characteristics; it has the same abundance, the same drive to propagate its goodness, the same urge to constitute its surroundings, the same promise of one day terminating violence and disorder altogether.

In Kant, then, we see a dialectic tale of subjection that posits man at the center of creation. First, reason (whether as pure reason or as understanding) constitutes our perception of nature (and the phenomenal self) through its epistemic-transcendental structure, then (as practical reason) it is alienated from the emerging historical-empirical reality the phenomenal self creates and is helpless in face of human animality. However, after the external conditions are ripe and reason has learned to recognize itself, it is able to subdue and mold the world according to its form. In the Kantian view, the state of being at home is a property of the future, the fruition of the successful overcoming of civilization, or man's double, and the Enlightenment—an age in which man finally becomes mature and unclouded by dogmas and unfounded beliefs—is a turning point in our destiny, a crossroads on our way home.

Frankenstein: Reason as the Instigator of Disorder

Jean Paul Richter, the early nineteenth-century writer, once described the refusal of Romantic poets to commit themselves to the representation of nature and reality as part of the "lawless, capricious spirit of the present age, which would egoistically annihilate the world and the universe in order to clear a space merely for free play in a void." In his view, artists denied their less than autonomous place in the world. But in an age when "God has set like the sun," Jean Paul added, "soon afterwards the world too passes into darkness. He who scorns the universe respects nothing more than himself and at night fears only his own creations."[47] This admonition seems to be directed towards Kantian and Fichtian idealism as much as toward those Romantics who glorified the poetic imagination, since both are driven by an uncritical quest for human omnipotence in the construction of reality. *Frankenstein, or the Modern Prometheus* (1818) expresses the same mistrust in human sovereignty, the same belief in its apocalyptic consequences.[48] Mary Shelley, in fact, turns the Kantian vision of reason-based order on its head, and demonstrates the breakdown of the self by suggesting that its doubleness has no remedy.

The novel, to begin with, uniquely captures the interrelation of two themes prevalent in the literature of its time. The first is the depiction of the self as divided and duplicated. This idea begins to appear in works such as William Godwin's *The Adventures of Caleb Williams* (1794), Jean Paul's *Siebenkäs* (1796), and several short stories by E. T. A. Hoffmann (see discussion in Chapter 4). Later this theme was embraced by German writers in the age of Poetic Realism, and it appears in the works of Otto Ludwig, C. F. Meyer, Gottfried Keller, and Wilhelm Raabe, among others.[49] In English literature, this motif had its heyday with works such as Robert Louis Stevenson's *Dr. Jekyll and Mr. Hyde* (1886) and Oscar Wilde's *The Picture of Dorian Gray* (1890). In many of these works, the relation between the self and its *Doppelgänger* is antagonistic, with the former representing rationality, goodness, and transparency, and the latter representing unbounded desire, evil, and unpredictability (the self and the *Doppelgänger* may also change roles). On one hand, this doubling could be viewed as a part of modern writers' endeavor to explore and celebrate the individual's psychological depths and multifaceted nature; on the other hand, doubling may reflect a crisis of identity, an interpretation supported by the common depiction of human life in nineteenth-century prose and poetry as devoid of a longed-for steadiness and wholeness.[50]

The second theme in *Frankenstein*, also present in other writings of its time, is that of creation and the dynamic between creator and created. Some of the most renowned writings of English Romanticism reveal a preoccupation with this notion, including Blake's *The Book of Urizen* (1794), Shelley's *Prometheus Unbound* (1819), and Keats's *Hyperion Poems* (1820). Inspired by humanism (especially in Shelley's case), these works aimed to revolutionize the common perception of the biblical and Greek stories of creation by redefining man's place and responsibility in the universe. As Paul Cantor suggests, these writers (with the exception of Blake) discredited the notion of God as the founder of the world "for the sake of exalting man's own creative powers."[51]

The originality of *Frankenstein* within this body of literature lies in the fact that it portrays the doubling of and division within the self as inherently intertwined with reason's Promethean task; the self disintegrates because of the misguided way it uses reason and attempts to create its own world. In contrast to Kant, *Frankenstein's* marriage of doubleness and Promethean consciousness generates neither the heightening of order nor the subsiding of otherness; rather, the autonomous constitution and transformation of human reality is possible only by envisioning a divided self whose parts are set against each other. For Mary Shelley, as for Kant, the creations of man are seen as objectifications of some aspect (reason in the former, inclinations in the latter) within himself. Yet in the novel this objectification is catastrophic: the creator (Frankenstein)[52] is haunted and destroyed not by an unfamiliar external reality, but by incomprehensible, internal forces that permeate his reason and that have been inadvertently materialized. Reason could perhaps fathom the laws of nature and calculate the ways this realm would unfold, but who would ken the nature of reason itself? As the social world becomes more "cloned," as it increasingly reflects human ingenuity rather than the naturally pregiven, this world also becomes more inexplicable: it is not easy to oversee or predict the reality the self has inaugurated precisely because it is a projection of poorly understood, yet clearly formidable, human powers—of the dark reason within. "I considered the being whom I had cast among mankind and endowed with the will and power to effect purposes of horror," says Frankenstein, "nearly in the light of my own vampire, *my own spirit* let loose from the grave, and forced to destroy all that was dear to me."[53]

Frankenstein opens with an optimism regarding the capacity of a limpid reason: it is able to explore the world, conceive obedient products, and create a social environment that embodies it. To begin with, Frankenstein is driven by a hunger for knowledge, and his reason will not rest until he discovers the essence of "things in themselves" or their true being. Indeed, Frankenstein wants to "pioneer a new way, explore unknown powers, and unfold to the world the deepest mysteries of creation."[54] The apex of such a quest is the making of another human being since, if man is indeed the creator of the social world around him, he will never be wholly sovereign until he proves to himself his capacity to create himself through deliberate, predictable, and technological design. Frankenstein's quest, however, is not entirely tautological and solipsistic, since he would like to elevate himself into the founder of a whole original class of beings: "A new species would bless me as its creator and source; many happy and excellent natures would own their being to me. No father could claim the gratitude of his child so completely as I should deserve theirs."[55] The young Frankenstein imagines that he can begin a new era, one that belongs to more blithe and able beings than ourselves; the second moment of creation is the beginning of an improved species of humans and of their distinct history. Hence, he understands his quest for omnipotence by virtue of his reason as intertwined with a general proliferation of goodness and well-being. Yet Frankenstein is also concerned with his own predicament and sees creative (rather than practical) reason as a way to elude aloneness and homelessness. The inventor expects to feel ultimate belonging and familiarity because he dwells in a world he has created: all creatures will be related to him, their entire makeup will be transparent to his eyes, and his presence in their lives will be their ultimate desire.

Yet this attempt to foster belonging through the constitution of a new social environment is ill-fated from the outset because of reason's *disembodied* nature. The construction of the monster is the culmination of a long, compulsive scientific pursuit in which Frankenstein becomes estranged from his surroundings and devoid of community. He is blind to the magnificence of creation and to his emotional bonds with others: "my eyes were insensible to the charms of nature. And the same feelings which made me neglect the scenes around me caused me also to forget [my] friends." He confesses that he "seemed to have lost all soul or sensation but for this one pursuit."[56] Since Frankenstein is stripped of all emotions and attachments, one could say that his *Doppelgänger* is being created through obsessional rational effort alone and embodies reason in isolation[57]—pure reason, if you will. If Frankenstein had accepted the human plurality inherent to the world, responded with receptiveness to its affective and aesthetic abundance, allowed himself to be shaped by and be dependent upon its contingent circumstances, and attempted to find his humble home within it, then perhaps he would not have needed to generate this world anew through a monological project. But scientific reason establishes a servitude to narrow causes at the expense of life; it is like a chronic disease that diminishes the self's bond to the environment into a single aspect: once knowledge "clings to the mind" and has seized upon it, it is "like lichen on a rock."[58]

The fruit of disengaged reason is aesthetically marred, even repulsive.

In contrast to the typical depictions of Enlightenment theorists of reason as the source of harmony and beauty, in *Frankenstein* reason is enmeshed with unattractiveness and dissonance, death and decay. The monster is composed of body parts taken from moldy vaults and bloody charnel houses; the outcome, indeed, is no less revolting than these origins. The monster's hands are in "color and apparent texture like [those] of a mummy." His face has an expression of "loathsome yet appalling hideousness." The monster is generally "uncouth and distorted in its proportions,"[59] a walking proof for his creator's negligent and disharmonized mind. This outward ugliness of the monster prevents him from social intercourse with (other) human beings; he gradually internalizes the meaning others attribute to his appearance and becomes governed by equally repellent emotions such as envy, revenge, and cruelty. The pathetic, unaesthetic shape of disembodied reason is eventually reflected in the monster's conduct—for whom evil "became my own good."[60]

The creature is not only ghastly, but also dangerously unpredictable. He reflects the emptiness of reason, since he lacks the character that makes an individual's actions intelligible and somewhat consistent throughout life. The monster lacks the substance and attributes that would make it possible to say *who* he is: at times he is benevolent and sentimental, as when he helps the De Lacey family anonymously by gathering firewood; at other times he appears perfidious, committing horrendous acts of murder without showing any sign of emotion. In his interactions with others, he shifts unexpectedly from a rhetoric of pleading to one of threats; at one moment he is consumed by a burning desire to wreck his creator, and at the next he vows to annihilate himself because of this desire. Overall, one gets the impression that he cannot be governed—not even by himself. This lack of character and direction is made especially destructive because of the superior powers (primarily physical, but also mental) of the monster. For Mary Shelley, it seems, reason produces its own unruly otherness, which then mirrors the capricious nature of reason itself.

The scientist's act of creation also fails because humans are unable to relate to and empathize with the creature; in *Frankenstein*, Mary Shelley establishes a complete divorce between reason and ethical conduct. In the course of the novel, the monster is consistently rejected and execrated by every human being he encounters: the De Lacey family, Frankenstein's brother William, Captain Walton—there is not a single exception. The ultimate ethical failure, however, lies within Frankenstein himself. He is unable to take responsibility for the monster's fate and does not attempt to make him an integral part of the human community, as any parent would. Frankenstein is even unable to undertake the most basic precondition for human intercourse: tolerating the presence of the other. "Accursed creator! Why did you form a monster so hideous that even you turned from me in disgust?" asks the monster.[61] In fact, Frankenstein's inability to harmonize his ethical conduct with his creative reason by treating his offspring with care, leads to the monster's murderous deeds in the first place: "I am malicious because I am miserable . . . why should I pity man more than he pities me?"[62] the monster wonders.

Conclusion

In *Frankenstein*, we witness how a wrongly motivated, aesthetically ill-conceived, and ethically mishandled act of creation leads to a turnabout in the relations of power between creator and created. As we have seen, the novel begins with a creator who is confident in his ability to constitute and doctor his environment. In the course of the novel, this confidence is transformed into despair and languor, as the monster strangles Frankenstein's best friend, his young brother, and his beloved wife. The ruin of these social attachments corresponds to a sense of perpetual dislocation: now the scientist feels totally homeless and peregrine in the world. His native city has become "hateful," and his wandering will "not cease but with life."[63] Not only are his emotional and spatial worlds shattered, but the creator also experiences the ultimate humiliation—the threat of subjection at the hands of his own artifact. Says the monster to Frankenstein:

> Slave, I before reasoned with you, but you have proved yourself unworthy of my condescension. Remember that I have power; you believe yourself miserable, but I can make you so wretched that the light of day will be hateful to you. You are my creator, but I am your master; obey![64]

"My reign is not yet over," proclaims the monster. "You [Frankenstein] live, and my power is complete."[65] This unmitigated subjection of the creator to his offspring and *Doppelgänger* may be seen as symbolizing a unique historical imagination, one stemming from an age when reality—whether in the form of living beings or in the form of social institutions—is seen as a human product that has gone out of control. Mary Shelley articulates the tragic facets of this historical imagination, suggesting that the power relations between moderns and their offspring are being inverted as human beings intensify the knowledge, planning, and audacity involved in the production of the social. Her novel inquires into the impending failure of reason to control the increasingly more impressive and complex products of the human mind and labor (represented by the pinnacle of human inventiveness, the conception of another intelligent being).

We can see, then, that Mary Shelley and Kant present us with opposing visions of modernity, visions that radically diverge because these authors have different understandings of rationality and the place humans occupy in the world. While for Kant reason (both as understanding and as practical) is a faculty marked by its uniform functioning and clarity of rules, for Mary Shelley reason is obscure and contingent. While for Kant the historical emergence of human reason signifies the advent of illumination, freedom, and self-reliance, for Mary Shelley the dominance of reason means a new human powerlessness and disorientation. While for Kant reason propagates unconditioned goodness, for Mary Shelley it is swarming with malevolence. While for Kant reason is able to arrest human inclinations and animality, for Mary Shelley it is reason itself that is desirous and capricious. Finally, while for Kant the rational order that is taking shape in modernity is the fruit of a marriage between unintended consequences and reason's intervention in history, for Mary Shelley rational, intended consequences produce the extreme and irrevocable disorder of this epoch. Indeed, these contrasting views of the human ability to generate order in a boundless world are perhaps constitutive of the modern imagination: when, on the one hand, we strive to establish a universal moral order (for example, by promoting peace around the globe through the peacekeeping forces of the United Nations, or enforcing the General Declaration of Human Rights through the International Court of Justice and the International Criminal Court), and when, on the other hand, we disrupt the existing natural order in respect to our biological makeup (for example, through genetic engineering and human cloning), we seem to be moving in an undefined world whose potentials and hazards were first discerned by Kant and Mary Shelley.

～ 2

Proto-Entrapment Theories

M ARY SHELLEY'S APOCALYPTIC CONCLUSION WAS an exception at the time—a privilege of the novelist, perhaps, and one denied to the social and political theorist. For most Continental theorists from the late eighteenth into the nineteenth centuries, the modern malaise of doubleness and hyper-order had a solution, whether in the present or in the future, the community or the individual. These "proto-entrapment" writers, as they could be termed, identified the normalization, the lack of control over social circumstances, the other-dependency, the fragmentation of experience, and other dehumanizing threats that were to haunt their twentieth-century followers; they maintained, nevertheless, that the prospect existed of overcoming modern social conditions through deliberate human action. In general terms, one can distinguish between two main strategies of such action.

First, writers such as Herder, Wilhelm von Humboldt, and especially Nietzsche urged us to rebuff normalization through the cultivation of authenticity and difference. As impersonal modes of conduct and thought penetrated modern society, so did the urgent flight toward expressive individualism. In lieu of engagement with and transformation of social institutions, this strategy highlighted the construction of a distinct self that would remain outside these institutions—or at least would be immune to their effects. Though these writers recognized the historic and generic role of man as the creator of civilization, they stressed even more the role of the individual as creator of himself. Second, writers such as Rousseau, Kant, Hegel (to a limited extent), and

Marx believed that selves should step outward, so to speak, bringing their civilization under their conscious, collective control. On the one hand, these authors portrayed history as miring individuals in subjection to and alienation from their social institutions; they proclaimed that, while our inferior or deformed aspects are enmeshed in the workings of civilization, the pith of our humanity remains external to it and is being neglected. But on the other hand, these writers countered their gloomy assessment with contemplations of a future when humans would become (or a present in which humans were already becoming) the masters of their social institutions. According to these thinkers, men and women could become autonomous and coexist with their surroundings in harmony—even if this ideal could only be approximated in practice. This strategy sought to constitute the identity of the self through a redefinition of its relation to other human beings as well as to collective institutions. It allowed adherents to picture a space of unity and mutual reflection, wherein selves recognize in themselves and in others some shared, essential characteristics; these selves, moreover, complement their conscious association by transforming their social environment to make it echo these characteristics. In this manner, the threat of chaotic history is overcome, and a solid block of overarching reflection in the void can be pictured.

My aim in this chapter is to illustrate how entrapment theorists—Weber, Freud, and Foucault (to be examined in depth later)—differ from proto-entrapment thinkers in their historical-political imagination. This chapter, accordingly, is divided into two sections. In the first, I portray in greater detail the two strategies of confronting the Otherness of civilization outlined above by sketching Nietzsche's and Marx's responses to this challenge. I take each of these thinkers to have epitomized a certain strategy and confine my interest to this aspect of their work. These great philosophers of the nineteenth century suggested opposing solutions to the same problem, pushing to the extreme a particular logic of confronting the problem of doubleness. In the second section of the chapter, I discuss Weber's critique of Marx's and Nietzsche's strategies and examine the transformation of historical-political imagination at this stage of modernity.

Overcoming Doubleness

Bounding the Self within a Space of Difference: Nietzsche

Celebrating our reason and fulfilling our collective autonomy, according to the Kantian vision, allows us sway over social institutions and

over civilization as a whole. Yet this mastery is achieved by a universalization of our identity and hence may be understood as enhancing the
very uniformity and sameness that are already imposed upon us
through the economy and the practices of work at the factory, the state
bureaucracy and its policing, shared social spaces, and public opinion.
If, in order to realize my freedom, I must affirm a practical reason
identical to that of others, join a society governed by a general will, or
celebrate my species-being and class identity, then in doing so I may
have relinquished my selfhood, and paradoxically, my chance at forming a substantive, unique existence. Taking these questions very much
to heart, the first strategy for overcoming doubleness that will be examined suggests that the individual confront the social matrix not through
an act of inclusivity, but by the cultivation of authenticity and distinctiveness. With Nietzsche, asserting our human worth no longer
demands that we transcend our particularity, since our worth is dependent upon the aesthetic exploration of this particularity. Like his predecessors since the late eighteenth century, Nietzsche rebuffs modern
society for denying this kind of exploration. From the perspective of the
entrapment problematic suggested here, however, the celebration of
difference is not motivated merely by a new vision of human beings, but
is also *a conceptual answer to the quandary of the doubles.* In a nutshell, the
rationale of this solution could be described as follows:

The menace that a civilization conceived as the Other, the menace
that a homogenizing social world poses to the self, could be mitigated
by the formation of a distinct identity that has internal order and
cohesion. History may lack an immanent plan and import, offering
no opportunity for the collective remolding of the shared social spaces,
promising no reconciliation between creator and created. But the
normalizing ills of civilization—as well as the consciousness of
doubleness—remains external to one who is well aware of oneself as
self-formed wholeness.[1] This self does not perceive social institutions as
a domain to which it is inherently connected, as a realm that it must
subject to its will and with which it must ultimately merge, nor does
it experience itself as divided between a universal core that embodies
its humanity, and a secondary aspect that is blindly absorbed in the
formation of civilization. Rather, the self can be complete and
well demarcated by placing itself at a distance from society altogether,
and by resisting the forces of homogenization. "A living thing," writes
Nietzsche, "can become healthy, strong, and fruitful only when
bounded by a horizon" (*"jedes Lebendige . . . kann nur innerhalb eines
Horizontes gesund, stark und fruchtbar werden"*).[2]

In modernity, Nietzsche observes, individuals seem unable to form such protective boundaries. He suggests that these individuals open themselves vertically, so to speak, absorbing into themselves unparalleled quantities of the past. They choose to be loyal to history and to its taxing demands instead of being truthful to themselves. Moderns believe that one is measured according to one's knowledge of preceding events, philosophies, religion, people, art, discoveries, and so forth— according to the degree to which one becomes a "walking encyclopaedia"; these individuals choose to dwell in a subjectivity overcrowded with the thoughts and deeds of past people. This penetrability, suggests Nietzsche, is fatal for one's personality, since it creates a "chaotic inner world"[3] and buries the self under a clutter of knowledge. Not only is the modern self unable to coherently digest these unlimited pieces of the cultural past, but the very act of striving to do so involves a twisted temporal vista: the self learns too early that every human project is relative and perishable, and thereby is aware of the passing away of its own existence before it has even begun to live. Finally, this jumbled and uncertain human existence must lead to an inability to form an intelligible and potent exteriority. Human action, believes Nietzsche, presupposes a well-ordered center; only if we ken and experience ourselves as possessing this center can we seek to assert ourselves outward.

The inability of the self to form an exteriority and conduct from within leads it to a submissive, horizontal exposure to its contemporaries. For Nietzsche, sameness is less the upshot of institutional practices than it is the result of a cultural malaise: according to him, "historical education" and an "identical bourgeois coat" are intermeshed.[4] Moderns are plagued by too much civility, politeness, and benevolence; they uncritically absorb into themselves codes of conventional behavior and thought that eventually become their genuine characters. As noted, Nietzsche believes moderns embrace this "external uniformity"[5] because it helps them cover up their own impoverishment and hollowness. However, this sameness is concurrently socially useful, since it serves the bourgeois priorities of increasing utility and fitting individuals into the "workforce," and because it provides a chimera of stability and predictability, while disguising the disorientation of a nihilistic culture. Because of this surrender to the social, Nietzsche sees a general "diminution" and "leveling" of European individuals. "We can see nothing today that wants to grow greater, we suspect that things will continue to grow down, down, to become thinner, more good-natured, more prudent, more comfortable, more mediocre, more indifferent, more Chinese, more Christian." This superficiality of individuals poses the greatest threat for Europe, which has lost trust in man and therefore in life itself. "The sight of man now makes us weary—what is nihilism today if it is not that?—We are weary of man."[6]

The surrender of the modern to the cultural past and the bourgeois present shapes a normalized self that does not dare "disturb the universe" (as T. S. Eliot would have put it), that lacks faith in itself because it is encumbered by Time and the expectations of society. But what is the reason for this porousness—and the nihilism that it generates—in the first place? In Nietzsche's view, this predicament evolved once the attempt to elicit meaning from the world and thereby to inject import into life had consumed itself. We do not know how to affirm an identity or how to affirm life itself without recourse to scaffolds that provide explanations for our fate and purpose. Man, says Nietzsche, has become "a fantastic animal that has to fulfill one more condition of existence than any other animal: man *has to believe*, to know, from time to time, *why* he exists; his race cannot flourish without a periodic trust in life—without faith in *reason* in life."[7] In the history of the West, the riddle of "Why?" has enticed humans to seek answers outside themselves: their scaffoldings have included Forms, God, Nature—and more recently, History and Nation. Each offered absolute values, overarching visions of meaning, a way to relate the self to the world. In modernity, however, all of these answers are delegitimized or about to be used up, and for the first time human beings encounter a total impoverishment of external sources of signification. They experience everything as worthless: the higher and the lower, the true and the false, the good and the bad—all are equalized in their nothingness.[8] Human life therefore becomes tumultuous and incomprehensible. "Is there still up or down? Are we not straying as through an infinite nothing? Do we not feel the breath of empty space?" (*"Gibt es noch ein Oben und ein Unten? Irren wir nicht wie durch ein unendliches Nichts? Haucht uns nicht der leere Raum an?"*).[9]

For Nietzsche, then, the modern age is characterized by hyper-order in everyday life and practices—but also by a harrowing cultural and internal chaos. He believes that the response to this predicament should be the creation of a differentiated and harmonious self. Now in espousing this path, he was not alone. Lionel Trilling sees the drive to form a bounded self as originating with Schiller, Wordsworth, and Rousseau. These three, he suggests, "are not concerned with energy directed outward upon the world in aggression and dominance, but, rather, with such energy as contrives that the center shall hold, that the circumference of the self keep unbroken, that the person be an integer, impenetrable, perdurable and autonomous in being if not in action."[10] Indeed, the concern with an "impenetrable" self runs through many of Rousseau's writings (in contrast to *The Social Contract*), especially *Emile* and *The Discourse on the Origin of Inequality.* In the latter work, Rousseau elucidates this notion of the self by juxtaposing the modern self with the savage. As seen above, he believes that the civilized self has lost its *"sentiment de l'existence,"* deriving its sense of being and worth from the approving gaze of others. Moderns are attuned to external expectations imposed through interactions in public spaces, and they are therefore deaf to authentic internal feelings and needs. Nevertheless, Rousseau's solutions were unsatisfactory in molding a bounded self: although his savage is independent and self-sufficient almost from infancy, this type of self is nonetheless devoid of significant distinctiveness. While Emile lives a secluded social life and his sense of being does not hinge upon the judgments of others, his personality is shaped by his educator and is wholly dependent upon the latter. Moreover, as a mature man he recognizes himself as the product of a pedagogical regime oriented toward harmonizing desire and need, freedom and necessity—rather than toward the independent cultivation of singular potentials.

Herder embarks upon the path Rousseau refused to take. He views difference as a given, yet as requiring individual cultivation over a lifetime. "The new creature," he writes, "is but the realization of a latent idea that was inherent in creative and forever actively thinking nature."[11] The core of identity that resides within me develops through an internal energy that animates my person. As a sentient being I have a vital power that is "innate, organic, and genetic," and which is "the inner genius of my being." External influences and material cease to be ominous for Herder, since they are shaped by this force that stamps everything with each individual's uniqueness. "Whatever the influences of the [external] climate," he writes, "every man, every animal, every plant, has its own climate. For every living being absorbs all the external influences in a manner peculiar to itself and modifies them according to its own organic power."[12] Man is the singular creator of himself, in this view, and he finds his freedom through this ongoing creation. As Charles Taylor suggests, Herder develops an "anthropology of expressivism," according to which a human life is the embodiment of an idea whose meaning one must clarify and define. Identity reflects both what was pregiven and the path one embarks upon in articulating the original idea. This path must be unique and suitable for me, since to exchange my own realization with that of another "is to lead myself to distortion and self-mutilation."[13] My dignity is conditioned upon my ability to form beliefs, feelings, character, and conduct, which have their source in me without being an imitation of others; only if I can see myself in the forms inhabiting my life can I be certain that the malignant forces of sameness have remained external to me, that I am not a porous being. The Herderian vision of the self, then, alleviates our doubleness and alienation, since it suggests that we are both the creator and the thing created, since both are united in a single human life.

The demand for a bounded individuality finds exemplary articulation in Nietzsche, who both continues the Herderian legacy and breaks away from it. Nietzsche agrees with his predecessors that human dignity commands the independent formation of internal order. "This is a parable for each one of us: he must organize the chaos within him by thinking back to his real needs" (*"Dies ist ein Gleichnis für jeden Einzelnen von uns: er muß das Chaos in sich organisiren [sic], dadurch daß er sich auf seine echten Bedürfnisse zurückbesinnt"*).[14] To vanquish the inward, identity-related chaos, one has to become engaged in a twofold operation. First, one must weed out anything that has been implanted within, anything that is being repeated without thinking or criticism, anything that is being accepted through membership in a democratic herd. Since we are lost in the nihilistic void, we are inclined to embrace the ethos of this herd, with its fear of deviance and its existential laziness; to regain self-respect and appreciation for our lives we must therefore cease to "seem like factory products."[15]

Next, the shaping of oneself calls for an uninhibited expression of one's will to power. By this Nietzsche usually does not mean a will that dominates others. The will to power entails assuming responsibility for one's life, consciously choosing how to live, and asserting abundance, vitality, and singularity. "The individual," he writes, "is something quite new which creates a new thing, something absolute; all his acts are entirely his own."[16] Strong individuals are self-sufficient and "want to form and no longer to have anything foreign about them" (*"wollen formen und nichts Fremdes mehr um sich haben!"*).[17] They would like to possess *Wahrhaftigkeit*—to adhere to their own values and needs instead of adhering to an external truth. This imperative of original self-generation—of values, conduct, style—is so important to Nietzsche that he even urges us to affirm those contingent events of the past whose imprints we invariably bear; in other words, we should master the effects of time. This yes-saying transforms past events from mere accidents and impositions into something willed by us; these events are now experienced as our own, rather than as something foreign that needs to be expunged from memory.

Nietzsche even sees the formation of strong individuals or overmen (*Übermenschen*) as the achievement that could render the tragic history of Western culture worthwhile. He emphatically rejects the notion that the meaning of history lies in the collective reconciliation between human beings and civilization. Instead, he writes that "the *goal of humanity* cannot lie in its end but only *in its highest exemplars.*"[18]

While in his quest for an enveloped identity Nietzsche builds on the Herderian tradition, he departs from it on a crucial issue: for Nietzsche the notion of innate genius or pregiven idea is an ontological fiction, a genealogical impossibility, and a psychological hazard. Nietzsche's epistemology presents truth as perspective dependent and as motivated by the will to power. He therefore denies a privileged position from which valid ontological claims can be postulated. Moreover, human identity is so complex that it is practically impossible to decipher its inner depth and to arrive at some pregiven, fixed core. A man is clouded, even to himself. "He is a thing dark and veiled; and if the hare has seven skins, man can slough off seventy times seven and still not be able to say: 'this is really you, this is no longer outer shell.'" Finally, a person who believes that his humanity and dignity depends upon the authentic articulation of a unique nature is harnessing himself, psychologically and existentially. Instead of transgressing what has been given by nature or insinuated through culture, this person remains committed to his or her constitutive effect. To such a person Nietzsche cries: "Your true nature lies, not concealed deep within you, but immeasurably high above you."[19]

Nietzsche, then, bids us to pursue an aesthetic exploration of the self. Life is an artistic, creative project in which we establish order within initial chaos by inventing an individual interpretation of the world and of ourselves.[20] This interpretation is not measured by "objective," universal categories, such as that of right and just action; rather, it is measured by its originality, creativity, beauty, and depth, as well as by the exertion it commands. We "*want to become those we are*—human beings who are new, unique, incomparable, who give themselves laws, who create themselves."[21] When the self realizes that it is essentially a will to power, it expresses this recognition by a Dionysian and vitalic generation of perspectives and forms to comprehend reality. Through this epistemological imposition, it is able to overcome nihilism and the quest for certainty that generated this state of being. The overman's interpretations are destined to be ever-changing and contingent; but it is precisely the transitory nature of oneself and the universe that he is able to celebrate—not merely to bear—as his own. Each moment in which the overman must confront the void is yet another opportunity to overcome himself *(Selbstüberwindung)* and his nihilistic tendencies—and this moment recurs eternally.

In sum, one may say that, in Nietzsche's case, a series of self-formed internal orders and bounded existences replaces the Herderian notion of a consistent and evolving order throughout life. These changing configurations allow the Nietzschean self to overcome the threats of both normalized existence and doubleness, since it recognizes itself as self-sufficient and distinctive—as different, to be precise, even from its former mold. Nietzsche insists that the decaying culture of modernity cannot and should not be confronted and prevailed upon by collective means, political or otherwise;[22] only circumscribed individuals—who are unique, strong, and intense—may accomplish this task. As the condition of European society becomes more desperate, Nietzsche is more strongly convinced that, for the overman, a new existential reality is destined to come; he is able to advance this individualistic vision, however, since within his theoretical frame civilization is mainly about culture and ideas that are shaped by singular persons, and less about social institutions and material reality. Since for Marx the latter sphere of existence is the fundamental one, he must offer a wholly different strategy for overcoming the threats of modernity. While sharing Nietzsche's quest to break away from the present, Marx's strategy aims at subjecting civilization rather than fleeing its effects, and it is founded on the trans-subjectivity of the poor masses, rather than the bounded horizons of exemplary and select individuals.

The Move Outward: Marx

"Even the need for fresh air," writes Marx, "ceases to be a need for the worker. Man reverts once more to living in a cave, but the cave is now polluted by the mephitic and pestilential breath of civilization."[23] In Marx's image, civilization is like a gigantic, half-living creature that contaminates, deforms, and dehumanizes the self; he sees the modern era as deepening and widening the conflict between self and civilization. This conflict occurs because individuals are dispossessed of their paths to self-realization through labor in a hyper-ordered environment. Marx follows earlier critics of modernity such as Smith, Herder, and Rousseau in viewing modernity as inaugurating new spaces—especially the factory—that homogenize individuals. "The technical subordination of the worker to the uniform motion of the instruments of labor," he writes, "and the peculiar composition of the working group, consisting as it does of individuals of both sexes and all ages, gives rise to a barrack-like discipline."[24]

Discipline is an external barrier for self-expression, establishing a rule-governed institution that is wholly indifferent toward the particularity of those who inhabit it. Beyond the human control in the factory (over the specific nature of productive activity, hours of work and time management, conduct and output, and more), the machine induces even more profound uniformity, since it is indifferent to the one who operates it and equalizes the labor power of individuals; with the machine, in fact, sameness penetrates even into the physical movement and internal rhythm of workers. Marx is troubled by this discipline more than by induced sameness in other spheres of modern life: he considers labor—the "life-activity" of humans—to be the genuine realm in which they may express and cultivate themselves. Through his interaction with nature, man changes nature and "simultaneously changes his own nature."[25] Our ontology dictates self-expression through work; this path, however, is open-ended. On the individual level, we transform ourselves by playfully conceiving objects, translating these images into practice, and mastering the determination and consistency needed for such labor; we grow as human beings through the objects we create, less by the ephemeral words we utter or the social conduct we display. The early Marx seems to have believed that this self-realization could occur even in the sphere of necessity—wherein human beings provide for themselves the shelter, food, clothing, tools, and so forth that are needed for survival—while the Marx of *Capital* suggested that self-realization could occur only outside the sphere of necessity. Even in the later case, however, the main thrust of Marx's concept of self-realization involves interaction with nature and concrete expression through work, while other forms of self-expression (literature, art, politics, science, and so on) remain marginal. "Man," he argues, "not only effects a change of form in the materials of nature; he also realizes [*verwirklicht*] his own purpose in those materials."[26]

In capitalism, however, relations of human beings to their objects are as perverse as human interrelations. Marx links the two themes examined above: the uniformity of selves is inherently intertwined with the conflict between selves and the civilization they bring about. In capitalism and its fetishism, human-made objects are dominant in shaping consciousness and action, but instead of articulating a person's distinctness, their production process involves the flattening of individuals. Moreover, in this economic system individuals enter into highly antagonistic relations with their objects. The latter ingurgitate the very essence of the self: the greater the object produced by the worker, "the less is he himself"; the more he invests himself in an object, the less substance he has left. While the entire physical energies of the individual are required for producing the object, it does not express his imagination, creativity, skills, or personal and social goals. Instead, the product begets wealth for another and therefore fosters the conditions that increase the worker's own subjection. "The worker," writes Marx, "places his life in the object; but now it [his life] no longer belongs to him but to the object . . . [T]he life which he has bestowed on the object confronts him as something hostile and alien," as an "autonomous power."[27] This hostile, half-living object incorporates a part of the self—his or her anonymous labor-power—which enters into the metabolism of the production process and renders the alienated object mighty in the first place.

Marx, then, echoes the historic imagination we saw in the previous chapter: First, throughout history, the human being has been divided and doubled, with a declining self on the one hand and a tangible and expanding object that gives external, yet alienated, form to the self on the other. These two parts stand in a conflictual relation (which capitalism has brought to a head), and the struggle of the self with the social world is also a struggle of the self with itself. Second, Marx echoes the Frankensteinian vision by presenting human beings as misguided creators, ones who generate a fecund world of objects that embodies their inventive powers, but who find that this world threatens to subject them precisely by virtue of these powers; the greater human ingenuity becomes, the greater our subjection grows. In capitalism, Marx observes, the "lord of his creation . . . [is] the servant of that creation" (". . . *dass der Herr seiner Schöpfung, als der Knecht dieser Schöpfung erscheint!*").[28] It is this helplessness and subjection—to the moderns' own products rather than to an external power—that underlies Marx's fury (as well as his optimism, since this particular predicament could be reversed). Finally, Marx resembles Mary Shelley in his suggestion that humans dwell in bedlam—that capitalism is unable to engender order from within itself—in contrast to the invisible hand argument, for example. Indeed, the "scientific" struggle to uncover regulative principles in capitalism is a mirage, and "the true law of political economy is chance" (*"Das wahre Gesetz der Nationalökonomie ist der Zufall"*).[29] The bourgeoisie may control the state, but even they are immersed in a recalcitrant universe colored by anarchy and arbitrariness. "So far," Marx writes, "association has been nothing but an agreement about those conditions within which individuals were free to enjoy the freaks of fortune [*Zufälligkeit*]."[30] Chance determines not only what one will produce in an arbitrary division of labor, but also whether someone will actually need this item in an anonymous market. Chance determines whether one will lose or gain in an economic exchange, and even whether the system as a whole will hold. Marx predicted that eventually the chaotic aspect of the capitalist mode of production would explode in a crisis of overproduction, failed credit and banking, shrinking markets, and high unemployment.[31] Modernity, for Marx, is a peculiar and cognitively mystifying age, since the extreme discipline and rationalization imposed on the worker in the factory is met by profound chaos at the macroscopic level of the system as a whole.

Marx thus urges human beings to bring civilization back "under their control"[32] and to eliminate both the hyper-order in practices of work and the disorder and chance that mark their existence as part of an irrational system. (Here, indeed, Marx is disclosed as a theorist of power almost as much as Nietzsche; he is interested, however, in the power humans exercise collectively upon social institutions, not in the power individuals unleash to remold themselves.) In this yearning for conscious and collective self-rule, Marx continues and radicalizes the Rousseauian-Kantian tradition that redefined the notion of human freedom. This tradition conceptualizes freedom as autonomy, and Rousseau is credited with being the first to declare that only "obedience to the law one had prescribed for oneself is liberty."[33] Both Rousseau and Kant reject adherence to external codes or conventions and believe that genuine moral action—regardless of its content—can only originate in ourselves. Moreover, these theorists suggest that human autonomy requires us to transcend our immediate desires and self-centeredness, the lower aspects of our being; both the republican citizen who espouses the general will and the noumenal agent of practical reason satisfy this condition of prioritizing a communal dimension of their identity. My main point is this: both these facets of the concept of autonomy—authorship over laws and generalization of identity—are necessary for resolving the agonism between self and civilization. Only when we conceive of ourselves as possessing a shared identity (as members of a particular political community or as similar rational beings) can we imagine that the rules and norms that originate in us would be reflected in social institutions. As unique selves with diverging interests, distinct identities, and incommensurable moral vistas, social institutions and laws cannot correspond to us. Most interpreters of this concept of autonomy assume that it is motivated by a new perception of human beings, their potentials, and their dignity, and that it is the main reason for the critiques of modernity that began with Rousseau.[34] From the viewpoint of the entrapment problematic suggested in this work, however, the essential role of autonomy lies elsewhere. The true value of this conceptual invention is that it enables the collective to imagine a way of gaining control over a dehumanizing civilization by redefining the bonds among and the universal-general essence of human beings.

Marx follows the insights of Rousseau and Kant, declaring that "in a real community, individuals obtain their freedom in and through their association."[35] He calls for collective self-rule over the entire social conditions of human existence, presenting a view of perfect order that counters the total disorder of capitalism; the messy, unfathomable, irrational, wasteful, short-sighted aspects of social life are contingent features of history that we are destined to overcome. Marx professes that this inauguration of intentional order will necessitate a new kind of collective self-consciousness. As atomized beings, workers encounter their material circumstances as something "over which they, as separate individuals, have no control."[36] In capitalism, he avers, individuals are separated from each other by their contingent self and class interest, and are tethered to a given occupational perspective; no overarching vision, political or otherwise, can inaugurate genuine unity. In the Hegelian, liberal state, individuals can forge only false and "unreal universality";[37] because of the multiplicity of stakes involved, this state becomes a reality to get along with, nothing more. However, such a mediating state and its centralized bureaucracy will not be necessary when the general interest shall genuinely resonate in each member of society. "The abolition of the bureaucracy is only possible by the general interest actually . . . becoming the particular interest, which is itself only possible as a result of the particular interest becoming the general interest."[38]

Marx insists, then, that we shall have the power to overcome the capitalist mode of production and its false symbols of universality only if we distance ourselves from our particularistic dimensions: "Human emancipation is complete only when the real individual has taken back into himself the abstract citizen, when as an individual, in his empirical life, in his work, and in his relationships, *he has become a species-being (Gattungswesen)*."[39] This change of self-perception will be reflected even in the character of work itself: while it is critical for Marx that we be able to express ourselves through labor in communist society, this individual expression must be subordinated to the general recognition of our social nature. In a communist society, people will produce the things society needs out of concern for the common good; in such a society, the product I produce will articulate "my authentic nature, my human nature, my communal nature." Evidently, for Marx, even the product reveals that the "essence of man is the true community of man."[40] By thus highlighting the universalist dimension of our identity—and suggesting that we can both become conscious of it and express it in practice—Marx is able to present self-rule as a shared human capacity that allows identity to be expanded outward and become reflected in the makeup of social institutions.

Control of a human collective over its civilization could be understood merely as an external relation. Yet Marx seeks to go even further by demanding a genuine unity of the two—*which is another way of saying that he longs for a coalescence of the self with itself.* At the most basic level, he argues that humans must not be called upon to create anything alien to themselves—that creators must be joined to their creations by a sense of purpose. In communism, the products we create will be "as many mirrors from which our nature would shine forth" *("ebenso viele Spiegel, woraus unser Wesen sich entgegen-leuchtete").*[41] Yet more generally, Marx famously suggests that communism is the "genuine resolution of the conflict between man and nature, and between man and man, the true solution of the conflict between existence and being, between objectification and self-affirmation, between freedom and necessity, between individual and species."[42] Such all-engulfing wholeness is possible because Marx presupposes that social reality is a totality in which all spheres of human existence hinge upon the material-productive sphere (that is, on the forces and relations of production). Once the latter is changed, family life, politics, law, religion, philosophy, arts and sciences, and all other spheres will be necessarily transformed as well. Marx must assume that the world has a "key" that opens the doors to every realm of human reality, since otherwise we would have little chance of introducing genuine unity among the various realms. Moreover, how could we exist in harmony with our creation when the latter suggests merely a multiplicity of spheres, each with its own rationale and driving force (as Weber would claim)?

Marx's concepts of wholeness and of the unity of creator and created rely not only upon an ontology of totality, but also upon an epistemological leap. He believes that epistemology is historically dependent and that moderns have arrived at a new stage of self-consciousness that can allow them to view history as formed solely by human endeavors. "The reality which communism is creating," Marx asserts, "is precisely the real basis for rendering it impossible that anything should exist *independently of individuals,* insofar as things are only a product of the preceding intercourse of individuals themselves."[43] Marx thinks that in order to defeat the Otherness of civilization we must not only transmute the present, but also first reexamine our relation to the past. Only a change of perspective on the totality of human endeavors to date could foster the audacity needed for becoming fully autonomous. Human history has been shaped by what humans produced, how and with what means they produced it, what kind of relationships they formed among themselves because of this production, and the ways their production introduced ever-changing needs. When we grasp that our present predicament is the upshot of the externalizing activity of human beings—that the present belongs to us because (as social beings) the past is profoundly related to us—we can claim ownership of the social world. When this authorship is demonstrated and internalized, we will no longer see the social world as a towering and reified reality, and the radical estrangement we feel toward our collective institutions will be revealed as a necessary stop on a meaningful historical path—rather than as the outcome of a capricious and impersonal force called "History."

The Marxian strategy of coping with the Otherness of civilization by outward expansion also requires a dual understanding of time. First, it relies upon a long teleological and dialectical development founded upon the material aspects of human existence. According to historical materialism, the forces of production are the engine of history that effects the relation of production and the superstructure (although the relation between these three spheres is not necessarily simple or unidirectional).[44] History is characterized by movement, which capitalism seems to have epitomized. "Constant revolutionizing of production, uninterrupted disturbance of all social conditions, everlasting uncertainty and agitation distinguish the bourgeois epoch from all earlier ones."[45] Modernity, according to Marx (and many of his contemporaries), is an age at a gallop. The future is consumed by a present that, whether consciously or unconsciously, wishes to be already "there."[46]

But the ideal of establishing mirroring relations between society and its institutions implicitly postulates a second type of time, a type that will begin after humans have achieved the dictatorship of the proletariat and the withering away of the state. The similarity among selves that Marx longs for—and the correspondence between them and their offspring (their self-made civilization)—calls for the introjection of a semistatic sort of time, required in order to keep the building blocks of Marx's society constant. Any radical modification in the defining fea-

tures of the individual's identity or in social institutions would introduce a new rift between creator and created. That Marx posits this form
of time is implied in the fact that, in communism, the possible effects of
new means of production upon the nature of social institutions is not
pondered, and the evolution of human nature from the universal
and socially oriented to something as yet unknown is also ignored.
Although Marx declines to prescribe a blueprint for the future, his
theory submits that a prolonged consonance between selves and civilization calls for the flattening of time, for rendering it horizontal. This
flattening explains how communism could be imagined as the "solution
of the riddle of history."[47]

To sum up this discussion of Marx and Nietzsche, we have seen that
both theorists view the modern age as distinguished by hyper-order in
everyday life and practices—but also as defined by a harrowing chaos.
Marx believes this disorderly world to be the upshot of the wasteful
organization of social institutions, while Nietzsche believes it to be the
outcome of a disintegrating culture and a porous self. Both theorists
profess that we have been inept creators, that our culture and institutions have failed us. For Marx, this failure is expressed in the ways we
produce things, determine who owns them, allow them to rule our lives;
for Nietzsche, this shortcoming is reflected in our values, our sources of
meaning, our concepts of truth. Moreover, both theorists—despite
their radically different theoretical frames and visions of the good
life—picture moderns as dehumanized, self-destructive, flat and hollow, mired in a world that blocks their paths for self-expression. But
while Nietzsche searched for ways to form a self (such as Zarathustra)
that is independent of society, Marx aspired to bind the individual to
this society; while Nietzsche longed for a self that would impose order
within itself, Marx sought to impose order upon the social-economic
world. (Nietzsche, incidentally, believed the socialist quest for order
would lead to the worst form of dictatorship.)[48] However, both these
strategies of coping with doubleness and the Otherness of civilization
are questioned by entrapment writers.

From Proto-Entrapment to Entrapment Theories

Notions of fixed beginnings are viewed today with suspicion—
especially those that coincide with a transition from one century to
another. Yet with Weber and Freud, a new understanding of modernity
and of the self's position within it does emerge. Suddenly, modern

culture and its institutions seem to become weightier, inescapable, fixed in their exteriority. The self is called to forgo a yearning for collective or individual transcendence, to accept its immurement within social reality and history. For these and other twentieth-century writers, the two strategies for overcoming the quandary of the doubles have failed: it is impossible to reorganize social institutions in a way that will render us autonomous and free, and the construction of a bounded self is an illusion, given the unconscious workings of internalized social norms. There are, of course, many contemporary theorists who do not accept this pessimism—Marcuse and Habermas come to mind. Nevertheless, Weber and Freud have helped to shape contemporary consciousness by arguing that discontent is constitutive of the modern, overcivilized predicament, that our victories over the forces of normalization are inescapably partial and transitory, and that we must confront this predicament with a new realism and prudence. These issues will be explored in depth in the subsequent chapters, but first one must grasp the transition from proto-entrapment to entrapment theorists. Analyzing Weber's critique of Marx and Nietzsche offers a succinct way to reveal the nature of this transition. (Later, in Chapter 4, I will discuss the ways that Freud criticizes the schools associated with Marx and Nietzsche.) To begin with, however, two general reasons for Weber's departure from nineteenth-century thought should be mentioned.

With Weber, a new type of self makes its appearance on the Western landscape: the "trapped" self. Individuals who dwell within the "iron cage" do not assume that a radical break with the present configuration of modernity is likely nor do they shape their lives in search of such a break. They forgo the idea of revolutionizing prevailing social institutions and their underpinning values because they view the existing social and economic cosmos as too powerful, too complex, and too fragmented to permit such remolding. Weber depicts the forces that promote calculable and rationalized human action, specialization, the shrinking of personal horizons, economic growth, and bureaucratization as too overwhelming. This sense of helplessness is enhanced by the fragmentation that gradually inheres in the progress of civilization: Weber contends that conflict is ever increasing among value spheres (for example, between the economic and the aesthetic, or the political and the ethical), and among the laws and demands that each sphere posits to the self. The independence and distinctiveness of each sphere, Weber argues, prove that human reality is not accountable to any one governing principle—be it theological, economic, historicist-idealist, or historic-genetic. No determining factor can be manipulated to bring about the birth of a new era. (With a different conceptual scheme, Foucault later takes this position of anti-ubiquity to its ultimate conclusions).[49]

Another reason that Weber relinquishes the quest for radical social change is that he lacks a clear, unequivocal ontological vision of the self. This essential precondition is also absent in the two other entrapment theorists studied in this work, Freud and Foucault. Weber clearly had some underlying essentialist notions about the self (otherwise, he could not have depicted the modern age in such bleak terms); nevertheless, he did not acknowledge these notions in general and in his preconception of the self as a hermeneutical creature in particular. Moreover, his philosophical anthropology attributes a central place to the contingencies of history in shaping the self. Weber's preferred self, the "personality," has Protestant origins and is marked by the aspiration for maximal projection of its core ethical values in daily life. Yet even this self is explicitly denied any superior moral status in relation to other types of selves—either within or outside Western culture. While Weber (in contrast to Freud and Foucault) maintains a moral language in discussing the self, his conception of it is too elastic to be translated into an ideology or a theory that would propel individuals to pursue a social or moral revolution. His proclaimed philosophical position could be characterized as Nietzschean perspectivism without the ontology of the will to power: any philosophical method (as he says of historical materialism) is only one outlook among numerous possibilities, and is always conditioned upon one's presuppositions. This standpoint cannot yield a credible foundation for demanding a radical transformation of one's environment, as Weber surely realized.

Weber's departure from nineteenth-century solutions to the problem of entrapment is manifest in his complex relation to Marx and Nietzsche. Weber's view of these two great nineteenth-century figures is demonstrated by a familiar story, according to which he once said that "the honesty of a contemporary scholar, and above all a contemporary philosopher, can be judged by his attitude to Nietzsche and Marx. Whoever does not admit that considerable parts of his work could not have been carried out in the absence of the work of these two, is only deceiving himself and others. The world in which we spiritually and intellectually live today is a world substantially shaped by Marx and Nietzsche."[50]

Weber's attitude toward Marx has been reevaluated in recent decades. In the past, Weber was perceived as a champion of an "idealist" interpretation of history in general and of modern capitalism in particular, thus proposing a counterview to Marx's historical materialism. More-over, according to this interpretation, Weber underscored the critical place of the state in determining social and economic structures, in contrast to Marx's playing down the role of this institution; he empha-sized the importance of status groups and nations as more attractive sources of identification than the merely economic category of class; he manifested the importance of the superstructure and culture in social life in opposition to the predominance attributed by Marx to the eco-nomic base—and so forth. However, contemporary literature has unraveled many of the ethical sensibilities, the methodology, and the overall picture of modernity shared by these two theorists.[51]

Most important to this study is the realization (to be developed in the next chapter) that Weber extends Marxist themes from the context of the factory to include modern institutions as a whole: armies, corpora-tions, state bureaucracies, universities, party machines, and more. By utilizing Marx's analysis of capitalist relations of production, Weber argues that in each of these institutions the concentration of ownership over the particular relevant means results in disciplinary conduct and in the impersonalization of human interaction, in objectification and the loss of freedom, and finally, in the frustration of any attempt to achieve a sense of meaning. Furthermore, Weber shares with Marx (and Freud) the insight that work is an essential activity for the modern individual, though his intellectual and spiritual sources in this matter do not derive from Marx.[52]

Nevertheless, Weber departs from Marx in his exploration of the potential routes of escape from the snares of modernity. Marxism, according to Weber, professes that a communist society will mark the end of the "the rule [*Herrschaft*] of things over man" and of "*all* rule by man over man."[53] This vision of absolute control over objects and of the demolishing of control among men and women is perceived by Weber as a twofold illusion. First, collective ownership over the means of production (or office) alters neither the basic circumstances of the individual, who still has to adjust to a given function within the existing division of labor, nor the situation of the specialist, who operates in an ethically neutral environment and with little control over the nature of her work. Marx's hopes—as expressed in *The German Ideology*—for a well-rounded and versatile individual who fully commands her environ-ment are a mirage. Second, as for people's domination over other humans, "It is the dictatorship of the official, not that of the worker, which, at present anyway, is on the advance,"[54] and in a socialist society this trend is only likely to escalate. With Weber, the sober realization that the socioeconomic world is immune to human autonomy dawns on the modern psyche. From their origins as servants of human needs, rationalized contemporary institutions take on an independent existence and become ends unto themselves, with humans serving their goals. For Weber, as Löwith says, "this reversal marks the whole of modern civilization, whose arrangements, institutions and activities are so rationalized that, whereas humanity once established itself within them, now it is they who enclose and determine humanity like an 'iron cage.' Human conduct, from which these institutions originally arose, must now in turn adapt to its own creations, which have escaped the control of their creators."[55]

What contributes to Weber's pessimistic outlook is his understanding of history as both chaotic and linear. From a specific constellation of contingent factors, history proceeds linearly in a certain direction until it is diverted to a different course by an unforeseeable factor, most often a new religious belief. (Modern capitalism, as Weber contends in *General Economic History*, results from a combination of diverse factors, such as the bureaucratic state, calculable law, citizenship, bookkeeping methods, and a business ethic that does not distinguish between community members and outsiders; this multifaceted analysis, however, complements rather than displaces his analysis concerning the key role Protestantism played in unleashing market capitalism.)[56] But precisely because history does not have a "plan" (and Weber rejects any notion of historical determinism), there is nothing to interrupt the indefinite amplification of instrumental and formal rationality. This fusion of order and disorder, of what could be termed arbitrary linearism, injects a new sense of doom into the post-teleological consciousness and marks the transition from the nineteenth to the twentieth century by reinvigorating a concern with the uninterrupted expansion of hyper-order.

Yet the difference between Weber and Marx goes even deeper. For Marx, the ramifications of the capitalist system of production included both the scarcity of essential goods and the impending of human creative and productive potentials. Human beings are makers, originators of objects who express themselves through interaction with nature. By engaging in "estranged labor," man, who is a "conscious being, makes his life activity, his being *(Wesen)*, a mere means for his existence."[57] In contrast, Weber views the central problem of modernity to be its giving birth to a new type of person, to "specialists without soul, hedonists without heart"; in other words, it brings about a problem of meaninglessness. Marx's anthropology propelled him to conceptualize the dehumanization of modernity chiefly in terms of the arrest of the productive capacities and overall advancement of humans; Weber's anthropology led him to see dehumanization in the frustration of any attempt to establish horizons of significance, and in the shrinking space within which an individual might act upon his or her "ultimate values" or vision of the good. Even if socialism were to succeed in introducing different notions of distributive justice, Weber insists, it is not likely to provide new sources of collective meaning or to inject ethical significance into specialized work within rationalized mass-organizations. Consequently, he could not consider socialism to be a solution to the modern predicament. But if Marx was wrong in advising individuals to immerse themselves in the collective transformation of objective conditions, Nietzsche, according to Weber, made the opposite mistake of advocating false withdrawal.

Weber seems to have been closer to Nietzsche in his response to the modern malaise, a response that centers on the individual. As we shall see, Weber believes that, because of the impoverishment of cultural sources of meaning and the normalizing and rational-instrumental nature of social institutions, the life of the modern has become flat and trivial. Like Nietzsche, Weber longs for potent and substantive individuals who would be able to confront this predicament, averring that each individual must be able to establish values for himself and "to decide which is God for him and which is the devil."[58] Weber concurs with Nietzsche that there is no exterior guide in such choices, and no force from within that impels us in a certain direction: we are all alone with the judgment, courage, energy, and commitment that we can muster. Furthermore, Weber follows Nietzsche in suggesting that life is a continuous struggle with others and especially within one's soul, and that suffering is inescapable, since no transcendental comfort is available for the self. Yet, while both point to the formation of a "strong" identity as a response to modernity, there are important differences between the two writers.[59]

We can approach some of these differences through Weber's discussion of the prospects for democracy in Germany (1917). There he condemns those who explore their individuality by setting themselves apart "from the 'far too many' (gegen die 'Vielzuvielen') as is maintained by the various and misconceived 'prophecies' which go back to Nietzsche." On the contrary, Weber says, if a person is to preserve his authenticity (Echtheit), he must do it "in the midst of a democratic world" (*"innerhalb einer demokratischen Welt"*).[60] "Inner distance" is a desirable quality in a person, but one that should be achieved through engagement and immersion in the existing social institutions—not by devaluation and departure from them. Weber rejected Nietzsche's denunciation of modern politics (especially nationalist or liberal-democratic ones), as well as the latter's attitude towards science and capitalism.

What is true for democracy, then, holds for modernity as a whole: Weber's personality strives to independently constitute its identity around a normative core within the rationalized world, its given life-orders and value-spheres; it reluctantly affirms modernity. In Weber's time, Nietzsche's aesthetic self was adopted by the poet Stefan George and his circle, who were inspired by Zarathustra in their choice of social seclusion and the formation of a poetic-formalistic conception of life.[61] Weber thought that George's flight was flawed not only because it was materially available to just a small, elitist group, but also because this disengagement from contemporary life-orders could have only a marginal impact on the human predicament. Therefore, from Weber's perspective, Nietzsche's work marks a dangerous move toward the valorization of inner experience and its expression in aesthetic forms at the expense of a confrontation with existing circumstances. Weber characterizes this move towards subjectivist culture as "the refusal of modern men to assume responsibility for moral judgments"; instead, there is a tendency to "transform judgments of moral intents into judgments of taste ('in poor taste' instead of 'reprehensible') (*"ethisch gemeinte Werturteile in Geschmacksurteile umzuformen* ['*geschmacklos*' statt: '*verwerflich*']."[62]

While Weber realized that, after Nietzsche, no common foundation for moral judgments exists, nothing is more foreign than this aesthetic turn to his ascetic concept of the personality, which relentlessly espouses the norms and demands of its vocation, whether by "objectivity" in science, "responsibility" in politics, or the like. The *Berufswelt* must be accepted as is: Weber adheres to the Protestant (and Jewish) tradition of affirming social reality, even if he discards the theological tenets that supported this view. Hence the Weberian self cannot be content with the Nietzschean, simplified notion of circumscribed identity, however pressing the need for such an identity may be; it must negotiate with the world, asserting itself only within existing social institutions and their objective claims.[63] Weber still searches fervently for a well-defined selfhood that is echoed in the mundane, but he is aware of the limitations of this project, and therefore also plays down the significance of the uniqueness of identity. Instead of striving for distinctiveness by living a life preoccupied with accumulating varied personal experiences and repeatedly reinventing values, we should sustain a continuous course, morally and professionally. Zarathustra, like the prophets Weber studied, flees from or devalues the world as we know it; soberly and religiously, so to speak, the Weberian self remains within it.

～ 3

Max Weber:
Between Homo-Hermeneut and
the Lebende Maschine

At the turn of the century, German philosophy both exhibited and helped to form a paradox that defined the Western understanding of the self thereafter. While Nietzsche's philosophy of nihilism shattered the last hopes for religious and metaphysical consolation, thereby suggesting the possible meaninglessness of human existence, Dilthey called for the hermeneutic understanding of human beings, arguing that they should be distinguished from all other creatures and from nature because they are able to generate meaningful interpretations of their lives and of the cosmos. As Nietzsche's philosophy pointed to the evaporation of import from the world and from human existence itself, hermeneutic theory asserted that the dignity and fulfillment of human beings lie precisely in their ability to generate such import. Nowhere is the tension between these two positions more manifest than in Max Weber's work.

Under Nietzsche's influence, Weber argues for accepting the irreversible disenchantment (*Entzauberung*) of the world. It is generally overlooked, however, that this state suggests a problem only for a specific type of self. The threats of disenchantment, of a rationalized social environment, and of meaninglessness dominate Weber's work because he views human beings as creatures who yearn for meaning and are able to invent it. In fact, Weber accentuates the modern paradox of meaning, since he posits in the midst of a radically objectified world a self within whom the demand for hermeneutical existence reaches an unprecedented height. This self (the "personality," as Weber terms it) emerged as the result of historical developments peculiar to the West, whereby a mixture of religious and psychological motivations gradually propelled the self to seek ethical import in all the departments of its life. Since he situated the personality in social and natural environments that are devoid of such import, Weber was inescapably led to deem modernity as a snare. Conceptions of the self—rather than being a vehicle for liberation and a source of hope, as in the works of proto-entrapment writers—become in Weber and Freud fertile ground for a gloomy outlook.

The aim of this chapter is to explore how Weber constructs entrapment as a problem of a hollow and ethically barren mode of being. In the first section I argue that some essentialist convictions about human beings underlie Weber's project, particularly in his sociology of religion. The most important of these is a vision of humans as *homo-hermeneut*, as beings that require a meaningful existence. This vision plays a central role in Weber's depiction of how the self has been gradually constructed through its religious experience, both in the Occidental and Eastern traditions. This historical-anthropological narrative describes the progressive shaping of a self characterized by its individualized needs, its quest for inner cohesiveness and certainty, and its universalized moral code. Weber contends that the continuous theological rationalization and the unwavering assay—evident throughout human history—to make sense of the world leads from naturalism to the construction of interpretive edifices, and finally undermines the prospect of eliciting any import from the cosmos. Thus, the contemporary Western crisis of meaninglessness has its origins in the internal movement of Occidental religions, and is aggravated by the self's existence within the objectifying environment of capitalism, bureaucracy, and science.

As noted, Weber suggests that the distinct, Western religious experience gave birth to the ascetic personality. This notion of cause-oriented and principle-motivated self is examined in the second section; it is argued there that while Weber calls for a well-defined and distinct notion of selfhood, he insists that the self must be involved in collective projects, and that an individually shaped, meaningful existence must be a part of a meaningful social world. In fact, the greatest danger for this personality, in Weber's view, is the advent of modern techniques of discipline and the disappearance of ethical import from the realms of civil society and vocational life. As demonstrated in the third section, Weber's critique of contemporary society in general, and of discipline in particular, may become fully intelligible only after we recognize that he approaches his studies with concern for the fate of a specific type of self; the disciplined self serves in his writings as the "double" (or *Doppelgänger*) of the personality.

More generally, Weber sees the disciplined self as part of the *great double*, since it shoulders the organizational facet of modern civilization. This self sustains the institution of bureaucracy through its bodily, emotional, and especially mental activities; indeed, it becomes an indispensable ingredient of the bloodstream of this *"lebende Maschine."* In operating a bureaucracy, Weber argues, the objectified and impersonal intelligence of the officials creates the reality that curtails the space open for individuals to live as "personalities" (for instance, the politician facing the party apparatus). Although Weber's account of discipline is one of the earliest among theories of modernity, insufficient attention is given in the secondary literature to the multiple dimensions of discipline in his thought and to their interdependence. A reconstruction of his observations about discipline reveals that he sees it as demanding the mechanical formation and adaptation of the self to a set of given external criteria, thereby rendering the forging of the "personality" and of meaningful existence an impossibility. In Weber, then, an intense conflict between self and civilization (whose origins we have seen in Kant and Mary Shelley) is framed mainly in terms of meaningful existence or its absence due to functional imperatives of contemporary social institutions.

The last section explores the fate of the self in the fragmented and disenchanted world of modernity. Weber sees the contemporary self as situated among various, increasingly conflicting domains of action and value. This state generates a sense of purposelessness and incoherence, since it jeopardizes the possibility of formulating guiding ethical principles and renders the preservation of unity in human life a tenuous project. (Weber, indeed, could be seen as a paradigmatic modern theorist confronting a postmodern predicament.) Weber celebrates politics and the human sciences as two domains of activity that advance a partial response to this quandary: these activities help shield culture—the only available source of meaning in modernity—by guarding the identity of the nation and inquiring about its dilemmas and challenges. The collective value of these endeavors is complemented by the rewards they offer to the participant, since they allow one to become a personality. Ways of life that do not support such a transfiguration of the self, especially the aesthetic and erotic, are rejected by Weber; the hermeneutic need can be met only through involvement with intersubjective projects and the assertion of the self through them, that is, through

what I will characterize as "redemptive realism." As Marianne Weber
writes in portraying the context of Weber's life, those who "had abandoned the old gods without turning to socialism or to the aristocracy of
artistry [Nietzscheanism] felt that they were in 'freedom's empty
space.'"[1] Insofar as Weber addressed himself to his contemporaries, it
was to those in this "empty space," suggesting to them a Sisyphean self
that relentlessly strives to cultivate a set of "ultimate values" to guide its
actions in a rule-governed and impersonal environment.

Weber's Anthropology

Weber's anthropology contains essentialist-hermeneutical presuppositions about the self, yet suggests an interplay between this essentialism
and specific historical-contingent narratives; an adequate understanding of this complex view of the self is necessary in order to fully
appreciate his discontent with modernity.[2] The convictions that underlie Weber's anthropology can perhaps best be reconstructed from
his studies in the sociology of religion. These include Weber's
well-known work on Protestantism, as well as individual texts on
ancient Judaism, Confucianism and Taoism, and on Buddhism and
Hinduism.[3] The best summaries of his main themes occur in two
essays from *Die Wirtschaftsethik der Weltreligionen*—"*Einleitung*" and
"*Zwischenbetrachtung*" (1915)—and both will be central to my interpretation of Weber.[4] It is important to note that Weber's works on religion
were written in different periods of his life and should be seen in the
contexts in which they were composed. Nevertheless, they do have
much in common, and what Weber says in *ES* holds true for all of his
studies in the sociology of religion. There, he says that the intention of
the study is not to provide an overall understanding of religion and its
"essence," but to "study the conditions and effects of a particular type of
social action." That is, the goal is to conduct the inquiry from "the
viewpoint of the subjective experience, ideas and purposes of the individual concerned—in short—from the point of religious behavior's
meaning *(Sinn)*."[5] Because they explore the inner lives of human beings,
as well as because of their comparative scope and complexity, these
works seem to provide a sound foundation for uncovering Weber's
anthropological claims, which he never clearly articulated or system-
atized.

Any reader of the "Author's Introduction" *(Vorbemerkung)* for the
GARS collection may think that the *distinguishing* characteristic of
Western civilization and culture is its tendency toward rationalization.[6]

This disposition for rationality has resulted in the development of modern capitalism, science and technology, unique forms of art and music, the formal-bureaucratic organization of society and state, and other phenomena. For Weber, however, rationality has many meanings and can take various directions, among which the Western ones are only a particular option. Rationality, in fact, is not culturally specific, but likely to be part of human life as such. "For the rationality, in the sense of logical 'consistency' of an intellectual-theoretical or practical-ethical attitude, has and always has had power *[Gewalt]* over man, however limited and unstable this power is and always has been in the face of other forces of historical life."[7]

Often, as in the passage above, Weber uses rationality in the sense of consistency or "systematic arrangement," a quest for order and interconnection among various phenomena such as natural events, ideas, and human conduct.[8] It is a form of thought that by itself is empty and can be imposed on any domain of life. Yet in each case, the *motivation for this rationalization must be preexistent:* a quest for mastery of the natural environment, a need for a meaningful interpretation of the world, or strongly held religious convictions. Therefore, if we would like to understand what steers rationalization in any particular direction, a deeper inquiry into the inner motivations of human beings is necessary. Here, we find that what underlies any such path of systematization are "interests." Weber uses this word in a very broad and ambiguous sense, and it includes both material or "this-worldly" interests (for example, health, long life, and wealth) and ideal ones (for example, salvation or understanding of one's predicament in the world). However, while each interest may point to a distinct form of rationalization of thought and conduct, the question of how the interests themselves are being formulated remains open. Interests, while inherently very potent, do not exist in the abstract, but are shaped within broader horizons of significance. "Not ideas," writes Weber, "but material and ideal interests govern directly man's conduct. Yet, very frequently, the 'world images' *[Weltbilder]* that have been created by 'ideas' have, like switchmen, determined the tracks along which action has been pushed by the dynamic of interests."[9]

We can grasp the origin and meaning of a particular interest for a person only if we understand the overall background and complex of meaning within which it has been conceived. To be sure, the relation between interests and world images is not unidirectional. Religion (as a world image) has an "elective affinity" with the "interest situation" of the class from which it originated.[10] Intellectuals are inclined to

embrace contemplative religions and to relentlessly construct a coherent and comprehensive view of reality, as exemplified by Buddhism and
Hinduism. Civic strata—artisans, traders, and small entrepreneurs—
are predisposed to espouse religions such as Protestantism, which
approve of their occupations and may endow them with ethical significance. In short, the preexistent interest situation of a certain stratum
will be influential in its acceptance or rejection of a religion, and the
given religion, in turn, is likely to both affirm and reshape these preexistent interests. However, such "elective affinity" does not always exist,
and in any event it would be a crucial mistake to reduce religions and
world-views to material, interest situations as Marx did. The religious
ethic, Weber insists, "receives its stamp primarily from religious
sources," and "religious doctrines are adjusted to *religious needs.*"[11]

The potency of religions in shaping history should be explained in
light of their ability to satisfy a need peculiar to the human species: the
emotional, intellectual, and spiritual quest for meaning. Behind every
religion of salvation "always lies a stand towards something in the real
world which is experienced as particularly 'senseless.' Thus the demand
has been implied: that the world order in its totality is a meaningful
cosmos, or could and should become one" (*"Stets steckte dahinter eine
Stellungnahme zu etwas, was an der realen Welt als spezifisch 'sinnlos' emp-
funden wurde und also die Forderung: daß das Weltgefüge in seiner Gesamt-
heit ein irgendwie sinnvoller 'Kosmos' sei oder: werden könne und solle"*).[12]
We shall see below what precisely can be experienced as "senseless."
But first we should note the decisive point that Weber makes: *that
human beings have the internal necessity, as well as the capacity, to interpret
their lives and the cosmos as a whole in a meaningful way.* "Man," in other
words, can be characterized as *homo-hermeneut.* The latter's quest to
make sense of his life is neither the result of, nor under the control of,
conscious and rational decision. Ratio is, of course, often the means
employed in this project, but underlying the search for significance and
import is an uncontrollable inner force and compulsion, a desire that is
none other than a desire for meaning.

The interpretations humans spawn of their lives and the world reveal
varying degrees of complexity, generality, abstractness, and consistency,
and begin with magical beliefs and practices. Magic, according to
Weber, emerged from the wish to sway and manipulate the external
and internal forces that shape human life—rain, war, illness, and
so forth. The concern of magical religions was with the possible
goods of *this world*, and an unwillingness to accept their seemingly
arbitrary and unpredictable nature. With religions of salvation (that is,

all world religions except Confucianism), the wish is less to influence supranatural entities than to make sense of the world from an ethical perspective.[13]

> All religions have demanded as a specific presupposition that the course of the world be somehow *meaningful*, at least insofar as it touches upon the interests of men . . . [T]his claim naturally emerged first as the customary problem of unjust suffering and hence as the postulate of just compensation for the unequal distribution of individual happiness in the world.[14]

The exigency to which religions must answer is the human experience that the fate of individuals and collectivities on this earth is contingent, unequal, and often unjust. Elaborate hermeneutical schemes of the world commence from this basic and unalterable human condition. Indeed, this inner necessity for interpreting and comprehending one's fate is shared by all: the rich, powerful, and blessed individual "needs to know that he has a *right* to his good fortune;"[15] the poor, the sick, and those who have suffered loss aspire to make sense of their unfortunate lot and look for alternative compensation, in this life or the life beyond. This latter group is naturally the most hospitable toward religions of salvation, though these religions do not necessarily originate among or limit themselves to members of this group.

The quest underlying salvation is therefore rather similar among all religions, but the specific nature it assumes depends upon the overall world-view.[16] In *ES* Weber discusses numerous conceptions of salvation and soteriology, but in the *"Zwischenbetrachtung"* and *"Einleitung"* he reduces them to the two most rational-consistent ideal types: innerworldly asceticism and otherworldly flight from terrestrial life.[17] Buddhism and Hinduism induce such flight from the world by leading the believer to *unia mystica*, a state in which he possesses the immanent holy through contemplation and thus becomes one with the cosmos. To that end, a certain conduct and attitude is required: detachment, passivity, and ultimate tranquility. This allows the believer to "empty" himself and to become a mere "vessel." Innerworldly asceticism as practiced in Protestantism leads in the opposite direction. Salvation is sought through mastering the world and making oneself into God's "tool." The believer must display God's glory in the world through continuous, methodical work and strict emotional and ethical self-control. One's vocation, therefore, attains religious significance, and success in the realm of the mundane is taken as a sign of salvation.

These diametrically opposed visions of mysticism and asceticism are the outgrowth of two specific paths of redemption rationalized to their extremes. Nevertheless, despite the differences, Weber argues that both evolve out of the same religious urgencies, and that the believer's hunger to be saved, once acted upon in a consistent way, tended to propel religions of salvation to follow three characteristic paths. First, the pursuit of redemption was progressively conceived in *individual* terms. The fate of the sib, clan, or local community could no longer be seen as directly and sufficiently related to that of the individual. Instead of these organic communities, new ones evolved which were founded on shared beliefs and were unfettered by personal commitments; the salvation of the believer—rather than that of the group—was at stake, and this held for the Eastern mystic, as well as for the Puritan.

Hand in hand with this individuation of salvation came the tendency to perceive salvation in terms of the inward, psychological needs of the devotee. The question was how to "put the follower into a *permanent* state which makes him inwardly safe against suffering."[18] To that end, both innerworldly asceticism and otherworldly mysticism freed the believer from dependency upon institutions or collectivities in his search for redemption, and showed how a "holy state" might be attainable solely through the systematization of the individual's conduct. Both Nirvana and methodical work in a vocation proved to be more effective in this respect than, say, occasional acts of good works. However, from Weber's perspective, the Puritan's way seems preferable, since here salvation can be experienced continuously in the totality of the believer's daily life; the mystic's union with God, in contrast, is by its very nature less enduring. This seems to be one reason why Weber, in his effort to redeem the modern individual from the crisis of meaninglessness, took up the Puritan as the paradigmatic figure for his concept of personality. (These issues shall be discussed further in the next section.)

Finally, the sublimation of religions of salvation in the direction of individual, inward needs also brought about the universalization of ethical obligations. The rationalization of faith in a God led to a sense—particularly potent in Christianity—that guilt was the only reasonable explanation for the human condition of misery. However, this recognition of the "natural imperfections of all human doings including one's own" pointed in "the direction of universalist brotherhood, which goes beyond all barriers of societal associations . . ."[19] Yet even in the ethical domain, what is at issue is the *salvation of the devotee,* not the well-being of the person to whom the charitable action is addressed.

Weber identifies in Protestantism a unique ethical conception that evolved out of this concern for the self: the ethic of ultimate ends or of conviction *(Gesinnungsethik)*, wherein the beliefs and intention of the believer, and not the consequences or success of her actions, were taken to be morally relevant. Since the world proved to be too complex, contingent, and uncontrollable, it was too dangerous to make judgments of the believer's conduct and prospects for salvation dependent upon such an environment. When Weber himself explores the options for overcoming the barrenness of significance in a secularized and disenchanted world, he considers how to satisfy inward, individual exigencies, but rejects the ethic of conviction as incompatible with such an undertaking.

~ I HAVE TRIED TO SHOW WHY, by the internal dynamic of the quest for meaning and by its gradual rationalization, salvation religions evolved that tended to have the three characteristics discussed above. But how does this cultivation of the desire for meaning take place? And what are the sources from which new world-views emerge? This is the point where Weber's charismatic leader, or prophet, comes into play. For the prophet, "both life and world, both social and cosmic events, have a certain systematic and coherent meaning, to which man's conduct must be oriented if it is to bring salvation, and after which it must be patterned in an integrally meaningful manner" *("Leben und Welt, die sozialen wie die kosmischen Geschehnisse, haben für den Propheten einen bestimmten systematisch einheitlichen 'Sinn', und das Verhalten der Menschen muß, um ihnen Heil zu bringen, daran orientiert und durch die Beziehung auf ihn einheitlich sinnvoll gestaltet werden")*.[20] The prophet "unlocks" the meaning of the world and opens it to the follower. He molds in some particular fashion the raw and *already present* human desire to make sense of life, but always does so by attempting to establish a comprehensive and consistent outlook on life. However, the prophet pursues this undertaking not through reason, knowledge or priestly teaching— but through the "charisma of illumination."[21]

Indeed, the prophet (and most directly the ethically-oriented one)[22] addresses the deepest set of questions human beings ask about the world and their position in it: Why was I born, why has my life ended up this way, and what will happen to me after I die? His ability (or perhaps presumption) to answer these and other questions is the reason for his allure and power: prophecies which provide spiritual nourishment may have far-reaching consequences for individual conduct and hence for human history as a whole. Rational bureaucracy may change human conduct "from the outside" by imposing certain rules and employing disciplinary methods. Charisma, in contrast, "manifests its revolutionary power from within, from the central *metanoia* (change) of the follower's attitude." It has the potential to be such a disruptive and unpredictable force because "instead of reverence for customs that are ancient and hence sacred, it enforces the inner subjection to the unprecedented and absolutely unique and therefore Divine . . . charisma is indeed the specifically creative revolutionary force of history."[23] Charisma, by speaking directly to the human demand for a world of ethical significance, breaks through the ossification of both traditionalism and bureaucratic rationalism.

The history of humanity, significantly shaped by the prophets and their comprehensive visions, is essentiality tragic. The search for meaning, observes Weber, "tended to progress, step by step, towards an ever-increasing de-valuation of the world."[24] This is true of both otherworldly mysticism and this-worldly asceticism: the former rejects any involvement with the goods of this world as an interruption of the acosmic union; the latter is engaged with the world, but for the sake of God and salvation, not because it values earthly lives in themselves. The outcome of both paths is therefore the ultimate disenchantment with the world and the rejection of any religious significance that may be embedded in it. Hence the dynamic, religious quest for meaning spawned the crisis of meaninglessness in modernity: it undermined itself, and discarded the traditional sources of meaning it helped to generate.[25] Weber believes that this disenchantment of religion set the stage for further disenchantment by the modern natural sciences, especially since the seventeenth century. These sciences explain reality in strictly causal terms within a closed system of the universe—stripping the natural world and humans as part of it from a magical dimension of being and eliminating the possibility of divine intervention (indeed, Deism and the advent of the natural sciences went hand in hand). As the ethic of conviction promised the believer a greater sense of control over her fate and salvation, so the new vision of science promised a sense of control over nature by using rigorously rational methods. In both cases, however, the price was distance from the world and a sense of homelessness that cannot be fully soothed through human action. (As we shall see in the next chapter, a profound sense of homelessness is also at work in Freud's theory.)

Underlying Weber's sociology of religion, then, are certain claims about human beings, particularly that a human being is a desiring *homo-hermeneut.* The crisis of modern culture is multifaceted, but is primarily the result of the impoverishment of the sources of meaning, which came about with the disenchantment and rationalization of the world. Thus, instead of generating meaning by interpreting the cosmos, our age "must rather be in a position to create this meaning itself."[26] Weber remained ambiguous in his political sociology as to whether charismatic political leadership in plebiscitarian democracy may provide a new source of collective meaning;[27] he is more explicit, however, in suggesting that the solution to the crisis of the modern self should be sought for "each person by herself." Weber's concept of personality is designed to address this challenge.

Weber's Concept of "Personality"

The disenchantment of the world, and the nihilistic state of mind which accompanies it, is a unique predicament of modernity, but it is clearly not the only problem faced by the modern self. The loss of horizons of significance coincided, in Weber's view, with other related threats: the growing division of labor and the demand for strict specialization, the dominance of instrumental rationality, the restriction of individual freedom, the impersonalization of human relations, and the conflict among value-spheres. These and other trials of the individual within modern culture seemed especially threatening in the German society of Weber's time, a society that subsequently underwent a failed attempt to adapt itself to modernity. His concept of "personality," which he first develops in *The Protestant Ethic* and adheres to throughout his life, is designed to address this plight of the modern self.[28] During the same period, however, Weber worked on his methodological essays, and his concept of personality bears the traces of these studies as well.

In one of these essays Weber defines the personality as "a concept which entails a constant and intrinsic relation to certain ultimate 'values' or 'meanings' of life, 'values' and 'meanings' which are forged into purposes and thereby translate into rational-teleological action."[29] The personality lives in light of ultimate values that are freely and consciously chosen; it creates a "center" of normative evaluations from which other beliefs and actions proceed. Such a self, of course, is only an option, but for Weber it is by virtue of these qualities that human beings are separated from nature and acquire distinctiveness and respect. "Certainly," he writes, "the dignity of the 'personality' lies in the fact that for it there exist values about which it organizes its life"

"([Und] sicherlich liegt die Würde der 'Persönlichkeit' darin beschlossen, daß es für sie Werte gibt, auf die sie ihr eigenes Leben bezieht").[30] Weber therefore founds his concept of the self upon the same anthropological presupposition that guides his sociology of religion, especially the notion of the individual as *homo-hermeneut*.

Weber's model of the self is based on the notion of a *coherent and intelligible narrative*. Life should not be an ensemble of inconsistent beliefs and unconnected decisions and actions; rather, each life in its totality should unfold from the "inner core" of the individual. This core would render meaning onto particular positions and actions taken in the course of life, since each incident would be part of a greater, continuous story. The personality may maintain its integrity throughout its life only by relentlessly struggling against both external and internal obstacles, by standing for the values it espouses "against the difficulties which life presents."[31] These difficulties, which Weber does not specify, are nevertheless familiar to all: temptations to compromise one's values, periods of self-doubt, insurmountable resistance by others and by objective external conditions, transient passions and desires that may sway a person from a chosen course. Lapses, to be sure, are as inevitable here as in religious worship. But what was true for the Puritan seems to hold for the personality as well. For the former, it was the "constant quality of the personality"—and not its possible occasional transgressions—that revealed its true nature and ethical worth.[32] Similarly, what counts for the personality is whether, in the final account, a common thread of some ultimate values inspired the story it forged out of its life.

In the creation of this narrative, the personality must rely on its will, both in choosing values and in acting consistently upon them. In this respect, Weber's notion of the self has Kantian foundations. For Kant, a "person" is someone who freely and autonomously chooses to follow the categorical imperative dictated by practical reason. Such a self must resist the empirical and natural aspect of humans; otherwise, it may follow contingent desires, or pursue its self-interest and happiness. Weber's concept of personality, at least in his early methodological works, seems also to be dichotomized between consciously chosen beliefs in the light of which the self governs itself, and jumbled decisions and actions not based on any enduring, rationally determined, normative foundation. But Weber departs from Kant in significant ways. The values adhered to by the personality are not simply moral and formal, but, on the contrary, take substantive stands with respect to the most meaningful and essential questions of life. The field of the ethically relevant is extended to encompass a person's entire existence: politics, science, art, and more. Furthermore, while embracing a set of ultimate values, the self does not follow any universal laws; it has to choose among numerous normative positions, steering a course of life that is marked by its aloneness. Consequently, the duties and obligations of the self are not to Humanity (as Kant would have it), but to what it has committed itself to be and do.

If Weber rejects the universality of the self on the one hand, he opposes the notion of the uniquely *given essence* of the self or its indissoluble bond with predetermined collective meta-narratives on the other. In Weber's time, such neo-Romantic conceptions of the self were held by members of the German Historical School. According to Weber, Knies (his former teacher and a member of this school) maintained that "the essence of 'personality' is above all to be an 'entity' . . . [which Knies] immediately transformed into the idea of a naturalistically and organically conceived *'homogeneity.'*"[33] Knies follows the Herderian tradition, suggesting that the self (and the *Volk*) unfolds like an organism from a predestined substance. Weber rejects this idea on the grounds that the self neither has a given essence or truth (except for its *hermeneutical* nature), nor is compelled from within to move in a certain direction. Weber's model is one of self-constitution and self-molding, rather than of the exploration of inner depths and organic growth.

But Weber seems to have taken something from the German Historical School after all. Knies believed that the essence of the personality determines its ethical, economic, religious, political, and social conduct. Weber, as I have pointed out, replaced the given essence with a freely chosen core—but one that nevertheless strives constantly for cohesiveness reflected in all departments of life. He clearly articulates this position in comparing the personality to the Confucian self:

> Genuine prophecy created a way of life from within, one systematically oriented towards a single scale of values; in light of such an orientation, the world is regarded as raw material to be shaped in ethical terms according to the given ideal. Confucianism was the reverse of this: it was an adaptation to external circumstances, to the various conditions in the land of the living. However, the well-adapted man . . . was unable to produce that *striving toward unity from within* which we connect with the concept of personality. Life remained a series of events, not a whole seen methodically in light of transcendent purpose.[34]

The Confucian self, according to Weber, lacked a center. The individual remained fragmented, following given conceptions of what is considered by social conventions to be the proper behavior in each case.[35] His goal was aesthetic: to make himself into a refined person, a work of art of beautiful deeds and articulations. His challenge was to carry himself properly in public and to fulfill the customary obligations towards others, especially parents and superiors. To achieve this, educated literati studied the canon, practiced the accepted manners, and suppressed personal desires. The Chinese, in other words, lost himself in the social world, forgoing any sense of distinct, integrated identity; he negated his selfhood, habituating his person to the traditionalist codes of the surrounding culture. To this type of individual the Western personality seemed barbaric and undisciplined: the Westerner allowed himself to "reveal his inner self in his conduct, gestures and expressions."[36] Furthermore, the personality directed itself to a narrow and specialized end (particularly a vocation), something the well-cultivated, multifaceted Chinese found repugnant. From Weber's depiction of the religions of the East, then, there emerges a common thread: as the Buddhist mystic, in his quest for salvation, emptied himself and strove to become "nothing" (Nirvana), the Confucian, while declining any notion of salvation, lost himself in the social world, forgoing any sense of a distinct and integrated personality.

Underlying Weber's conceptualization of the self is a recurrent dichotomy: on the one hand, there is the self without a center, such as the follower of the Eastern religions (especially Confucianism and Buddhism), the bureaucratic-rational official, or the traditionalist. On the other hand, there is the self that seeks agonistically a clearly demarcated and unified inner core, the Western personality. This core is constructed, as Hennis puts it, "by the fact that such a person is capable of a complete and inwardly motivated personal 'dedication' . . . to a cause (Sache) that transcends individuality."[37] One establishes an enduring sense of distinct selfhood by serving ends that go beyond oneself and hence have less of a fragile and transitory nature. The cause may differ—it may be a religious command, a nation, humanity, or what is vital for the modern self, a specific vocation—but it must in all cases be embraced whole-heartedly, passionately by the individual. Because of this *constituted* individuality and distinctiveness, the Occidental self was able to break through the uniformity of tradition and to pursue "what is peculiar precisely and only to this individual, in opposition to all others." Weber, it seems, believes that only social openness to the assertion of individuality provides the inner motivation to "drag oneself by the forelock from the morass and make oneself into a 'personality.'"[38]

The dedicated service of a cause requires a vigorous, energetic, and methodical-rational type of conduct. The Western ideal is of an engaged self, a "busily active 'personality' relating his activity to a center, be it other-worldly and religious or be it this-worldly."[39] In order to facilitate such conduct, it is necessary that the "totality" of a person's endeavors gain ethical significance. As we saw above, this was precisely the goal of ethical prophets (such as Jesus and Calvin) who wished to secure in the believer a constant feeling of salvation. To that end, the *Gesinnungsethik* was gradually introduced, as well as an ascetic-active way of life. The Buddhist mystic fled from the world, and thus had no use for placing ethical value in the mundane; the Puritan remained in it and could therefore rescue his life from the fear of damnation only by ethically "charging" his everyday activities, by regarding the world "as a raw material to be shaped in ethical terms." This also meant that the individual was formed into a personality only in a *social context*, in which beliefs revealed themselves through one's relations to others: family members, neighbors, friends, and the community as a whole.

The concept of the personality, Weber realized, may have value in contemporary society only if it can be secularized, especially as far as the value and meaning of work is concerned. In *The Protestant Ethic*, Weber argues that work, which lacked any religious significance in Catholicism, became for the Puritan a "calling" or "vocation" (*Berufung*). The Puritan viewed work as the arena in which he must manifest his religious virtue, since "divine providence has prepared for everyone without distinction a particular *calling*, which he must recognize and in which he must work . . . [since it is] a commandment by God to the individual to work to His glory."[40] However, the Puritan was not exclusively concerned with God's glory; he also yearned for the immediate psychological reassurance of eternal salvation. Methodical work in a calling, especially if it brought proof of virtue through material success, fulfilled this need in a permanent present.

But for "us," things are different. "The Puritan wanted to be a man with a calling: we are compelled to be." Yet "the idea of 'duty in one's calling' haunts our present life like the ghost of our former religious beliefs."[41] In modern capitalist and bureaucratic societies, narrow specialization and the renunciation of any hope of overcoming this confinement is the fate of all. Nevertheless, if the "totality" of life is still to have ethical meaning, it must manifest itself in the working lives of modern individuals, not only because they are "forced" to spend their lives in occupational activities, but also because this is the main sphere within which the modern self may establish personal identity and gain a sense of self-worth. In a secularized world, however, turning an occupation into a vocation with ethical import requires at least two conditions. First, the *this-worldly* ultimate values of a person must be related to her vocation, which means that it is the intrinsic qualities of the vocation that matter to the secularized self, and not the symbolic role of work as a tool for salvation. Second, the external conditions of a vocation must allow enough "free space" (not merely in the private sphere!) for the individual to practice and act upon her beliefs. The predicament of the modern, disciplined self fails to fulfill both of these conditions.

The Disciplined Self and the Rights-Protected Space

Weber's delineation of discipline is one of his most important insights into the fate of the modern self. Except for a short chapter dedicated explicitly to this subject,[42] Weber's reflections are scattered throughout his studies; to facilitate my discussion, these need to be grouped together and reconstructed. In order to make manifest the implications of his critique for contemporary social and political thought, I will juxtapose (in a rather schematic fashion) the disciplined self not only with Weber's concept of "personality," but also with its prototype—that is, with the liberal self.

Liberalism, especially in its rights-based variant, introduced the distinction between the public and private spheres, the latter being a space insulated by a cluster of rights in which the individual can foster and practice her notion of the good life without social and state interference. According to Isaiah Berlin's well-known interpretation, the shared and fundamental conviction among the otherwise diverse liberal views that evolved since Occam and Erasmus, and later developed by theorists such as Smith, Mill, Constant, and Paine, is their demand for a "minimum area of personal freedom." Individual rights are designed to protect a *range of possibilities* open to the self, and thus the crucial question is: "What am I free to do or be?". This type of freedom "from," or "negative" liberty, is the mark of "high" civilizations; it originates from "the desire not to be impinged upon, to be left to oneself."[43] In Berlin's view, this desire, as well as the wish to develop one's individuality, is likely to appear only with a certain level of socioeconomic and cultural development. Modernity is not only compatible with greater personal freedom and diversity, therefore, but in fact enhances the demand and provides the necessary external conditions for accomplishing them.

We can see liberalism, at least in its Berlinian interpretation, as demanding that each person will be conceived of as possessing around her a three-dimensional space: physical, emotional, and mental. She is free to the extent that her movements and the uses of her body are not restricted; her attachments to others (or lack thereof) are not imposed upon her or shaped by external institutions in any way, and her thoughts, deliberations, and expressions of views are not interfered with. The fact that none of this is characteristic of contemporary civil society and its occupational structure is taken by liberalism as essentially nonproblematic: it tacitly assumes a dualistic self that is allowed to change identities when moving between the private and public spheres. For Weber, to whom the personality is "a whole," such distinctions are an evasion: the self shaped in the rationalized life-orders is identical to the one that moves within the "insulated" private sphere. Weber's portrayal of the disciplined self therefore offers us an opportunity to examine critically and to contextualize some liberal assumptions about the self and its present circumstances. As we shall see, Weber's critique of modern society implies that in each of the three-dimensional liberal spaces the self is forged and molded by "the outside." This does not mean that he considers insignificant the notion of individual rights and . the political structure that guards them. "It is," Weber writes, "a piece of crude self-deception to think that even the most conservative amongst us could carry on living at all today without [the] achievements from the age of the 'Rights of Man.'"[44] Nevertheless, Weber thinks that rights have limited usefulness as far as the self-formation of identity is concerned.

The disciplined self (that is, the strictly habituated human being such as the soldier, official, or worker) is the mirror image of the personality. Externally, there are some resemblances. Both work methodically on a given task, display control over their emotions, and act in a rational-instrumental manner. This is not surprising, since self-discipline as a personal trait first emerged from monasteries into mundane life with the Protestants. As a strategy of mass control, discipline was perfected in armies governed by Calvinist and Puritan principles and beliefs, such as those of Maurice of the House of Orange and Cromwell. Progressively, however, disciplinary conduct remained, while the internal and personal motivations underlying this type of deportment faded.

The difference between the disciplined self and the personality is thus essentially an *internal* one, and it can perhaps be captured best by the interpretive methodology of *verstehende* sociology. Precisely because from an external-descriptive point of view no fundamental change can be discerned, this science is called for by our time: it inquires into the relation between observed conduct and the motivations behind it, and illuminates the continuous impoverishment in the inner lives of modern selves. Weber's study of "social action," especially in life-orders such as capitalist markets and bureaucracies, reveals a flat and hollow human environment where individuals must adapt themselves to the impersonal demands of their given functions. These functions are determined by the goals of the mass-organization, not by the needs of those embedded within the institution or by the interests of particular persons at its head. For these reasons, as well as because of their sheer magnitude, we can say that modern mass-organizations are highly *anonymous* in nature. Thus, while the Puritan's self-discipline was inspired by God, contemporary discipline is essentially without a "subject," and its maxims are internalized as such. This is crucial for any understanding of the special character of modern discipline. However, before we examine the typical characteristics of this human behavior, its preconditions should be enumerated.

The human deportment that follows disciplinary rules emerged and became widespread throughout the modern institutional matrix because of two important processes. First, "the separation of the warrior from the means of warfare and the concentration of the means of warfare in the hands of the warlord have everywhere been one of the typical bases of mass discipline," explains Weber. "And this has been the case whether the process of separation and concentration was executed in the form of *oikos*, capitalist enterprise or the bureaucratic organization."[45] This concentration of means (of warfare, production, and office) made the individual materially dependent upon the owner. Moreover, it legitimized obedience to imposed regulations of conduct according to the shifting external and functional necessities. (Weber thus agrees with Marx that this process of concentration of means is one of the sources for the enslavement, alienation, and dehumanization of human beings, but sees the sphere of production as just one part of a larger trend.)

Second, the segregation of workplace from home was decisive for the advent of discipline, since sexual and erotic needs no longer interfered with the execution of tasks, and the energies of the individual were at the complete disposal of the organization. Furthermore, this separation allowed for a change in relations of domination, because obedience now followed formal and hierarchical lines instead of patriarchal or feudal ones. The operation was freed from personal commitments and could abide, without disruption, by the standards of efficiency and calculability. Under these conditions disciplinary conduct evolved. Weber defines such conduct as follows:

> The content of discipline is nothing but the consistently rationalized, methodically trained and exact execution of the received order, in which all personal criticism is unconditionally suspended and the actor is unswervingly and exclusively set for carrying out the command. In addition, this conduct under orders is uniform.

> *Sie [die rationale Disziplin] ist inhaltlich nichts anderes als die konsequent rationalisierte, d.h. planvoll eingeschulte, präzise, alle eigene Kritik bedingungslos zurückstellende, Ausführung des empfangenen Befehls, und die unablässige, innere Eingestelltheit ausschließlich auf diesen Zweck. Diesem Merkmal tritt das weitere der Gleichförmigkeit des befohlenen Handelns hinzu.*[46]

The disciplined self, in contrast to the personality, obeys commands that have exterior sources; it is governed by the "outside" rather than by its self-created center. The official is reduced to being "only a single cog in an ever-moving mechanism which prescribes to him an essentially fixed route of march."[47] As such a "cog," he is discouraged from exercising any personal judgment or reflection, especially in matters of substantive values. Even when he is not blindly following given rules, his discernment is restricted to cases requiring calculative, instrumental rationality. Indeed, the type of knowledge accumulated by the disciplined self is concerned with means-ends and costs-effects estimations, as well as with the rules of the system and its modes of operation. To sum, the vision that guides discipline as a technique of control is twofold. First, discipline is devised to achieve the "optimal economy of forces"[48] and the complete utilization of individuals—even of their mental activities. The second, and related goal is to intentionally fashion human beings in a similar manner, to achieve "rationally uniform" conduct that is utterly predictable and therefore efficient. This permits the "mechanism" to continue operating even if the individuals within it are replaced.

Now we can see why the induced uniformity and the utilization of human powers infiltrate each of the liberal rights-protected spaces.

This is manifested, to begin with, in the contrived objectification of the body. The purpose of military drills and training is to achieve homogeneous movements governed by a rationally determined strategy. What made Cromwell's army unique was not its weapons, but "that after the attack they [his soldiers] remained in close formation or immediately realigned themselves." Indeed, "the kind of weapon has been the result and not the cause of discipline."[49] In the factory, however, the type of inner motivations that guided the Puritan soldiers were no longer necessary, since the human body was now called upon to adapt itself to predetermined, objective, and external requirements. In the industrial plant, "the psycho-physical apparatus of man is completely adjusted to the demands of the outer world, the tools, the machines—in short to an individual function." The body is no longer seen as a whole, but as composed of numerous parts, each of which can be manipulated separately; it thus acquires a "new rhythm through a methodical specialization of separately functioning muscles."[50]

The emotional lives of human beings are not exempt from discipline either, contends Weber. The bureaucratic organization operates under the principle of "*sina ira ac studio*. It develops the more perfectly the more the bureaucracy is 'de-humanized,' the more completely it succeeds in eliminating from official business love, hatred and all purely personal, irrational and emotional elements which escape calculation."[51] The Puritan controlled his emotions and his irrational behavior for the sake of salvation; the official is forced to do so by the very rationale of the organization. She is trained to be a contained, unexpressive, and unspontaneous self, and hence capable of being wholly anticipated. This bureaucratic ethic of affective suppression is the complete reversal of the feudal one; the feudalist social structure was grounded in feelings of "purely personal loyalty of the members of the administrative staff."[52] The emotional relationship between lord and vassal was the very foundation of the bond that held the medieval bureaucracy together. For the modern official, however, personal commitments and feelings are taken as irrelevant and disruptive; if any sense of loyalty exists, it is to an impersonal mass-organization. Similarly, the modern military rejects "individual hero-ecstasy or piety" and "spirited enthusiasm of devotion to a leader as a person," and commands instead cool "matter of factness" and a *rational* allegiance of an "objective character."[53] Discipline therefore enhances the powerful disposition of the capitalist market to introduce emotion-free human intercourse.

But it is the standardized employment of human mental and intellectual capacities that most alarmed Weber. The bureaucratic organization cultivates the instrumental and formal rationality of individuals; it is an institution that is blind to personal-distinctive characteristics based on ultimate values, personal experiences and memory, cultural background, and so forth. As noted, modern mass-organizations are guided by the principles of predictability, calculability, and efficiency; these can be followed—ideally—in the same manner by any person. Bureaucratic discipline has a profound leveling effect since it eliminates difference where difference is perhaps most important (that is, in our normative, rational existence), and since it inculcates procedural-universal modes of thought. Weber deemed this habituation of the mind as the most elusive and hence the most dangerous form of discipline, arguing that it is on the rise in modernity because the entire functioning of society depends upon the smooth operation of social institutions. Indeed, the bureaucracy is an "animated machine" *("lebende Maschine")* the product of a "reified intelligence" *("geronnener Geist")*.[54] While Marx was concerned with the relation of the self to its produced object and the subjection of the former to the latter, Weber is concerned with the mental-institutional reality individuals establish, and with the manner in which these individuals subject themselves to the intangible creations of their own powerful minds; doubleness, for Weber, is mainly an antagonism between the instrumental, objectified, and embodied facet of the mind and the value-rational facet of the mind, which guides the personality.

Weber's picture of the self as disciplined in its bodily activity, affective life, and mental functions leads him to use mechanical metaphors repeatedly in reference to the modern self. However, Weber does not seem to view this uniform discipline and the de-assertion of selfhood as simply "imposed" from outside. A closer look at the inner motivations and meanings of the soldier, the worker, and especially the official does not necessarily reveal a coerced individual.

> An official who receives a directive which he considers wrong can and is supposed to object to it. If his superior insists on its execution, *it is his duty and even his honor to carry it out as if it corresponded to his innermost conviction*, and to demonstrate in this fashion that his sense of duty stands above his personal preference . . . This is the ethos of office.
>
> *Ein Beamter, der einen nach seiner Ansicht verkehrten Befehl erhält, kann—und soll—Vorstellungen erheben. Beharrt die vorgesetzte Stelle bei ihrer Anweisung, so ist es nicht nur seine Pflicht, sondern seine Ehre,*

sie so auszuführen, als ob sie seiner eigensten Überzeugung entspräche,
und dadurch zu zeigen: daß sein Amtspflichtgefühl über seiner Eigen-
willigkeit steht . . . So will es der Geist des Amtes.[55]

In contrast to the politician, the official finds his sense of self-worth
precisely in the *renunciation* of his person. His sense of identity is based
upon his ability to internalize and identify with goals that have an
impersonal and anonymous nature for him, and on his willingness to
turn himself into a "tool" of the organization rather than of his own
ultimate beliefs. Weber's account of the official is one of the first depictions of a self that internalizes and acts upon "masterless" maxims and
imperatives, and in this respect it resembles Freud's analysis of morality
and the agency of the superego, as well as Foucault's discussion of
Bentham's Panopticon.

The disciplined self, as I have noted, serves in Weber's thought as the
double of the personality; discipline not only eliminates the possibility
of conducting oneself in light of a freely chosen normative core, but it
even curtails the cultivation of those human potentials that would make
such a project possible in the fist place. Only with Weber's notion of the
personality in mind can we understand his conceptualization of discipline and why he saw it as a "dehumanizing" phenomenon. But if the
personality can be seen as only one variant within the broad spectrum of
liberal notions of the self, its fate in the modern social matrix may be
seen as a generic case that illustrates the failure of liberal theory (especially of its rights-based variant) to take discipline into consideration.
Perhaps most critical in this respect is the assumption of most liberal
theorists, at least since Kant and Mill, that each person is capable of
choosing by herself some notion of the good (or in Weber's formulation, a set of ultimate values). In order to espouse this individual vision
of the good life, the liberal self must have attributes such as experience
in deliberation over matters of values, courage, a sense of independence, and most important perhaps, an inner motivation to embark
upon this liberal project. Yet it is an open question whether the self can
actually be characterized by these attributes, and this question should
be examined within *specific historical and cultural contexts*. As we have seen
above, the official—the predominant disciplined character in contemporary society—is trained to lack all of these qualities, and liberal theorists generally fail to explore the implications of this training for their
view of the self as a free agency capable of normative choices.

Liberalism, however, not only neglects to explore the ways in which
the self is being disciplined and constituted in its daily activities, but

also fails to observe how the domains in which personal visions of the good may have impact are continuously shrinking. The increasing density of bureaucratic regulations, the demand for specialization, and the progressively more impersonal human relations—these and other such factors make the human environment ethically and normatively neutral and immune to any notion of the good. The unwillingness of liberal theories to contextualize the potentials and motivations of the self, is complemented by their reluctance to inquire into what could be called the range of the "space of the good," the extent of those life-domains in which the individual's conception of the good is relevant. (The "personality," of course, wishes that this space would include its entire existence.)

These two shortcomings of liberal theory lead us to the following conclusion. Liberal theorists view our age as one of increasingly pluralistic and unique identities, partly due to the variety of moral alternatives that exist in general, and in concepts of the good life in particular. While to a certain extent this view is accurate, it may also be misleading. Weber's argument shows the crucial aspects in which the socioeconomic orders of modernity operate in the reverse direction, enlarging the domains of uniformity in each self's identity—despite the ever-increasing role of individual rights in contemporary political discourse and practice. It is therefore simplistic and pointless to ask which is on the rise in modern societies: pluralism and difference or homogeneity and sameness; the significant question is their relative weight within the constitution of identities.

The Fragility of Meaning

Can the modern self still find a sense of purpose and value in a world governed by instrumental rationality and the discipline of mass-organizations? Weber's answer is complex. He warns against the anti-rational and aesthetic sources of meaning that are increasingly embraced by modern selves in response to their rationalized environment. Weber believes that a more fruitful response to modernity would be to take on particular types of vocation, ones that may help us overcome the contemporary forces of uniformity and that may also help to secure the collective source of import—culture. This source gains unprecedented importance, since with the disenchantment of the world the self is faced with a new challenge: it must construct this-worldly sources of meaning. According to Weber, this undertaking begins only after we have recognized the unique structural demands made upon the modern self and must involve a conscious, deliberate, and resolute choice among value-spheres. The religious believer was relatively exempt from such choice, but today the individual has to contend with the increasing clash among the life-domains within which meaning may be sought.

> For the rationalization and the conscious sublimation of man's relations to the various spheres of values, external and internal, as well as religious and secular have . . . pressed towards making conscious the *internal and lawful autonomy* of the individual spheres; thereby letting them drift into those tensions which remain hidden to the originally naive relation with the external world.[56]

This well-known sentence from the opening pages of the *"Zwischenbetrachtung"* is followed by a discussion of five value-spheres (the economic, political, aesthetic, erotic, and intellectual-cultural), each of which is examined from the point of view of its incompatibility with the value-sphere of religion (and especially the ethic of brotherly love).[57] The conflict among the value-spheres is inescapable because, as Brubaker says, they are "not created by individuals: they exist independently of and prior to the individuals who participate in them. Value-spheres have an objective existence, based on the objective requirements of particular 'forms of life.'"[58] As such, they provide a preexistent context within which meaning may be generated. As long as Christianity served as an overarching *Weltanschauung*, it provided ways, however tenuous, of reconciling the claims of these different value-spheres. (Like any other religion of salvation, Christianity presupposes that the world can be harmonized into a meaningful totality.) This changed with the process of secularization on the one hand, and the cultivation and increasingly autonomous weight of each sphere on the other, since now even the *hope* for harmonizing the different life-domains had to be relinquished. In order to overcome the likely *internalization* of this extrinsic predicament of conflict, which threatens to leave the self divided and full of inner strife, one must make a decisive choice among the value-spheres.

This recognition by the self that it should espouse a certain value-sphere (and the related choice of a specialized vocation) at the expense of others, calls for a heroic renunciation: not all the possible human goods of this world are open to us, and in order to achieve some we must deliberately and consciously forgo others. Accordingly, one may establish a unified identity and become a personality only by accepting a human condition that is the antipode to the *eudaimonia* of the Aristotelian self. The personality realizes that it cannot pursue within one life span such diverse goods as contemplation and pursuit of culture, active citizenship and political engagement, cultivation of moral virtues, deepening of intimacy and love, and economic well-being. Only by devotion to a particular sphere of activity, and by accepting that sphere's binding norms and practices, may the individual forge a life of enduring significance, if not of true happiness.

Weber rejects otherworldly salvation as a mere chimera, yet he recognizes the exigency behind it and when bidding us to make a choice among value-spheres he searches for this-worldly redemption. Value-spheres (except the economic-instrumental) offer routes to earthly salvation and opportunities for the defeat of meaninglessness, though not every route holds the same prospect for such salvation or serves equally well as grounds for turning oneself into a personality. Despite these differences, they hold something in common that distinguishes them from any concept of salvation within theodicy: because in all spheres the source of meaning is this-worldly, entangled with human affairs and endeavors, it is by its very nature uncertain and contingent. Invariably, the trapped self's existence is accompanied by a heightened awareness that the meaning of its life is, to a certain degree at least, fragile.[59]

The rationalization of religions of salvation, we saw above, was propelled by an attempt to escape exactly this kind of contingency and fragility. By making the ethical conduct of the individual the foundation of salvation, and by introducing a particular type of ethic *(Gesinnungsethik)*, the individual may gain a permanent and secure feeling of salvation. Under the imperative of brotherly love, which most salvation religions hold to, it is the intentions of the believer—and not her actions or their consequences—that are considered religiously relevant. However, since the allure of this highly demanding ethic rests in the inner assurance of the otherworldly salvation it grants, secularized versions of it (such as Kant's) fail to provide sufficient motivation to follow them. While from his Nietzschean philosophical position Weber must accept the *Gesinnungsethik* as a valid possibility, his empirical assessment of human life as highly conflictual[60] implies that this ethic is inadequate for anyone who wishes to live *in* the world and in accordance with "the demand of the day" *("Forderung des Tages").*[61] For while this ethic can no longer generate otherworldly salvation, it jeopardizes the worldly human goods still accessible to the individual.

(In this respect, Weber follows a Western critique of Christianity that goes back to Machiavelli's *Discourses*.)

Eroticism and Art

One of these worldly goods is the realm of erotic relations. These evolve within human civilizations once there is a "gradual turning away from the naive naturalism of sex." Since the Medieval period, sexual relations in the Occident have gradually transcended their reproductive and physical functions, and turned into an erotic bond "raised into the sphere of conscious enjoyment (in the most sublime sense of the term)."[62] Eroticism implies the sublimation of primal desires and emotions, and in general of the irrational aspects of human beings. Because it involves the feeling of the ultimate uniqueness of each person to each other and of their union, this bond is characterized by its exclusive and uncommunicable nature. Furthermore, this "direct fusion of souls to one another," this loss of the self in the singular other, is accompanied by an experience of elation: through erotic love one feels that one adjoins the stream of life, the "kernel of the truly living which is eternally inaccessible to any rational endeavor."[63]

In an age where instrumental and formal rationality reign, the erotic sphere becomes an essential refuge. Erotic relations, in fact, offer "the specific sensation of an *innerworldy salvation* from rationalization."[64] Perhaps more than any other source of meaning, they bring a person to affirm the value of *life itself*. Erotic experience allows one to recover what has been buried by the rationalization of modern culture: the world is reenchanted through the beloved other. The bewitchment of the world, however, also makes this source of meaning highly unstable: ultimately, erotic relations are a passing "euphoria," and their powerful intensity cannot last. (In fact, the sudden absence of love may result in an unprecedented crisis of faith in the value of life.) Hence, the usefulness of the erotic bond in endowing life with significance is rather limited. Weber, however, had additional reasons to criticize a way of life that promotes eroticism as the primary route toward innerworldy salvation: eroticism leads to seclusion and to a life of inaction, which are rebuked by the ascetic. Such a life certainly lacks the type of values that may allow an individual to become a personality.[65]

Another possible source of meaning in Weber's view is art; like eroticism, it "takes over the function of this-worldly salvation."[66] In art, a person can explore her true, authentic self, thus expressing her individuality in the face of a world that rejects it. Art may very well be the realm that most conflates the distance between the self and its vocation (and, more generally, the totality of its life). This explains its great appeal for the self and its emergence as the symbol for the assertion of subjectivity in contemporary culture. Art ceased being "conducive to the community formation"[67] and serving collective goals, but became identified with the individual's needs for inner growth and self-expression. This does not mean that the work of art cannot transcend the subjective. On the contrary, it may communicate emotions, experiences, and a sense of beauty, which can be shared by others—but *qua* individuals, not as a group.

Weber, recognizing the appeal of art as a path for personal fulfillment, maintains that it could be a basis for transforming oneself into a personality. Like the scientist, the artist may become a personality by serving "his cause *(Sache)* and only his cause,"[68] not by turning life itself into a work of art. Moreover, art has advantages over other domains of meaning, since a "work of art which is a genuine 'fulfillment' is never surpassed; it will never be antiqued."[69] The artist, more than the scientist or the politician, may attain immortality. Nevertheless, the artist is not one of Weber's heroes, and one can only speculate why. First, it seems, the artist is not fully engaged with the existing life-orders of modernity, but tends to remain outside of them. Moreover, the aesthetic creation (like the erotic relation) is founded upon the irrational forces of life, which are transitory in nature, both in form and in content. The contemporary artist is guided chiefly by the shifting grounds of the psyche and less by consciously held values. One has little control over these grounds, and consequently the life of the artist cannot be assembled into a meaningful totality; it remains, rather, a composite of fragments governed by an unconscious master.

Redemptive Realism: The Place of Politics and Science in Modernity

There are two other sources of this-worldly meaning discussed by Weber, both of which are essential to his thought and person: politics and science (as reflecting on and contributing to culture). Both of these activities combine self-fulfillment with the engagement of social and collective concerns, the incessant presence of the self with its transcendence; in both vocations personal values are essential since no policy or inquiry can be launched without them, yet these values must be subordinated to the particular ethos of the profession. Both vocations require distance from oneself, because an ability to examine reality objectively is vital for successful political conduct and for worthy research, and while both vocations promise the individual considerable freedom in choosing lines of action or research, it is precisely this freedom that increases the imperative of responsible performance. Now, despite the importance Weber ascribes to politics and science, it should be mentioned from the outset that they cannot wholly satisfy the basic quest of *homo-hermeneut* as presented by Weber in his sociology of religion. The human preoccupation with justice among members of a community, the meaning of bodily and psychological suffering, chance and uncertainty, aging and death—in short, with one's entire fate—cannot be adequately addressed by political ideologies or scientific means. Politics may reduce injustice, but cannot explain why some are more successful and happier in life than others; science may explain why an individual is sick, but cannot give meaning to her misery. Moreover, religions often advanced the idea of compensation either in this life or in afterlife, thus suggesting that even if happiness and well-being elude us at the moment they may still appear in the future. But for Weber, neither politics nor science offers such a state of abundant happiness: they involve personal sacrifices and dutiful responsibility at the present, without the prospect of assured or full compensation in the future. In Weber's thought, tragedy hovers over the modern's existence, since he could not find a genuine solution to the self he believes emerged in the West: a religiously-shaped self devoid of religion.

Nevertheless, Weber does make an attempt to view politics as offering a solution to at least one fundamental question that troubles humans: the meaning of their death. Weber was troubled by Tolstoy's observation, according to which "for civilized man death has no meaning." The continuous and unprecedented advance of culture does not allow any cycle of life to be completed: "there is always a further step ahead of one who stands in the march of progress. And no man who comes to die stands upon the peak which lies in infinity."[70] As we shall see, Weber believed this view is accurate especially in the case of science, where every research question is bound to become anachronistic at some point, and every finding surpassed by subsequent findings. But in this context Weber posits politics in opposition to culture and science. Weber sees politics as a distinct human activity because it involves a struggle for power and the possibility of resorting to violent means; for him, however, this use of force is not merely a necessary evil. For many people who have experienced a war or lost loved ones as a result, national causes and slogans for armed conflict became an empty shell behind which there is only infinite, private sorrow. But Weber claims that only the individual soldier who may die on the battlefield "can *believe* that he knows he is dying for something" *(". . . daß er 'für' etwas stirbt")*.[71] On the loss of his own brother, Karl Weber, in the battlefield, he wrote to his mother that Karl "had a beautiful death in the only place where it is worthy of a human being to be at the moment."[72] While Weber's ardent nationalism surely underlie these perplexing statements, his longing for meaning plays no less an important role. He suggests that war—the characteristic collective practice of the political sphere—is the sole *modern* path for redeeming death from insignificance and arbitrariness, because behind it stands a community (nation or otherwise), a cause that endures in Time and transcends the fetters upon the individual's life span.

But what about politics as a source of meaning in life itself? What about politics as a vocation? Weber sees numerous dangers for the "soul" of a person dedicated to this vocation, since the external-structural conditions of modern politics introduce new "human types" into this sphere. These include those politicians who live "from politics" rather than "for politics," the party bosses and political entrepreneurs who recruit votes merely out of lust for profit and power, and obedient and uninspiring officials both in the state and the party apparatus.[73] Nevertheless, the politician who is able to resist becoming one of these characters is Weber's hero, for she, more than anyone else, may overcome the rule-governed environment and shape the world in the light of her innermost beliefs. These convictions, not merely subjective or individualistic, are social-collective in nature and thus promise effects that will last through time. For example, one may embrace "national, humanitarian, social, ethical, cultural, worldly or religious" causes, all of which are a "matter of faith."[74] Nevertheless, conviction alone is not sufficient for the politician: together with "passion," she must also have "a feeling of responsibility *(Verantwortungsgefühl)* and a sense of proportion *(Augenmaß)*.[75]

The "political personality" thus ought to foster a balance between strongly held beliefs on the one hand and a capacity for cool, distant observation of itself and the world on the other. It should be able to assess external conditions objectively, and then to determine rationally how to advance its causes—or be willing to admit that these causes are unrealistic. For Weber, the responsible politician is a cultural symbol, because she understands that ultimate values can be upheld and acted upon only through negotiation with the rationalized world and its orders. In contrast, the politician who adheres to the ethic of conviction, and strives to realize her ends despite all costs and secondary implications, misconstrues the nature of politics and its special requirements in an age when the political sphere clashes with the religious-moral one.

The responsible politician walks fine lines: between ultimate values, without which politics is only a pointless game of power, and the need to make compromises or even abandon causes too costly to realize; between the imperative to use violence as a constitutive element of politics, and the excessive and unjustified use of such means; between the attempt to express the inner soul in the public arena and the prospect of corrupting the soul because of evil deeds necessitated by circumstances. Perhaps the hardest challenge is to cope with the fact that the "final result of political action often, no, even regularly, stands in completely inadequate and often even paradoxical relation to its original meaning."[76] But it is chiefly in light of these sometimes unexpected and uncontrollable results that the politician is judged. In politics, therefore, the paradox of this-worldly salvation is the greatest. From one perspective, politics offers the person who engages in it the best prospects for redeeming her life from meaninglessness through the struggle to realize ultimate values on the largest possible scale; in politics, an individual may channel her entire existence into the service of supraindividual causes and influence the fate of society and its culture. Yet the inescapable dependency of political endeavors upon the contingencies of the world—a dependency that grows in direct proportion to the scale and importance of the political—makes it a highly fragile source of meaning, especially when the use of violence is involved. In politics salvation and damnation are intertwined, and one can never be certain which will eventually prevail.

There is a natural affinity, according to Weber, between the politician and the cultural scientist. The former aspires to advance the power of the state, especially in a world where great powers are engaged in an imperialist struggle; this political structure, however, is also necessary to preserve and solidify cultures, particularly in an age when the interpenetration of cultures threatens the distinct existence of each one. Weber contends that countries such as Germany are drawn to becoming a *Machtstaat* because they are legitimately interested in guarding their ways of life and traditions. Indeed, he suggests to his fellow Germans that they have a "responsibility before history" (*"unsere Verant-wortung vor der Geschichte"*)[77] to become such a state and to engage in such guarding (in contrast to small countries such as Switzerland, which cannot become the representatives of a major European culture). The scholars, and more generally the intellectuals, are not particularly interested in *Machtpolitik*; but because they are ardent believers in what Weber calls the "specific cultural mission" of the nation, they are obviously inclined towards nationalism and the politics it entails.

"By intellectuals," Weber says, "we understand a group of men who by virtue of their peculiarity have special access to certain achievements considered to be 'cultural values' and who therefore usurp the leadership of a 'cultural community.'"[78] Any person who embraces this-worldly values and constructs a personal *Weltanschauung* does so within a cultural context, since culture is the immense container of meaning.[79] This is why "worldly man has recognized [the] possession of culture as the highest good."[80] Yet only the cultural scientist, the paradigmatic man of culture, has the tools, the skill, the external conditions, and the internal dispositions to cultivate a coherent world-view that relentlessly aspires to be all-encompassing. From this latter vantage point he can grasp the social events, phenomena, processes—which remain obscure and senseless to all around him—within an overall intellectual and normative framework.

The cultural scientist is not only the greatest beneficiary of culture, but also its devoted guardian. Through his studies he contributes to its evolution and vitality. His investigations are designed to answer questions and illuminate problems relevant to his time and society. As researchers, we select "only a *part* of individual reality," a part that "is interesting and *significant* to us, because only it is related to the *cultural values* with which we approach reality" (*"für uns Interesse und Bedeutung hat, weil nur er in Beziehung steht zu den Kulturwertideen, mit welchen wir an die Wirklichkeit herantreten"*).[81] Each scientific endeavor is anchored in a specific cultural context, but is also *individually* formed: it is the "values in the prism of his [the scientist's] mind" that give direction to the investigation and in light of which he determines what is significant. The scholar does not simply grasp the dilemmas and challenges of his age and place, but helps to redefine them. The "values to which the scientific genius relates the object of his inquiry may determine, i.e., decide, the 'conception' of a whole epoch, not only concerning what it regards as 'valuable' but also concerning what is significant or insignificant, 'important' or 'un-important' in the phenomena."[82] The science of culture, then, is such a cherished this-worldly activity because it allows an individual to construct the most comprehensive world-view, to pursue the latter through ascetic work of research, and perhaps even to shape the ideas and deeds of fellow members of society. For Weber, then, engaging in the study of culture is the exemplary way to turn oneself into a personality.

Conclusion

Weber's answer to the crisis of the disenchantment and rationalization of life-orders is the immersion of the self in intersubjective causes and complexes of meaning. Yet this solution ultimately fails because of the unique nature of modern culture: even scientific activity—which is relatively insulated from the contingencies of the world or from the instability of the irrational forces of life—may seem pointless. There are a number of reasons for this predicament. To begin with, the economic rationale that penetrates the university (first in the United States and later in Germany and elsewhere) entails that the prime objective of the profession becomes the training of the workforce needed by the economic-social sphere; with the means of inquiry being concentrated in the hands of the university rather than in those of the individual researcher, there is an increasing drift away from the intellectual-critical role of academic life toward a more functional one. Perhaps even more alarming for Weber are the increasing obstacles the cultural scientist encounters in developing a comprehensive *Weltanschauung* and therefore in adequately answering his calling. (The politician faces the same problem.)

> The perfectibility of the man of culture in principle progresses indefinitely, as do the cultural values. And the segment which the individual and passive recipient or the active co-builder can comprise in the course of a finite life becomes the more trifling the more differentiated and multiplied the cultural values and the goals of self-perfection become. Hence the harnessing of man into this external and internal cosmos of culture can offer the less likelihood that an individual would absorb either culture as a whole or what in any sense is 'essential' in culture . . . It thus becomes less and less likely that 'culture' and the striving for culture can have any inner-worldly meaning for the individual.[83]

The expansion, production, and progression of modern culture are so immense that no person is able to absorb and integrate this culture into his being. It becomes impossible to establish world-views that will not be composed of small and somewhat *arbitrary* segments of the cultural cosmos, or even to make sense of the constant change. Certainly, a strict specialist, as Weber thought any scientist ought to be, cannot achieve such a goal. Weber must have realized, but could not admit, that while scientific endeavor demands strict specialization, it depends nevertheless upon a much wider understanding of social conditions: only on the basis of such an understanding can the scholar frame significant questions. Moreover, the scholar's "findings" are not likely to have lasting effect, given the dynamic changing of society (that would render these findings irrelevant), as well as the proliferation of knowledge (that would render them anachronistic). From both ends, then—from his diminishing ability to construct an inclusive world-view and therefore to ask questions that are significant for his culture, and from the questionable endurance and relevance of his research—the scientist has to combat the futility of his vocation. Finally, Weberian logic points to the tapering of the academic community—without which research remains a cloistered task without an addressee. The narrow specialization of modern science results in the formation of multiple academic communities that become ever smaller, ones that find it difficult to share their research interests and conceptual language with other communities. The cultural scientist, the prototype of the *Kulturmensch*, is therefore a tragic hero; indeed, "the advancement of cultural values appears the more meaningless the more it is made a holy task, a 'calling.'"[84]

The cultural scientist exemplifies the modern paradox of meaning: an investigator of the colonialization of social life by instrumental and economic maxims, he is nevertheless the prototype of the Occidental self because of his heightened quest for meaning. By studying how meaning flees from the world, both in the natural and social realms, Weber grappled with what he thought was the most crucial question of his age, while at the same time inquiring into the foundations and prospects of his own vocation. Like the politician, Weber's cultural scientist has a distinct ethos and responsibility: he must illuminate the predicament of his culture, point to its pressing dilemmas without endangering the objectivity of his own research. But with his diminishing ability to do so, the greatest danger commences—not simply the disenchantment of the world or the increasing rationalization of life-orders, *but the disappearance of the consciousness that perceives this predicament as problematic.* Furthermore, since Weber believes that any objective inquiry must commence from questions that are related to the values of the researcher himself, we can say that he positioned himself in a singular temporal juncture. On the one hand, many of his studies examine how a self such as himself—one that strives for meaningful existence in this (academic) world—was constructed in the midst of the religious history of the West. On the other hand, the same researcher who narrated this (self-) construction also inquires how contemporary social institutions—including the universities—are becoming ones that form new types of selves, for whom "personalities" like Weber are incomprehensible. In his work, the history of the Western self is at odds with its present, the *homo-hermeneut* that was gradually cultivated by this history beholds its hollow contender. It is not clear from Weber's writings how he thought this struggle would evolve, since the complexity of his account of the self (which couples this self's hermeneutical essentialism with its equally baffling malleability) leaves open the question of whether full and unchallenged adaptability of individuals to modern social institutions is possible.

To conclude, then, in Weber the conflict between self and civilization is formulated in a new way, acquiring a new intensity. On the one hand, Weber radicalizes the view of hyper-order theorists by suggesting that in modernity instrumental rationality, calculability, rule-governed conduct—in short, systematic order—take hold over increasing domains of life, from the *Betrieb* called the state to the account books at the factory, from the composition of music to modes of legal arbitration. Modern organizations and offices epitomize this quest for order. Referring to his fellow Germans' admiration of bureaucracy, he says it is "as if we were deliberately to become men who need 'order' and nothing but order, who become nervous and cowardly if for one moment this order wavers, and helpless if they are taken away from their total incorporation in it." Men and women are supple "cogs" who only aspire to become bigger cogs in a machinery (or double) that they themselves have created; this machine utilizes their skills and energy by disciplining their bodies, emotions, and minds, while operating completely "soullessly."[85] What makes this predicament especially tragic is that the modern order is diametrically opposed to the deepest spiritual and existential needs of the self as they evolved in the West (evolution that is both part of a continuous progression of the Judeo-Christian tradition and the upshot of unexpected religious developments within this tradition, such as Protestantism). In the West, the essentialist desire of *homo-hermeneut* to overcome senselessness was combined with specific historical developments within theology that eventually led the self to search for an all-engulfing, systematically explicable, innerworldly sense of meaning. The tension between the personality that was formed in this journey and longs for meaning in the totality of its life, and a world that is increasingly concerned with smooth and predictable fulfillment of functions wholly indifferent to such human import, is the main reason for Weber's view of modernity as a stymieing trap. Part of what makes him one of the most respected thinkers of the twentieth century is that he combined the verve in criticizing the normalizing practices and ethos of modernity with a sober and steadfast refusal to outline an escape from its grip.

~ 4

Freud and the Castration of the Modern

I T IS HARD TO THINK OF TWO contemporaneous authors who differ as much as Weber and Freud. They seem, in fact, to pose a fundamental threat to one another, given their diametrically opposed views of human agency: while the Weberian "personality" is ruled by a desire for meaning, the psychoanalytic self is motivated, at least in its original constitution, by instincts that struggle for "discharge" and are oblivious to meaning. The personality, as we have seen, is characterized by its capacity to consciously choose ultimate values and by its relentless effort to act upon them in the world; Freud questions the autonomy of consciousness in relation to other psychic systems, as well as the notion of free will and the motivations for embracing particular ethical ideas. Weber, who had read some of Freud's works, was aware of the challenge psychoanalysis posed to his views; he recognized that the theory and the treatment it recommends could endanger the future of normative discourse. Weber claims that while "Freudian therapy is simply a revival of *confession* with somewhat different techniques," Freud neutralized from this religious practice any moral significance and instead invented a novel type of self-indulgence. "Someone who is deceiving himself and wants to deceive himself," writes Weber, "and who has learned to shut from his memory those things in his life which he has to be ashamed of . . . is not going to be helped *ethically* by lying for months on end on Freud's couch and allowing 'infantile' or other shameful experiences which he has 'repressed' to be called to consciousness."[1]

Weber acknowledges that psychoanalytic therapy might help a person from what he calls a "nervous hygienic" point of view (by curing hysteria, for example). But he is alarmed by the possible transformation of value systems that the new discipline could inaugurate in society. If mental health were to become the prime value, would there still be a place for a "'heroic' ethic," one that demands "man's endless *striving*"?[2] If Freudians were to follow Otto Gross, they would recommend the avoidance of any sacrificial deeds, since renunciation of instinctual satisfaction could bring about repression and neurosis, and events such as war could result in trauma and permanent anxiety. Weber recognizes that Freud himself is careful not to associate psychoanalysis with any particular normative *Weltanschauung.*[3] Yet psychoanalytic treatment steers the self *inward*, the latter's heroism consisting in its pursuit of self-knowledge and its struggle with unconscious psychic forces; the personality is oriented *outward*, actively engaged in collective projects, and it is measured by its willingness to adhere steadfastly to its values. It is therefore surprising that despite these profound differences, Weber and Freud share an earnest, critical attitude toward modernity: both believe that the institutions of contemporary society impose escalating demands for normalization and eradication of individuality, and that their age is witnessing the inescapable frustration of fundamental human needs—whether defined by hermeneutical or instinctual presuppositions. Notwithstanding this critique of modernity, both theorists adamantly refuse to view the entrapment of the self as legitimizing radical, collective political solutions.

The aim of this chapter is to explore the Freudian conception of entrapment and thereby to juxtapose the "psychological iron cage" with the disciplining, meaning-free social universe of Weber. I begin by expounding upon the Freudian critique of social institutions in general and of bourgeois culture in particular. This critique is based on Freud's theory of instincts and the economy of their distribution: he criticizes bourgeois society for employing human instincts in optimizing productivity, predictability, and security—for preferring the good of humanity as a whole over the individual's well-being. This gradual domination of the interests of the collective is reflected in the overrestrictive and hypocritical sexual mores of bourgeois culture, and in the empty universalization of ethical commitments among the members of civil society. Modernity, then, is the age when historical processes of normalization have been intensified, and, as a result, neuroses such as narcissism, melancholia, masochism, and hysteria are mushrooming. From this perspective, Freud views modernity as differing from other epochs simply in the quantitative degree of instinctual repression. Most of Freud's interpreters take this economic approach[4]—which centers on the forces and mechanisms at work in the system unconscious—as the heart of Freud's social-political critique of modernity.

The interpretation suggested here goes beyond this reading. In the second part of the chapter, I shall argue that implicit in Freud's writings there is a view of modernity as begetting a new type of trap for the self: he regards the modern self's plight as especially dire because it experiences an uncanny *(unheimlich)* mode of being. By this mode I mean an eerie encounter with tradition and the repressed memories associated with its formation, an encounter that leads moderns to question both the contents of and sacrifices demanded by their revered myths, customs, and practices, their ideals of the good and the moral. According to Freud, moderns suspect that these are merely external impositions, the introjected voice of society within as embodied in the superego; they develop an experience of estrangement from the contents of their own beings. More specifically, Freud depicts modern selves as facing a unique trial of homelessness because they have become homeless in their own home(s): neither their individual minds nor their culture promises a sense of belonging or a ground. It is argued below that Freud believes this predicament to be unprecedented, despite the fact that he most often presents the superego in universal and atemporal terms. For Freud, certain characteristics of the superego remain constant in all cultures and at all times: it is always instituted in the mind at an early stage of childhood, it is always the fruition of a psychosexual dynamic within the family, it always employs the energy of the death instinct, and it always fulfills similar functions, such as prescribing ethical norms, judging conduct, and inflicting guilt. Nevertheless, Freud seems to be suggesting that modernity is a unique epoch, *wherein the normalization induced by the super-ego has intensified to an unprecedented degree, while its hold on the self has become fragile and its position is no longer taken as "natural."* I shall argue further that Freud feared that such selves, being aware of their homelessness, would become semipsychotic, rejecting their superegos and normative attachments to society; indeed, World War I, which entangled Europe in a dance of destruction, exemplified for Freud exactly such a rejection and rebellion against modernity. Yet Freud did not believe that we could go back in time to a state of naive embeddedness in tradition nor that we could silence the friction between self and society. His position could be characterized as a unique type of communitarianism, one that calls on moderns not only to accept their inherited norms and notions of the good, but also to recognize that these should be regarded ambivalently, as an intrusion and not simply as a given of their own identities.

In the third part of this chapter, I explore Freud's response to the threat of psychic disintegration in modernity and his rejection of the possibility that moderns shall expel the superego from their mental makeup. This position, I will argue below, is implied in Freud's psychology of the self—especially in his theory of the Oedipus complex. The complex breeds a new psychic agency, the superego, which thereafter represents social demands for conformity and decisively limits the freedom of self-formation. The superego has the essential role of directing, motivating, inhibiting, and censuring the individual according to imposed expectations and prohibitions; the Oedipus complex, in fact, could be seen as a generic narrative that defines normalcy in terms of the symbolic subordination of the ego to the superego, and of the self to its civilization. More precisely, while Freud condemns certain aspects of modern civilization, *his psychology of the self categorizes the escapes from its grip as pathology.* Freud, in other words, does not share the prevalent anticipation of nineteenth-century theorists for a radical (social and individual) metamorphosis: he insists that we should, in principle, embrace social reality and its effects upon the individual, that we should help the self adapt to its communal circumstances rather than shape them anew.

In order to demonstrate the novelty of this view, then, it is essential to examine Freud's position in the intellectual context he was writing—especially in comparison to the claims of his two famous predecessors, Nietzsche and Marx. First, Freud presents as mentally dangerous and socially destructive those attempts to liberate the self by eliminating its historically constructed duality and by overcoming inner aggression. In contrast to Nietzsche, Freud believes that the self must contain ongoing contention and rift, must accept the sea of negative and devitalizing feelings such as guilt, shame, and contrition—and must amplify the voices of anonymous others within. Second, Freud spurns notions of society as an intersubjective domain where individuals recognize their common humanity and become liberated by interacting with each other on the basis of their self-determined and rational values. In contrast to Marx (and the tradition that began with Rousseau), Freud insists that human beings harbor constitutional forces that mar solidarity and fracture communication: social intercourse is colored by pervasive rivalry, hostility, and frustration—and the attempt to eradicate these feelings is even more dangerous than their contained presence. While Nietzsche and Marx viewed their age as deeply distorted and inimical to the self, they still perceived an opening for a radical transfiguration of individual and/or communal existence. These harsh critics of the bourgeois order and culture nevertheless celebrated modernity too, because they believed this epoch could be *eclipsed*, because they divined a flight from the present configuration into a future situation promising a wholeness of being. Freud's theory of the self introduces a different view, a new historical imagination that under-scores the immanent and embedded nature of human existence, the inability to defeat normalization, and the imperative of coping with this unhappy predicament.

While exploring the shift in historical-political imagination between Marx and Nietzsche on the one hand and Freud on the other, the third part of the chapter questions the prevailing view of the Freudian critique of modernity as simply an application of the insights gained through the psychoanalytic study of the self. According to the latter interpretation, Freud initially developed notions such as the instincts, repression, and the superego (or conscience) in order to explain the psychic apparatus; only gradually did he apply these concepts to the study of society, since he realized that the individual cannot be understood without reference to a historical context and that methodological individualism is flawed. There is a chronological basis for this claim, since Freud wrote his main sociopolitical writings rather late in life, after the bulk of his conceptual innovations had been established. (For example, "Civilization and Its Discontents" was published in 1930; "The Future of an Illusion" in 1927; and "Group Psychology" in 1920. "Totem and Taboo," published in 1913, is an exception, but its subject is not modernity.) Most of Freud's interpreters differ only in their valuation of this extension from micro to macro: while some view it as deepening our understanding of phenomena such as leadership and political order, others are more skeptical, seeing this extension as specu-lative and not sufficiently coherent.[5]

Yet this line of interpretation is incomplete. If we accept Freud's claim (see below) that political philosophy must be based on sound psychol-ogy, then the picture of the self that Freud advances even in his early works (where he inaugurates the notions of the Oedipus complex and autoerotic stages) contrasts with and has bearing upon fundamental ideas of nineteenth-century models of the self in the sociopolitical context. Rather than perceiving the social critique in Freud's work as simply an extension of his psychology of the self and as a secondary, speculative addition to the main body of his work, I would like to show that his conception of the self is already an event in the historical context of such critiques, since Freud redefines the relation between the self and (modern) civilization. To be sure, Freud intended his theory of the self and its psychosexual development to be a universal and a historical narrative of individual growth; nevertheless, this narrative could also be perceived as a parable about collective maturity, about moderns being summoned to shun their illusions of transcendence.

Two further, introductory points: The themes of homelessness and psychic subjection to civilization discussed below illuminate an essential aspect of entrapment in modernity. For Weber, as we saw in the preceding chapter, culture was the essential container of values, of patterns of life, of accumulated human experience; submersion within it allowed an individual to rationally construct a meaningful course of life and to find a haven from disciplinary institutions. But Freud depicts culture as imperious to and virulent toward the self; he fosters the distance and skepticism of the self toward the past it bears and the shared understandings of its community. Weber heralded the disenchantment of the world, the present discomfort of humans in what was once an orchestrated, interwoven cosmos; Freud extends this theme of homelessness, stripping the self of what Weber thought were the last anchors and refuges of belonging. In seeking to fathom the predicament of the modern self, then, we must explore both the Weberian and Freudian understandings of estrangement within spheres of normalization, since each presents only one aspect of the trapped self's dilemmas and challenges.

Finally, a clarification of intent: The scientific validity of psychoanalysis is not at issue here, in contrast to much of the current literature.[6] My critique of Freud rests not only upon the understanding that normative presuppositions are inescapable in the social and human sciences,[7] but also upon the conviction that it is necessary to read these presuppositions in their historical-political context. Needless to say, Freud never suggests that his theories of the self and society reflect a particular historical horizon or that they rely on an unarticulated background of normative judgments. But as a science and therapy whose subject is human beings, psychoanalysis inevitably contains valuations about the desired psychic state of the self and the latter's proper relation to social reality. These preferences and convictions are reflected both in the selection of facts, of what is considered relevant and irrelevant, and in the construction and internal organization of the theory. This study seeks to go beyond Freud, while remaining faithful to him—to uncover the normative presuppositions of psychoanalysis and to show how they express the entrapment imagination.

Freud's Theory of Instincts and the Origins of Discontent

Freud (similarly to Weber) grounds his discontent with modernity in a view about the predispositions, needs, and potentials of the self. Freud holds a semi-biological conviction, according to which instincts are central to human motivation, conduct, and being; his observation that there is a "hostility" between humans and their civilization rests on the claim that "civilization is built upon a renunciation of instinct."[8] In each person's development and in civilization's advent as a whole, these "powerful" instincts undergo repression, diversion, and sublimation, and the self that emerges is increasingly alienated from its organic constitution. Although Freud's theory of anthropological-historical development, which is based on the economy and vicissitudes of instincts, cannot be compared to complex and rich theories such as those of Hegel or Marx, he does put forward an original perspective. Moreover, one must grasp his picture of the dynamics between instincts and civilization in order to penetrate the far more interesting aspects of his thought: his critique of modern self and culture.

The Freudian instinct should be viewed in the context of a Western, mechanistic conception of human beings first suggested in the seventeenth century. Writers such as Descartes, Gassendi, Boyle, Borelli, and Hobbes advanced a physiological theory that presented the self as willing and acting only in response to immediate and disconnected stimuli stemming from the internal flow of material particles, such as "blood and animal spirits."[9] This involuntary vision is echoed in Freud's definition of the instinct *(Trieb)* as "a concept on the frontier between the mental and the somatic, as within the organism and reaching the mind, as a measure of the demand made upon the mind for work in consequence of its connection with the body."[10] The instinct, which may originate in various bodily organs, is experienced by the mind as an "excitation" that requires some type of *activity* to alleviate the inner tension it has established. The self cannot flee these excitations, as it can flee external sources of tension, threats, demands—sources of displeasure. "Toward the inside," writes Freud, "there can be no . . . shield."[11]

Yet if an instinct commands irresistible activity, the specific nature of this activity is undetermined. The Freudian instinct has two important characteristics: irresistibility and high fluidity. In *Three Essays on Sexuality* (1905), Freud distinguishes between the source, aim, and object of an instinct, showing that while the first may be relatively fixed, the last two are susceptible to complex vicissitudes. For example, while the original aim of an instinct may be a discharge of aggression on an external object (sadism), this object may be displaced by one's own body (masochism). The aim of an instinct may undergo more radical alterations. Relief from an internal stimulus can be obtained through a sublimated expression, such as work, or it can be denied discharge altogether, in which case repression would follow. Freud's theory of instincts went through some significant changes. He first distinguished between sexual and ego instincts, then suggested the existence of only one instinct, and finally introduced in *Beyond the Pleasure Principle* (1920) a new pair, Eros and Death. This late theory serves as the primary basis of his social critique in "Civilization and Its Discontents" (1930).

The formation of civilization, argues Freud, is based on the utilization of instincts. The development of social institutions, systems of production, arts and sciences should be explained through biological-psychological categories. The energy (libido) of the instinct Eros obeys an economy of a zero-sum game, and the significant question historically has been the relative distribution of this fluid energy. Eros is first oriented toward unspecified, immediate sexual discharge that is not loaded with emotions and commitments. But desire sets in motion a mechanism that is self-defeating. From the point of view of phylogenesis, this self-defeat began with the onset of civilization: the brothers, speculates Freud in *Totem and Taboo* (1912), murdered their father and entered into a semicontractual association in order to achieve access to women and instinctual satisfaction; their sexual desire forced them to invent morality and an enduring collective organization. However, once the germ of civilization was established, society became a distinct entity with its own interests. Communal goals often contradict the wishes of individuals, who are gradually forced to divert their libido into conquering nature and producing wealth. To ensure its continued success and to maintain its existing achievements, society progressively introduces more restrictive and universal norms.

According to Freud, then, constraints on sexuality and immediate physical pleasure without commitment opened the way for the dual sublimation of Eros. First, this instinct is utilized for labor and cultural production; it provides the energy both for physical and mental work and for the cultivation of complex human capabilities. This means that Eros undergoes a temporal transformation, since instead of seeking immediate satisfaction it serves deferred satisfaction and the long-term perspective required of both the individual and the group. Freud sees this generation of civilization through continuous and prolonged exertion not as historically contingent, but rather as a necessity that springs from biological and psychic needs. In "On Narcissism" (1914), Freud quotes Heine: "Illness was no doubt the final cause of the whole urge to create. By creating I would recover; by creating I became healthy."[12] Freud concurs: internal tension caused by the sexual instinct compels humans to reach beyond themselves,[13] to create, not only through love and biological reproduction, but also through begetting the social. (This latter theme becomes more prominent with the introduction of Eros instead of the sexual instinct *per se*.) While originally humans were not engrossed in the establishment of the social world, they are progressively forced to become so. The formation of the first social organization by the brothers instituted a new dialectic: normative prohibitions propel humans to discharge their Eros through economic and cultural production, yet this process generates more mutual dependency and hence new prohibitions, which, in turn, call for an even greater discharge through sublimation. Because of the irresistible and fluid qualities of instincts, then, the construction and cultivation of civilization becomes an *internal compulsion*, a last resort for avoiding sickness and insanity after the purely sexual channels for expressing Eros have been blocked.

Second, Eros is sublimated into universal love or affection. In higher forms of civilization, Freud suggests, people are disposed to see any other person as an object that concerns them and deserves their empathy. In such societies, exclusivity is displaced by the flattening of human relations, differences in the attachment to others is displaced by general affability. The spirit characteristic of commercial society—where trade and common economic projects necessitate cooperation and trust among strangers—could not have been sustained without a redistribution of libidinal energy and an enlargement of object-relations. According to Freud, the utilization of Eros to extend human libidinal bounds cements the social matrix in ways that shared norms and interests cannot: the foundation of order is sexual. But Freud believes that our instincts can only be manipulated to a degree. While Eros can be diverted and sublimated, another part of this instinct is inescapably repressed. Freud's theory of instincts seeks a delicate and somewhat elusive balance, recognizing the extreme malleability of the self but at the same time its inescapable constitution; ultimately, he suggests, a full and satisfactory sexual life cannot be dispensed with without a price. Despite the flexible quality of Eros, then, history for Freud is a narrative of denied wishes and of sacrifices, of growing distance from our bodies and psyches, and of the increasing loneliness of the individual submerged in the expanding ocean of universalism.[14]

The repression and forced rechanneling of Eros is one reason for *das Unbehagen in der Kultur.* The other reason is the fate of the Death instinct. Despite the bonds established by Eros, the social order contains catastrophic and unruly forces. "Besides the instinct to preserve living substance and to join it into ever larger units [Eros], there must exist another, contrary instinct [Death] seeking to dissolve those units and to bring them back to their primeval inorganic state" "*(es müsse außer dem Trieb, die lebende Substanz zu erhalten und zu immer größeren Einheiten zusammenzufassen* [Eros], *einen anderen, ihm gegensätzlichen geben* [Death], *der diese Einheiten aufzulösen und in den uranfänglichen, anorganischen Zustand zurückzuführen strebe)*".[15] The Death instinct is marked by a "compulsion to repeat," to return to its original state of nothingness, and hence there is an inexorable conflict between union and dissolution in human life, between forming more complex social organizations and returning to a parochial, unregulated condition. In combating the Death instinct, the community establishes legal and coercive means, defines the legitimate occasions and goals for using them, and ensures that humans will not destroy what they have accomplished collectively throughout the ages. But these external mechanisms of control are insufficient. Freud suggests two other strategies employed by society to control the Death instinct. First, this instinct undergoes sublimation, so it can be expressed externally in civil society.[16] The human predisposition toward aggression is channeled into constructive paths, in addition to less benign outlets such as conflicts among nations. Aggression in the sphere of civil society can be beneficial if translated into competition in the market, arts, and sciences; civilization fosters the displacement of the physical struggle for domination by a monitored rivalry that promotes collective progress. From a psychoanalytic perspective, it is no accident that the increasing curtailment of overt aggression in human relations (whether in deeds or in words) coincided with the penetration of *competition* as the fundamental, regulative maxim of our collective institutions.

A second strategy of defense is even more important: society protects itself against the Death instinct by a dialectical psychic mechanism that directs the belligerent acts of the individual against him or herself. Freud seems to agree with Nietzsche's well-known claim that "all instincts which are not discharged outwardly *turn inward,*" and that in the course of civilization "those instincts of the wild, free, roving man were turned backwards, *against man himself.*"[17] For Freud, the potentially destructive Death instinct is transformed into a vehicle of civilization; it governs humans internally and represents the collective

interest in obedience and civility. To make the political order less vulnerable to human passions, there has to be a shift in the balance
between sociopolitical and psychopolitical coercion, between overt and
covert sanctions. "It is in keeping with the course of human development," writes Freud, "that external coercion gradually becomes internalized" (". . . daß äußerer Zwang allmählich verinnerlicht wird").[18]

As we shall see below, the outcome of the Oedipus complex (both
collectively and individually) is the institution of the superego, a psychic
agency characterized by its imposition of moral imperatives upon the
ego and by its harsh internal policing of possible transgressions,
whether in thought or action. While the contents of the superego are
variable and culture-specific, the means for imposing them is uniform:
the antagonistic energy of the Death instinct. "The institution of the
super-ego," writes Freud, "introduces a garrison, as it were, into
regions that are inclined to rebellion" ("Die Einsetzung des über-Ich . . .
bringt gleichsam eine Besatzung in die zum Aufruhr geneigte Stätte").[19] In
the course of history, this "garrison" becomes increasingly armed and
watchful, so that "the price we pay for our advance in civilization is a
loss of happiness through the heightening of the sense of guilt
(Schuld)."[20] Freud deems this price indispensable. The "strengthening
of the super-ego is a most precious cultural asset in the psychological
field," he writes. "Those in whom it has taken place are turned from
being opponents of civilization into being its vehicles."[21] Yet despite
this psychic mechanism, Freud remains leery. He sees an endless interplay of Death and Eros: the progressive, human odyssey within time is
highly fragile, and primitive existence is not only something of the past,
but something that could lurk in the future. The notion of the Death
instinct and its possible circularity betray Freud's post-teleological
uncertainty about the direction of history. "In consequence of [the] . . .
primary mutual hostility of human beings," he writes, "civilized society
is perpetually threatened with disintegration."[22]

While the metapsychological theory of instincts is central to psychoanalysis and to Freud's critique of modernity, it is rather speculative in
nature; psychic instincts, after all, are not subject to empirical observation and verification. Freud acknowledges this problem. "The theory of
instincts," he writes, "is so to say our mythology."[23] Like any other
mythology, it is evaluated by the insights it provides about the human
psyche and social behavior, not by its empirical status. Freud often seeks
to support his mythology with selected excerpts from other sources,
such as philosophy, poetry, and, of course, Greek mythology and plays.
In order to reinforce the plausibility of his (final) theory of instincts,

Freud cites, on different occasions, two very distant philosophers, Plato and Schopenhauer; this mixture of epochs gives the theory an apparently universal, timeless standing.[24] Whether or not this is so, by elaborating the early modern, mechanistic conception of human beings, the theory of instincts introduces innovative concepts and mechanisms for explaining the dehumanizing process that preoccupied proto-entrapment writers. Freud presents human beings as obeying an economy that makes them into internally forced, regretful creators of the social. While recognizing the possibility of catastrophic reversal, Freud does not attribute the erection of the overcivilized state to any contingent, historical factor; in contrast to the prevalent belief of the nineteenth century, he argues that human discontent is intrinsic to life in a social order *as such*.

My aim in this chapter, however, is to go beyond the common perception of Freud's sociopolitical critique of modernity and of the place repression occupies in this critique. Although Freud believes that modern social institutions induce an especially high level of instinctual inhibition, he downplays qualitative differences in this process across both time and place. The unique challenge to moderns according to the Freudian vista, I would like to suggest, is not the need to contain the misery of repression *per se*; rather, it is the far more difficult task of *deliberately accepting* and *ingeniously coping* with their homeless mode of being and imposed social selves. I open the discussion by examining Freud's well-known essay "The Uncanny," an essay whose import for the self-civilization relation in Freud is most often neglected.

Modernity and *das Unheimliche*

Human history, Freud is reported to have said during a discussion on Marx at the Vienna Psychoanalytic Society (1909), contains a paradox. "On the one hand, it is a question of an enlargement of the consciousness of mankind (analogous to the coming into consciousness of instincts and forces hitherto operating unconsciously); on the other hand, progress can be described as a repression that progresses over centuries." When placed next to each other, continues Freud, "these two characteristics seem to be entirely contradictory to each other, for with the progress of repression, more and more should become unconscious, and not the other way around. But then comes the liberating thought that these two processes are the condition for each other: *the enlargement of consciousness is what enables mankind to cope with life in the face of the steady progress of repression."*[25] Modernity in general, and Freud's day in particular, present an unprecedented challenge for the self: on the one hand, the self recognizes itself as repressed and neurotic, as estranged from powerful and unconscious regions within its own mind; on the other, its heroism consists precisely in the ability to grasp through reflection the inevitability of this predicament. Freud, in other words, professes that the modern self is called to embrace what could be termed a state of psychic homelessness.

Homelessness has been commonly understood as a condition wherein one does not feel belonging either to a dwelling place or a geographic location—in short, to a spot on the earth. The dynamic pace of modern life, in particular, creates selves that have numerous "homes" in the course of their lives but not a "Home"; we have become, in Agnes Heller's words, "geographically promiscuous."[26] Others have extended the theme of homelessness, arguing that the homeless person is one who feels distanced from the norms, habits, memories, foods, music, and other elements of the surrounding culture. Such a person stands outside her milieu, hearing herself think and talk even if she has mastered the native language; she is damned by a continuous need for translation in the most taken-for-granted spheres of existence. Still others have gone a step further, suggesting that homelessness refers to our relation to the entire cosmos, to our estrangement from a disenchanted and objectified nature that we can conceptualize well—but are unable to relate to without rational mediation. But Freud adds perhaps the most interesting aspect of homelessness in modernity: he drives this theme to its ultimate conclusion by suggesting that even the individual's own mind and his/her native tradition cannot be genuine homes; in modernity, he seems to be claiming, both inner and outer modes of being are permeated with feelings of not belonging.

"Nothing [more] . . . is meant by our talk about uncanniness," writes Heidegger, than the "existential 'mode' of the *'not at home.'*"[27] Although Freud does not make such an explicit statement, his discussion in "The Uncanny" [*"Das Unheimliche"* (1919)] leads to the same conclusion. Freud begins his discussion in "The Uncanny" by suggesting that *das Unheimliche* "is that class of the frightening which leads back to what is known of old and long familiar."[28] This interpretation seems at first contradictory: how can something with which we are well acquainted be transformed into a cause for terror? In its common usage, the word "uncanny" is employed when we feel uneasy and bewildered because we have encountered something foreign, eerie, incomprehensible. But Freud claims etymological justification for his twist of the prevalent understanding of *das Unheimliche*.

Normally, the word *heimlich* is associated with what is homelike and thus safe, expected, agreeable, and intimate. Home is not only an environment to which we are well accustomed, but also one that allows us to get reacquainted with ourselves, a place where inner and outer familiarity reinforce one another; it is therefore the ultimate metaphor of belonging. Yet home, or hominess, can have completely different connotations. *"From the idea of 'homelike,' 'belonging to the house,' the further idea is developed of something withdrawn from the eyes of strangers, something concealed, secret (geheim)."*[29] The place that is homelike *(heimlich)* to me, that encloses my life, may seem impenetrable, mysterious, and even inhospitable to others, and in this case *heimlich* approximates the common usage of *unheimlich*. Taking this a step further, Freud seems to find the true meaning of *unheimlich* in that state in which an assured feeling of belonging is displaced by or juxtaposed with a new sense of estrangement precisely from what we thought most our own, when what we have concealed or forgotten in the house suddenly comes to light and transforms our experience within it. The home then becomes an incomprehensible and hostile space, not for strangers, but *for its own inhabitants*.

For psychoanalysis, the mind is our home (house), or, indeed, it was until this theory arrived on the scene. After Copernicus, proclaims Freud, humans had to recognize that they inhabit only a peripheral fragment of a vast universe. "The second blow" was Darwin's discovery that humans are descended from primates. "But human megalomania will have suffered its third and most wounding blow," writes Freud, "from the psychological research of the present time which seeks to prove to the ego that it is not even the master of its own house" *(". . . es nicht einmal Herr ist im eigenen Hause")*.[30] This experience—the consciousness of helplessness—is the outcome of the ego's encounter with two psychic systems that function as otherness within the mind: the id and the superego. While these two unconscious systems have an overbearing power within the self, their dissimilar natures and origins can provoke very different psychic reactions from the ego.

The id is a semi-biological system constituting the substratum of our psyche. "Originally, to be sure, everything was id; the ego was developed out of the id by the continuous influence of the external world."[31] Even in adults, the id continues to be infantile in character: chaotic and contradictory, unreasonable and impatient. This id is the realm of instincts, where somatic excitations become psychic wishes; these wishes remain unconscious and inaccessible to us, except, for example, in dreams. Because of their semi-biological and infantile character, the contents of the id are not represented in language or organized in time. Language and time are formed through our interaction with others, and the id is a realm impermeable to communication. In fact, the circumstances of the external world are irrelevant to the ravenous id, which is solely interested in the economy of its pleasure. "The id," writes Freud, "knows no judgments of value: no good and evil, no morality. The economic or, if you prefer, the quantitative factor, which is intimately linked to the pleasure principle, dominates all its processes" (*"Selbstverständlich kennt das Es keine Wertungen, kein Gut und Böse, keine Moral. Das ökonomische oder, wenn Sie wollen, quantitative Moment, mit dem Lustprinzip innig verknüpft, beherrscht alle Vorgänge"*).[32] In addition to these pleasurable desires, the id contains impressions from the external world, especially traumatic memories that remain forever embalmed. While psychoanalysis contends that the power of these desires and memories over the mind could be disarmed by a hermeneutic technique, the theory also acknowledges that the self must accept its random banishments from the mental zone of rationality and purposeful action. The self cannot fully master and comprehend its own psyche, cannot fully articulate the ontology of its own being. This predicament cannot be changed, because the id is the primary psychic system and the one most intimately connected to the body; the self simply cannot eliminate this system or ignore its taxing claims.

But things are very different with our second, acquired otherness: the superego. This agency has exterior sources, and the ego may eject it in attempting to restore a homelike, harmonious mode of inner existence. The modern self, who kens itself as a historically constructed being and therefore as permeated by normative contents that are contingent, may well wish to disclaim the psychic agency that represents a devitalizing tradition and repressive social institutions. Yet psychoanalysis adamantly disallows this prospect. The Freudian panacea for our conflicted psychic existence calls for increasing self-awareness and rational control over the superego (and id)—without attempting to deny its independent existence or resorting to nostalgic efforts to overcome the mental self-estrangement. The theory's narrative, on both the ontogenetic and phylogenetic levels, designates the plight of homelessness as a *constitutive*, ineradicable condition of the modern self. While Freud's theory, then, may have helped to shatter the Western sense of home within the self, a sense based on a Cartesian and Kantian tradition that viewed rationality and consciousness as characteristic of human agency, it employs these very attributes in its search for a *modus vivendi*. A rebellion against this condition is seen as mentally chaotic, even potentially psychotic.

∾ THE SUPEREGO, "THE VEHICLE OF CIVILIZATION," generates two types of homelessness: the first is experienced by the ego within the mind, the second by the self within culture/civilization. While these two types are interwoven, for explanatory purposes they will be discussed sequentially. In *"Das Unheimliche,"* Freud defines the uncanny as "nothing new or alien, but something which is familiar and old established in the mind, and which has become alienated from it only through the process of repression."[33] More precisely, the uncanny is the experience of repressed material suddenly coming back to consciousness and inducing terror. To illustrate this point, Freud cites a Romantic literary source, E. T. A. Hoffmann's short story "The Sandman." Hoffmann is well known for creating multiple doubles, as well as for mixing supernatural and realistic motifs; "The Sandman" is no exception. This tale depicts a young man, Nathanael, who cannot escape his traumatic childhood memories and the self-destructiveness these memories have implanted within him. As a child, Nathanael was occasionally expelled from his father's study when the footsteps of a mysterious stranger were heard approaching from outside. He was told at these times that the "sandman" had arrived and that he must go to sleep. "The sandman," a maid explained to him, "is a wicked man who comes to children when they refuse to go to bed and throws handful of sand in their eyes till they bleed and pop out of their heads. Then he throws the eyes into a sack and takes them in the half-moon as food for his children."[34]

Terrified by the sandman but compelled to know more about him, Nathanael hides one night in the study. To his great surprise, he learns that the sandman is the lawyer Coppelius, a person whom he knows well, but abhors. For a while he is able to watch his father and the visitor, who are engaged in a mysterious undertaking with a hearth, but finally he is discovered and seized by Coppelius. The latter would have thrown red-hot coal into Nathanael's eyes had his father not intervened. A year later, during one of Coppelius's visits, an explosion occurs in the father's study; while Nathanael's father dies, Coppelius disappears. Nathanael suffers his first nervous breakdown then, and suffers a second as a student, when these memories are reactivated in him. Hoffmann ends the story with a scene that occurs when Nathanael is about to get married (an act that would have symbolized a full recovery). Without warning, Nathanael is seized by madness and attempts to throw his fiancée from a tower; when he fails, he jumps to his own death. Among those who gather near the body is Coppelius, who has suddenly reappeared in town.

The story's uncanny effect, according to Freud, originates in a series of repetitions echoing a repressed, unresolved Oedipus complex. In psychoanalytic vocabulary, fear for one's eyes represents a fear of castration, and the father is seen as the potential victimizer. Yet the emotional attitude of a child to his father is always ambivalent, a mixture of feelings such as terror, hate, love, and admiration; images of persecution may coexist with images of paternalism and benevolence. From this perspective, Nathanael's father and the evil Coppelius are one and the same. Freud's interpretation here is supported by the text. While his father was sitting together with Coppelius in the study, Nathanael felt that "his mild and honest features seemed to have been distorted into a repulsive and diabolical mask by some horrible convulsive pain. He looked like Coppelius."[35] Nathanael's inability to contain and reconcile the dualistic images he had of his father—especially the castigating, evil facet—led him to project these images outward and to embody them in others, such as Coppelius; the repressed Oedipus complex is then played out through the self's relations to its surroundings. Nathanael's paranoia can therefore be understood in terms of a miscarried incorporation of the superego.

The "normal" resolution of the Oedipus complex, during which the male child relinquishes his sexual desire for the mother, demands the institution of the superego as an integral part of the self. This happens through an identification with the father, who symbolizes for the child the imperatives of the external world. As soon as the child is old enough to see life from the viewpoint of the other, to recognize the feelings and interests of the other, he takes the other's inner world into himself and establishes it as the foundation of his judgments. In "The Uncanny," Freud characterizes this introjected agency as one "which has the function of observing and criticizing the self and of exercising a censorship within the mind, and which we become aware of as our conscience."[36] The superego, in other words, is a persecuting agency that governs the self through the infliction of self-condemnation and self-hate. In psychotic cases such as Nathanael's, this agency rages relentlessly, its pressure intensifies, and the ego even suffers from "delusions of being watched." The self may defend itself against this painful awareness by a process of *psychic disintegration:* it expels the superego so that this agency becomes "isolated, dissociated from the ego" (*"isoliert, vom Ich abgespalten"*),[37] its menacing effects projected outward to objects in the surrounding world.

According to Laplanche and Pontalis, by "projection" (*Projektion*) Freud refers to a mechanism of defense "whereby qualities, feelings, wishes or even 'objects,' which the subject refuses to recognize or rejects in himself, are expelled from the self and located in another person or thing."[38] They point, however, to an ambiguity in Freud's use of the term. In one sense, projection simply signifies an operation whereby the self's refusal to acknowledge internal sources of displeasure leads it to *pretend* these sources are external. In another sense, however, projection of the superego is an attempt to redefine one's entire mode of being by repudiating the expectations and claims of the external world. Here projection "means a *quasi-real* process of expulsion: the subject ejects something he does not want and later rediscovers it in outside reality. One might say schematically that projection is defined in this sense not as 'not wishing to know' but as *'not wishing to be.'* The first meaning confines projection to the status of an illusion, while the second roots it in a *primal division between subject and outside world.*"[39]

In its radical form, projection signifies a liberation of the ego from its double, the superego; it is a strategy for acquiring, or rather regaining, a *monolithic psyche.* Following Otto Rank's study, *Der Doppelgänger* (1914), Freud suggests that the idea of the "double" originated in ancient societies that distinguished between body and soul in their attempt to maintain an illusion of eternal life.[40] Doubling was in this case a mere fantasy, a sign of primitive immaturity. "But . . . this stage has been surmounted [and] the 'double' reverses its aspect," writes Freud. "From having been an assurance of immortality, it becomes the uncanny harbinger of death" (*"Aber . . . mit der Überwindung dieser Phase ändert sich das Vorzeichen des Doppelgängers, aus einer Versicherung des Fortlebens wird er zum unheimlichen Vorboten des Todes"*).[41] This harbinger, the scolding voice of conscience or superego, is no longer a mere invention, as is the soul, but constitutes a concrete psychic reality. By projecting this agency, the self can recover its primary narcissism, a monolithic, psychosexual stage that precedes the introjection of the superego and is characterized by the concentration of libidinal energy in the young ego, unhindered by significant object-relations.[42] This effort to overcome the double through projection and regression—and thereby to restore a more conflict-free, home-like existence within the mind—acquires a different import once we recall that, for Freud, the superego is the mental representative of tradition and cultural norms. From this perspective, the self's expulsion of the superego betokens a rejection of its chief rival, civilization.

～ WE MAY NOW EXPLORE THE SECOND, social dimension of homelessness in Freud. The mental discomfort of the modern self cannot be explained without a broader analysis of the changing relations between the self and the shared world of meanings it inhabits, changes leading to an estrangement from tradition and to what could be termed the disenchantment of culture. "More than anything," Freud writes, the superego represents "the cultural past" ("*die kulturelle Vergangenheit*") and is the mediator through which "the present is changed into the past" ("*Gegenwart in Vergangenheit umgesetzt wird*").[43] This cultural continuity is achieved through a minute shaping of identities. As Freud writes, the superego "play[s] the part of an external world for the ego, although it has become a portion of the internal world. Throughout later life it represents the influence of a person's childhood, of the care and education given him by his parents, and of his dependence on them." This identification with the parents is a gateway to a much more extensive world of influences: "It is not only the personal qualities of these parents that are making themselves felt, but also everything that had a determining effect on them themselves, the tastes and standards of the social class in which they lived and the innate dispositions and traditions of the race from which they sprang."[44]

To be sure, the superego could also be interpreted as essential to human autonomy and freedom from traditional authority. Autonomy, as understood by Rousseau and Kant, demands that we live according to rules that we have prescribed for ourselves and that these rules be issued by the rational aspect of the self—a part disengaged from spontaneous desire, the mechanisms of the body, and egoistic interests. In conceptualizing the superego, Freud partly follows this tradition. First, the institution of the superego allows the self to conduct itself according to an inner legislator and to see itself reflected in its own actions. Second, the superego helps to free the self from the reign of instincts, since it presents to the ego courses of action that are motivated by what is considered worthy, good, and future-oriented, and not merely by what is pleasurable, value-neutral, and immediate.[45] (To be precise, Freud believed that the ego must find a balance between these two contradictory orientations within the mind.) Only with the superego, then, can we become fully capable moral agents and worthy members of a human community.

But to stop here would be misleading, since the superego also secures continuity in the constitution of social identity across time. The child's superego "is in fact constructed on the model not of its parents but of its parents' super-ego; the contents which fill it are the same and it becomes the vehicle of tradition and of all the time-resisting judgments of value which have propagated themselves in this manner from generation to generation."[46] Through the superego, the collective and impersonal become part of the self and are experienced as particular and private, as what is most one's own. This is achieved (as we have already noted above) through a twofold operation. On the one hand, the superego sets positive moral and social ideals ("ego ideals") to which the individual strives to conform in her deportment and activities; it steers the individual's efforts at sublimation by designating worthy activities and achievements and by furnishing the motivation necessary to engage in such undertakings. On the other hand, the superego has a negative aspect as well: it acts as a penalizing machine each time the ego fails to accomplish these goals, and renders a failure to follow an external, social norm into a personal failure. Since Freud attributes to this agency such a fundamental position in molding identities, it is fair to say that he views the individual's life story as unintelligible without a grasp of the collective narratives of which that individual is a part.

The sacrifices demanded by these collective narratives and the emotional effects of the superego remain most often unaccounted for. "[I]t is very conceivable," writes Freud, "that the sense of guilt [as well as anxiety] produced by civilization is not perceived . . . and remains to a large extent unconscious, or appears as a sort of *malaise* [*Unbehagen*], a dissatisfaction, for which people use other motivations."[47] But Freud felt that with contemporary processes of secularization and intensified self-reflection, modern selves might finally be able to uncover some of their unconscious regions and identify the societal reasons for their dissatisfaction. The maxims of civilization and tradition that underlie the bourgeois order—productivity, deferment, restraint, civility, and so forth—are increasingly exposed as exterior and foreign to the self,[48] and while psychoanalysis calls the self to accommodate this exteriority, it also recognizes the prospect of its expulsion from the mind. In fact, Freud feared that such a collective process might be in the making, and that what Laplanche and Pontalis describe as projection in the sense of "not wishing to be" could become manifest at the social level.

In *Civilization and Its Discontents*, Freud asserts that "the community, too, evolves a superego under whose influence cultural development proceeds." He depicts the relations between this communal superego and that of the individual as follows:

> We come across the remarkable circumstances that the mental processes concerned [guilt, anxiety, etc.] are actually more familiar to us and more accessible to consciousness as they are seen in the group than in the individual man. In him, when tension arises, it is only the aggressiveness of the super-ego which, in the form of reproaches, makes itself noisily heard; its actual demands often remain unconscious in the background. If we bring them to conscious knowledge, we find that they coincide with the precepts of the prevailing cultural super-ego. At this point the two processes, that of the cultural development of the group and that of the cultural development of the individual, are, as it were, always interlocked. For that reason some of the manifestations and properties of the super-ego can be more easily detected in its behavior in the cultural community than in the separate individual.[49]

By the "cultural super-ego," Freud seems to designate two interrelated aspects of the individual's superego: that which is unconsciously shared by the community and concerns collective life, and that which is "objectified" through public discourse, legal codes, religious and philosophical teachings, and cultural production as a whole. If psychic disintegration of contemporary selves is impending, it will announce itself (according to Freudian methodology) through ominous communal attitudes toward these dual aspects of the shared superego. In Freud's view, these attitudes might have already begun to surface, because of the collapse of two traditional sources for legitimizing and enforcing social norms: leadership and religion. The decline of leadership is interwoven with the rise of modern, mass democracies. In *Democracy in America*, de Tocqueville pointed out that individuals in an egalitarian society dominated by a middle class do not possess the economic independence, the cultural breeding, or the social prestige to express beliefs and positions that would command particular attention from their fellow citizens. The demise of aristocracy boosted atomization, since now no one could presume to enjoy natural authority and to articulate the shared concerns and vision necessary for maintaining a sense of community.[50] Freud expresses a similar apprehension, believing that leadership is essential for a group's formation and continued existence. In

Group Psychology (1921) he defines "primary group" as "a number of individuals who have put one and the same object [the leader] in the place of their ego ideal, and have consequently identified themselves with one another in their ego."[51] A group is founded upon horizontal equality and libidinal bonds that are synthesized with a singular, hierarchical relation based on love, admiration, and emulation. Their shared introjection of the leader into the superego (as ego ideal) allows group members to identify with one another and cements their communal cohesion. Moreover, such an introjection is a means for internalizing the cultural norms represented by the leader. Without a leader to facilitate such formation of a collectivity, society is prone to "the danger of a state of things which might be termed 'the psychological poverty of groups.'" By this concept Freud presumably means a state in which the libidinal ties among the members of the group are weak, and the members have few ego-ideals in common. Freud seems to dread the imminent prospect of this overdemocratized state. "The present cultural state of America," he writes, "would give us a good opportunity for studying the damage to civilization which is thus to be feared."[52]

But the chief reason for the delegitimization of existing social norms is the final erosion in the status of religion, an erosion which Freud nevertheless strongly supported. While a leader may personify some of the values underlying the social order and induce group members to heed these values, it is religion that has always been the prime guarantor of the extension and intensification of moral and social norms. "Through some kind of diffusion or infection, the character of sanctity and inviolability—of belonging to another world, one may say—has spread from a few major prohibitions on to every other cultural regulation, law and ordinance."[53] This infiltration of religions to culture at large springs in part from their ability to provide theological justifications for the assaults of conscience that ensue when the self transgresses rules and expectations. For Freud, religions veil the true causes of human discontent with social organizations, since instead of exposing instinctual repression and the resultant mechanisms of psychic self-punishment, they "claim to redeem mankind from . . . [the] sense of guilt which they call sin."[54] But Freud also suggests numerous other arguments to account for the hold that religion has had over the human unconsciousness throughout the ages. The traumatic memory of killing the father in the primal horde, leading to totemic practices that are the womb of religion, is one such argument; human weakness, which establishes a longing for a sheltering and all-powerful father (God) in the face of nature, is another. Whatever its source of power, religion has now lost its credibility for many; with the emergence of critical and scientific thinking in general and psychoanalysis in particular, the allure of religion for the unconscious and the infantile motivations for embracing it have been unveiled. In Freud's formulation, modern individuals must "honestly admit the purely human origin of all the regulations and precepts of civilization."[55] For the cultural elite, this admission is unproblematic, he claims, since they are enlightened and able to govern themselves by following rational considerations and calculations of utility.

> But it is another matter with the great mass of the uneducated and oppressed, who have every reason for being enemies of civilization. So long as they do not discover that people no longer believe in God, all is well. But they will discover it, infallibly, even if this piece of writing of mine is not published. And they are ready to accept the results of scientific thinking, but without the change having taken place in them which scientific thinking brings about in people. *Is there not a danger here that the hostility of these masses to civilization will throw itself against the weak spot that they have found in their task-mistress?*[56]

With the death of God and the breakdown of traditional ways of legitimizing authority and rationalizing injustice, the Freudian proletariat might engage in a *deliberate* repudiation and expulsion of the cultural superego—the cement of civilization. Moderns, who are disposed to celebrate a critical attitude toward their own identities and to "enlarge their consciousness," might become aware of the external and imposed nature of their positive ideals, of the social sources of their most private feelings of guilt and self-hate, and of the connection between their existential unhappiness and sexual repression. Hence, the repressed and neurotic self might turn into a *"semipsychotic"* one: it might announce its unwillingness to abide by the identity imposed upon it by civilization via the superego. Modernity is a decisive crossroads in the history of the West (or of civilization in general). Secularization, the ethos of reflection, the natural and human sciences: all these have contributed to the formation of a self that is well aware of its own psychological makeup and the internal mechanisms by which it obeys social rules. Hence the self may choose to eject the voice of society within, a response that would signify the end of the civilization project. Freud shuddered at this prospect. "How ungrateful, how short sighted, after all, is it to strive for the abolition of civilization! What would then remain would be a state of nature, and that would be far harder to bear. [Nature] destroys us—coldly, cruelly, relentlessly . . . and possibly through the very things that occasioned our satisfaction."[57] Freud perceives this return to a precivilized state—motivated by a longing for a more autonomous, harmonious psyche—as a regression to the childish abyss of narcissism (a stage prior to the institution of the superego). His dilemma then becomes how to ensure that moderns will not embrace this destructive option, while still recognizing that in modernity the self can no longer be wholly situated in tradition. However, before examining Freud's response to this dilemma—a response that hinges on the Oedipal complex—a number of additional comments on Freud's vision of community and tradition are warranted.

◇ FREUD, AS WE HAVE SEEN ABOVE, presents us with a complex view of the relation between self and community, a mixture of critical distance and embeddedness. This conception of homelessness *in* tradition and of conditional membership in community might help us illuminate some of the quandaries faced by modern selves; in particular, Freud's conception is valuable as a critique of and amendment to the notion of identity prevailing in contemporary communitarian theory. From a Freudian perspective, it seems, the communitarian attempt to reanchor the self in tradition and to seek a harmony between the self and its social environment is misconceived. While Freud's vista of the self as being submerged within tradition (via the superego) establishes an affinity between his own views and those of communitarian political philosophers, he is skeptical about the nature of the self's attachment to its social environment. These differences are highlighted through a comparison of Freud with the communitarian philosopher Alasdair MacIntyre.

According to MacIntyre, "we all approach our own circumstances as bearers of a particular social identity . . . I inherit from the past of my family, my city, my tribe, my nation, a variety of debts, inheritances, rightful expectations and obligations. These constitute the given of my life, my moral starting point. This is in part what gives my life its own moral particularity."[58] There is no epistemological point of view that is context-free, an archimedean position from which we can conceptualize and fathom the transcendental attributes of the self; to be human means to be placed in social and cultural settings that provide the particular moral language through which we comprehend who we are and who we yearn to be. From this descriptive argument MacIntyre proceeds to claim that without such languages, traditions, and pregiven roles, the self would not be able to construct a meaningful narrative of its life and to evaluate the completeness and coherence of this narrative; life without the horizon of tradition would be impoverished, without direction, arbitrary.

Before we examine how Freud differs from this position, it is important to note what he shares with MacIntyre and other communitarians. Freud agrees with such theorists that tradition (via its psychic delegate, the superego) implants in the self certain notions of the good and social rules, certain motivations, and even emotions. His picture of the self disagrees with the liberal suggestion that the individual could be insulated from society: Freud insists that the self is formed through involuntary, psychosexual interactions with others, and that its attachments to loved ones shape its character in a profound way through the Oedipal complex. (From this Freudian perspective, the entire liberal vocabulary of rights, which seeks to draw a firm line between the private and public, the autonomous individual and the pressures of society, is an ideological fiction; rights, while valuable, concern only the superficial level of human relations.) Without these attachments, the self's rationality and capacity to choose—facets celebrated by liberals as its distinguishing characteristics—would lack a ground within a particular normative and cultural context, rendering the self empty and clueless. Moreover, Freud concurs with the communitarian view that a community (or group) could sustain itself only by possessing shared values, ideals, and symbols (though, as we saw above, he believes a leader to be necessary for that type of cohesion). Freud even suggests that the existence of community hinges on the dispersion of Eros, so that each member directs this instinct toward another; Eros, indeed, could be present in a multiplicity of human relations and not necessarily be limited to the intimate ones. In this sense, there is an affinity between the classical republicanism of Aristotle—according to which friendship among citizens is essential for preserving a polity—and Freud's recognition that communal relations are often more than a legal contract among atomized, self-interested, and mutually indifferent individuals.[59]

Nevertheless, from a psychoanalytic standpoint, the communitarian picture of the relation between self and tradition is romanticized and inadequate. To begin with, according to the psychoanalytic view the imperatives of civilization and tradition—and the identities these imperatives forge—never become incorporated fully into one's being. The superego remains a particular department within the mind, an introjected otherness that can be expelled. We conduct ourselves in the world under constant threat of such reversibility, since "the primitive stages [of the mind] can always be re-established; the primitive mind is, in the fullest meaning of the word, imperishable."[60] The identity that emerges from embeddedness in tradition is a superimposed layer of the self, a coat that could be cast off: this identity does not epitomize who we are, only who we were made to be.

While Freud suggests, then, that community is essential to identity and psychic health, he also recognizes that modern selves could *choose* whether to remain concocted in this fashion.[61] His position is closer to Rawls's claim in *Theory of Justice* (1971) that the self is prior to its ends than to the communitarian claim that, by our very nature, we are constituted by tradition in an irreversible manner.[62] This is not merely a theoretical debate, since it is translated, in Freud's case, to a demand that the community can expect the self to adhere to its central values and notions of common good only if the community benefits the private individual (especially by advancing distributive justice, and ensuring wider access to the scientific and cultural fruits of civilization).[63] In other words, while in the past communities could take for granted the immersion of the individual in their collective projects because of these individuals' psychological makeup, in the age of psychic homelessness and contingent identity we must think differently. In modernity, community is not taken for granted, but is constantly on trial: it is not the individual who must justify why she desires to escape from society's normalizing grip, but the community that must constantly explain why the individual should not follow this alluring path.

Freud differs from current communitarian theory not only in his depiction of the fragility of human identity, but also in his analysis of the mechanisms through which tradition operates in the self. For communitarians, tradition is the essential container of values, of patterns of life, of accumulated human experience; submersion within it allows an individual to rationally construct a meaningful course of life and to find a haven from mass-organizations and economically based relations. Freud, in contrast, depicts tradition (and culture) as imperious and virulent toward the individual: a constant inner surveillance of the superego is joined with the employment of emotional sanctions, such as guilt, self-hate, and anxiety. Rather than merely enriching the self and infusing its life with meaning, the visit of cultural norms within the mind is colored, in Freud's view, by the most destructive forces in human mental and emotional life, which threaten the self with psychic pathologies.

There is an inevitable struggle between the needs of the self and the contents of tradition, a struggle that has intensified over the centuries with the process of civilization and its inevitable by-product of normalization. Indeed, in contrast to communitarians, who seek harmony of purposes between the individual and the community, Freud deems the duality of the self (that is, the rift between the ego and the superego) psychically healthy and the related, contentious relation between self and society as constitutive of the human world. Freud therefore affirms the distance and skepticism of the self toward the past it bears and the shared understandings of its community. In modernity, being in concert evokes a new sea of feelings, ones that have less to do with spontaneous warmth and the happiness of being together, and more to do with ambivalence and conditional attachments. As Zygmunt Bauman has recently noted, in contemporary conditions "identities cannot but look fragile, temporary, and 'until further notice.'" In fact, these identities are "devoid of all defences except the skills and determination of the agents to hold them tight and protect them from erosion."[64] Perhaps, then, it is precisely this *emotional distance* that generates good citizens: ones who are willing to relentlessly announce the imperfections of their community without feeling that they violate primordial loyalties, ones who are aware of their individuality and are circumspect about compromising it for dubious collective goals, and ones that cannot be manipulated by the political menaces of (distorted) communitarianism in our times, such as tribal nationalism and even unreflective patriotism.

Narrating the Modern's Subjection: Freud's Theory of the Oedipal Complex

While psychoanalysis approves of the self's emotional distance from the community, surely Freud's main concern was that such distance, if taken to the extreme, could result in the total expulsion of the superego; in other words, that the modern self might rebel against the yoke of tradition and social institutions, seeking to radically assert its autonomy and transform itself and/or its environment. The import of the Oedipal complex, I would argue, is that such an expulsion is pathological and would give birth to semipsychotic, self-destructive, and delusional selves; Freud's scientific observations define normalcy in such a manner that excludes certain political visions and affirms others. In particular, Freud's theory of the self criticizes the dominant spirit of the nineteenth century and expresses a new historical-political imagination that is suspect of "total revolutions" (to use Bernard Yack's apt term): he insists that we should in principle embrace modern culture and institutions and their effects upon the individual, that we should help the self adapt to its circumstances rather than shape them anew. In other words, his vision of the relation between self and society repudiates both the Nietzschean and Marxian visions. To understand the originality of the Oedipal complex from a historical-political point of view, then, we must first compare Freud to his two eminent predecessors, and examine his critique of their theories of the self.[65]

Freud and Nietzsche share a profound interest in the emotional fabric of human beings, yet they differ in their definitions of a healthy one. In particular, both are intrigued by the dynamic of inner dialogue and the emotion that engenders it. Emotions such as shame, remorse, and guilt are powerful motivations for engaging in reflection on one's actions and their meanings. But is this type of reflection desirable? According to Nietzsche, guilt was the fundamental psychic tool of slave morality, and still stands at the center of the modern self's malaise. To some extent, this malaise emerged with the first social organizations: "I look on bad conscience as a serious illness to which man was forced to succumb by the pressure of the most fundamental of all changes which he experienced—that change whereby he finally found himself imprisoned within the confines of society and peace."[66] Guilt emerged as soon as humans made commercial and legal commitments to one another,[67] and was originally purely functional, helping monitor mundane, human affairs. Social life is sustained by a peculiar mechanism whereby the self learns to exercise its own will upon itself, to master its own power *(Macht)* for internal reproach. Instincts oriented outward such as "animosity, cruelty, the pleasure of pursuing, raiding, changing and destroying—all this was pitted against the person who had such instincts—that is the origin of 'bad conscience.'"[68]

For Nietzsche, then, guilt introduces a vicious conversation within the self: armed with the energy of repressed instincts and with social norms that define legitimate venues for action, the self seizes itself as an object of reflection and punishment, dividing itself into an acting self and an observing self. Guilt inaugurates a rent between what was done and what should have been done, between the past as it was and the reflecting present that wishes this past would have been different. "The will cannot break time and time's covetousness, that is the will's loneliest melancholy,"[69] suggests Nietzsche. The self wishes to amend the past, but this correction eludes it. "Thus the will, the liberator, took to hurting; and on all who can suffer he wreaks revenge for his inability to go backwards. This, indeed, this alone, is what revenge is: the will's ill will against time."[70]

Guilt, a natural outgrowth of living in society, was heightened by and turned into a fundamental principle of the Jewish and Christian faiths. In slave morality characterized by *ressentiment*, weak and hostile individuals utilize guilt as a psychological tool against the assertive and noble. The marriage of guilt and monotheistic religion is the ultimate strategy for leveling individuals, since the believer inevitably minimizes herself in the face of God; she is a meek, feeble creature confronting a mighty creator to whom she owes her existence. This primary indebtedness and the lingering inability to adequately fulfill ideals such as brotherly love or humility implant a consciousness of sin—and consequently introduce self-hate, self-denial, and self-sacrifice. Yet Nietzsche does not see guilt as a necessary and irreversible feature of the self. Not only had the Greeks been able to attenuate the effects of guilt and be at peace with their existence, but the decline of the Christian religion also contains the seeds of a promise. "We should be justified in deducing," writes Nietzsche, "that from the unstoppable decline in faith in the Christian God there is, even now, a considerable decline in the consciousness of human guilt; indeed, the possibility cannot be rejected out of hand that the complete and definitive victory of atheism might release humanity from this whole feeling of being indebted towards its beginnings, its *causa prima*."[71] The termination of the internal, conflictual conversation is precisely the goal of the *Übermensch*. This life-affirming and powerful self must possess internal wholeness, and its first step is to master the doubleness induced by regret and shame, self-hate and guilt. The self can overcome these feelings only by eradicating everything foreign or accidental within it, everything in the past that does not let go and demands internal revenge. The new, higher individual will be able to say "yes" even to this past, to embrace this disagreeable and coincidental part within the circumference of himself. "All 'it was' is a fragment, a riddle, a dreadful accident—until the creative will says to it: 'But thus I willed it.'"[72]

Freud sees this strategy of coping with doubleness and self-critique as narcissistic. Not only does he view philosophy as a narcissistic enterprise—and Nietzsche in particular as a narcissistic personality[73]—but he believes that the *Übermensch* is a regressive personification of this type of character. The higher individual envisioned by Nietzsche is, in Freud's lights, an attempt to achieve inner unity and a sense of potency that requires detachment from one's social surroundings, including its emotional bonds and moral commitments. For Freud, the notion of the *Übermensch* is not a prophetic projection into the future but part of our shared memory; it presents an archaic phase of our existence rather than a utopian one. The figure most resembling the *Übermensch*, avers Freud, is the father in the primal horde: "[h]ere, at the very beginning of the history of mankind, was the 'superman' whom Nietzsche only expected from the future."[74] This powerful and independent individual ruled the horde purely according to his instinctual wishes. The primal father was not answerable to secular or divine authority, tradition or custom, public bodies or positive law. In particular, the autonomy of this father translated itself into a complete monopoly over sexual intercourse and procreation, and he conducted himself sexually as in all other spheres—according to his enjoyment and needs. Guided purely by the "pleasure principle," the primal father avoided dependency and frustration in relation to external objects: he had no permanent libidinal ties and was in love solely with himself; he infused his ego with erotic energy, and this narcissism, in turn, made him megalomanic, intoxicated by his own powers.

According to Freud, then, the primal father had no notion of guilt or shame and could therefore idolize himself. He had no social rules to internalize, no inner voice to second guess his actions. There was no one who could evoke in him feelings of remorse, and no addressee for such emotion; he existed on a plane of his own, so to speak, without normative interlocutors. Civilization, Freud suggests, can begin only when this father has been surpassed by primal patricide, when instincts are no longer exercised freely in the world without consideration of others. The aggressive instincts "make human communal life difficult and threaten its survival. Restriction of the individual's aggressiveness is the first and perhaps the severest sacrifice which society requires of him."[75] Social life demands an inner conversation whereby the self is able to behold itself through the eyes of others and to heed their judgments. The termination of this conversation and the disregard for the voice of others within would herald the end of civilization, rather than the onset of a new and higher one. *"Fear of the super-ego should normally never cease, since, in the form of moral anxiety, it is indispensable in social relations,* and only in the rarest cases can an individual become independent of human society" *("Die Angst vor dem Über-Ich soll normalerweise kein Ende finden, da sie als Gewissensangst in den sozialen Beziehungen unentbehrlich ist, und der Einzelne nur in den seltensten Fällen von der menschlichen Gemeinschaft unabhängig werden kann").*[76]

Nietzsche seeks to overcome the morbid effects of inner dissent and aggression; Marx aspires to foster collective solidarity and autonomy. These two goals are interrelated, since genuine human fellowship is viable only when the values and rules guiding relations among individuals have been freely and consciously determined. According to Marx, solidarity has been unattainable throughout history because the structural, material conflicts among individuals and classes have generated divisive and skewed moralities. Morality is part of the ideological superstructure that legitimizes hegemonic economic powers; it merely serves material interests, and is forced upon individual actors by their mode of production and its corresponding class stratification—both of whose origins elude human control. But bourgeois morality is especially repugnant for Marx, since it degrades human relations and represents a new nadir in the collective's ability to determine these relations. Though this morality may profess to uphold equality, mutual respect, and universality, in capitalism, humans are in fact submerged in their individuality, forced to exploit and objectify one another in their economic war for survival. In the bourgeois order, our profound impotence in shaping our material conditions and satiating our needs is echoed by our total inability to shape the way we interact with and care for one another.

Marx declares that only with "the abolition of the basis, private property, with the communistic regulation of production (and implicit in this, the abolition of the alien attitude *[Fremdheit]* of men to their own product), the power of the relation of supply and demand is dissolved into nothing, and men once more gain control of exchange, production, and the way they behave to one another."[77] In communist society, the individual will be salvaged from his or her conflict with fellow members of society, since the economic basis of this predicament will no longer exist; values and rules will no longer be conditioned by want and class interests, but will be determined freely and rationally. The new, unconditioned basis of morality will allow individuals to become wholly socialized, wholly susceptible to transcending their particularity. Nietzsche aspired to overcome the voice of society within; Marx hoped to *magnify* this voice and ensure its domination over other internal voices. "Under human conditions," writes Marx, "punishment will really be nothing but the sentence passed by the culprit on himself . . . he will see in other men his natural saviors from the punishment which he has imposed on himself."[78]

According to Freud, Marx's critique of modernity is seriously flawed, since it lacks psychological depth: it positions "man" at the center of its theoretical and practical concerns, without ever examining this creature's emotions and psyche. Marxism "has mercilessly cleared away all idealistic systems and illusions," but "it has itself developed illusions which are no less questionable and unprovable than the earlier ones."[79] In particular, the notion that animosity and heartlessness in human relations are a function of contingent historical circumstances suggests that, in essence, humans are benevolent, innocuous beings. "The communists believe that they have found the path to deliverance from our evils. According to them, man is wholly good and is well-disposed to his neighbor; but the institution of private property has corrupted his nature."[80]

This is a dangerous chimera, admonishes Freud, since the belief that an otherwise pure human nature is corrupted by society could lead to the most radical and savage political action. (As noted, from the Freudian perspective the conflict and competition that are ingrained in capitalism are more compatible with and hospitable to human nature than the communist economic and political vision.) Aggression—whether in word or in deed, whether addressed toward the body or toward the dignity of another—cannot be eradicated from human intercourse. Violence towards others is a deep-seated and *pleasurable* need, and the more one attempts to curtail it in ordinary life, in daily interactions at the work place and in public spaces, the more likely it is to erupt in unexpected and horrifying manifestations (such as World War I). "It is clearly not easy for men to give up the satisfaction of the inclination to aggression," observes Freud. "They do not feel comfortable without it."[81]

More generally, Freud does not share Marx's belief that we can simply decide which norms we want to embrace, that we can emancipate ourselves from our customs and ideals. We are engrossed in the past, a fact materialists are especially inclined to ignore. "It seems likely that what are known as materialistic views of history sin in under-estimating this factor [of tradition]. They brush it aside with the remark that human 'ideologies' are nothing other than the product and superstructure of their contemporary economic conditions. That is true, but very probably not the whole truth. *The past, the tradition of the race and of the people, lives in the ideologies of the super-ego . . . independently of economic conditions.*"[82] From this perspective, individualism and universalism, moderation and the cultivation of privacy, and other bourgeois values are not an epiphenomenon, and their domination does not derive from any particular mode of production. Freud believes that the ideals and values by which we live evolve very gradually, irrespective of specific technological, material, political, and social circumstances. The cultural superego displays remarkable continuity, one that cannot be explained by historical materialism. This continuity of moral and cultural ideas springs (in part) from the constitutive elements in our nature, and especially from the continuous necessity to combat instincts (which remain unrelenting throughout history) with the aid of the superego. In Freud's view, the existence of instincts constitutes the underlying reason for the implausibility of the Marxian call for the annulment of social sanctions and state violence. "The attempt to replace actual force by the force of ideas seems at present to be doomed to failure," writes Freud. "We shall be making a false calculation if we disregard the fact that law was originally brute violence and that even today it cannot do without the support of violence" ("*Es ist ein Fehler in der Rechnung, wenn man nicht berücksichtigt, daß Recht ursprünglich rohe Gewalt war und noch heute der Stützung durch die Gewalt nicht entbehren kann*").[83]

Freud's critiques of Nietzsche(anism) and Marx(ism) seem like mirror images: Nietzsche is rebuked for seeking psychic unity, Marx for seeking a communal one. Nietzsche erroneously longs to eradicate inner aggression, Marx—equally erroneously—to eradicate conflictual human intercourse. Nietzsche celebrates the mirage of individual freedom and autonomy in shaping ethical values, Marx the mirage of unconditioned, rational, and emancipated community. Given this intellectual context, psychoanalysis is distinguished by its attempt to ensure the reign of the "*reality principle*" (echoing Weber's call to heed "the demands of the day").[84] This entails, as an *a priori* maxim, the acceptance of the self and society as they are: structurally disharmonious, mired in aggression, hardly liberated, and only partly autonomous. To embrace reality means to accommodate ourselves to these circumstances in a rational-instrumental fashion, to endlessly and agonistically negotiate between the different departments of the mind and between the self and its surroundings.

Freud's conception of the self—especially of its psychic development during the Oedipal stage—implies that, despite their marked differences, both Nietzsche's and Marx's thought contain elements of immaturity, of an inability to bear the complex cultural and institutional conditions of modernity. I do not propose that in developing his theory of the self, Freud was preoccupied with political philosophy and was deliberately grappling with its contemporary dilemmas. Indeed, one might even question whether it is appropriate to juxtapose philosophy and psychology, and to use the psychoanalytic theory of the self to criticize Nietzsche and Marx. But Freud insisted that "it is not permissible to declare that science is one field of human mental activity and that religion and philosophy are others." Philosophy, in fact, "behaves like a science and works in part by the same methods,"[85] but is often based on mere intuition and requires sciences such as psychoanalysis to correct its mistakes. More specifically, Freud claims that any body of thought that advances assertions about the individual and his or her relation to society contains at least a minimalist theory of the self and thereby dwells in the territory of psychoanalysis. "Strictly speaking," he proclaims in his discussion of Marx, "there are only two sciences: psychology, pure and applied, and natural science."[86]

〰 IN FREUD'S LAST MAJOR PUBLISHED WORK, *An Outline of Psychoanalysis* (1938), he writes that "if psychoanalysis could boast of no other achievement than the discovery of the repressed Oedipus complex, that alone would give it a claim to be included among the precious new acquisitions of mankind."[87] This discovery is essential to Freud's theory, since the dispositions and character of the self cannot be fathomed without a picture of psychic development, and the latter is shaped principally by the complex. Freud believes that the Oedipal stage "forms the nucleus of . . . neuroses,"[88] since the myriad processes that the child undergoes can fail in various ways. Masochism, sadism, narcissism, melancholia, euphoria, phobia, hysteria—all these and other psychic phenomena originate in the collision of the family triangle. The fact that Freud celebrates this narrative as the core of his ontogenetic theory and as the etiological source of neurosis invites questions about the symbolic-historical import of the Oedipus complex and the stages that precede it.[89] To be sure, there have been numerous attempts to interpret Freud's theory of the complex contextually: it has been explained as part of a false ideological-bourgeois construct that attempts to mask the role of capitalism in bringing about mental illness;[90] as expressing a contingent, patriarchal social order where the mother is in fact the powerful figure whom the boy seeks to flee;[91] as continuing a German Romantic, nineteenth-century intellectual tradition that celebrated myth as helping to illuminate human phenomena;[92] as expressing the modern, anomic collapse of the family wherein the father has been positioned—in an impossible fashion—as a figure to be both emulated and feared.[93] But these and many other contextualizing interpretations fail to see the new historical imagination that the complex introduces, its role as an alternative to "the longing for total revolution" that griped Freud's predecessors.

The Oedipus complex is essentially a narrative of individuation and subjection, wherein the self both acquires its circumference and internalizes a shared cultural world. According to Freud, in the pre-Oedipal period the boundaries between self and environment are blurred: there is no separation between subject and object, between perceiving consciousness and perceived world. In other words, this period is distinguished by *oneness*, both within the self and in its relation to external phenomena. This holds particularly true for the oral stage, in which the child strives both to merge with and to master the world through an act of incorporation: sucking. Rather than being a mere activity of nourishment, sucking is emblematic of the relations between child and surroundings. The child has no clear sense of being a distinct entity at this period and wants to "contain" the objects around her—to deny their separateness and independence. (In psychoanalysis the word "object" refers to a human being, but the use of a word commonly denoting inanimate things is not accidental, and the relation of self to other could be seen as influencing the self's relation to its environment as a whole.) "During the oral stage of organization of the libido, the act of obtaining erotic mastery over an object coincides with that object's destruction," writes Freud.[94] This annihilative consumption (of the toy, the nipple, the mother—in short, of the animate and inanimate surroundings) brings the child a sense of both security and erotic pleasure. And although the mouth is the prime organ for this devouring activity, Freud totalizes its presence in the infant to such a degree that he even sees the eyes that behold the world as fulfilling a similar function of incorporation.

During the anal phase, however, the child turns peevish in her relation to the world. She begins to ascertain the limits of her position, but wishes to violate them through sadistic maneuvers. The denial of the independence of objects becomes aggressive and deliberate, manifested by efforts to control things by positing herself as their sole *generator*. The excretion of faeces simulates birth: "they acquire the meaning of 'baby'—for babies," writes Freud.[95] Through games of retention and release by the anus, of creating things and then dissolving them at will, the infant gains a megalomanic sense of herself. While objects must now be recognized as extraneous, the infant insists that their origin remains herself. In the transition from the oral stage to the anal one, then, the child shifts from a desire to incorporate the world to an urge to engender it, from a primal desire to be one with the world to an urge to stand above it. Perhaps the most crucial point for Freud is that the child's false sense of self-sufficiency and autonomy is boosted in the oral and anal phases, because both are autoerotic: in these phases the child finds sexual satisfaction without a need for others, solely by stimulations of the erotogenic zones (mouth and anus). At this stage of primary narcissism, only one's own ego (or body) is cathected; because there is no investment of human objects with libido, no dependency or constraint is imposed by bonds with others.

The Oedipal stage symbolizes the radical termination of these misconceptions of oneness and omnipotence. At this stage the child goes through crucial developments, such as the adoption of a sexual identity and the centering of sexual activity in the genitals. The process that concerns us here, however, is the changing relationship of self to others. To begin with, the *male* child[96] undergoes a redefinition of his place in the world, since after making his first object choice, he is forced to renounce it completely. During this so-called phallic period, the child develops a sexual attraction toward his mother, replacing a dependency based on nourishment with a dependency based on eroticism. The wish to become her lover is joined with a more complex effort to prolong his reign over the world. Transcending his efforts at mastering the motor movements of the anus, the male child now orders and manipulates his new sexual object as evidence of his governing powers. As a consequence of this new interest in his mother, the boy's attitude toward his father becomes a mixture of love and hostility, the latter due to a sense of competition. The child may endure these confusing and paralyzing feelings toward his parents for some time, but ultimately they demand resolution. The turning point, according to Freud, occurs after the child views the genitals of the female sex and imagines the possibility of losing his penis. The fear of castration—an act he believes may be carried out by his father—induces him to relinquish and repress his desire for the mother and to identify with the presumably all-powerful figure that threatens him. The positioning of the father within the self desexualizes the relationship to the parents, generating a structural, psychic change: the institution of the superego. For Freud, this change represents *"the most important characteristic of the development both of the individual and of the species."*[97]

The superego transforms the ongoing, judgmental dialogue between self and parents (or society) into an interior one. "External restraint is internalized and the superego takes the place of the parental agency and observes, directs and threatens the ego in exactly the same way as earlier the parents did with the child."[98] In order to do this, the superego must utilize the aggressive instinct of the self and cultivate the human capacity for feelings such as shame and guilt. These feelings are nourished by our multilayered, temporal existence: we regret in the present things we have done in the past; we shape impending events through lenses colored by our older, regrettable traumas. We live the past in the present; we view the present through the past. Because of this temporal and emotional labyrinth launched in the Oedipal period, anguish lingers. "A threatened external unhappiness—loss of love and punishment on the part of the external authority—has been exchanged for a permanent internal unhappiness, for the tension of the sense of guilt."[99] The origin of contrition is the child's sexual history, his wish to remove the father and gain monopoly over his first sexual object: he cannot forget these wishes of parricide and incest, nor forgive himself for having been possessed by them. Freud suggests that the guilt that arises out of erotic yearning has the potential of turning into more intricate, behavioral and moral guilt;[100] although the latter is essential for preserving the social order and civilization, it is essentially parasitic, a continuous replay of an emotional pattern formed by desire.[101]

The establishment of the superego symbolizes the independence and autonomy of the child. He acquires a sense of distinct agency, and becomes responsible for controlling his own desires and engaging with society according to its rules.[102] But in order to obtain this selfhood, the child must (unconsciously) accept that, instead of incorporating, begetting, and mastering the surroundings as he did in pre-Oedipal stages, he is now inevitably shaped by social norms and tradition. At first, the superego speaks in the name of the father, his particular expectations, prohibitions, admonitions. But as the self matures, this agency gradually becomes impersonal, its contents representing ideas of teachers and leaders, religious precepts, and cultural idols. What began as a sexual episode within the family and the introjection of an intimate and beloved person concludes with the formation of an anonymous, harsh social voice within. This bellowing voice, whose introjection is wholly involuntary and devoid of conscious criticism, exercises power over the self throughout life. The "mature ego remains subject to its [the superego's] domination. As the child was once under a compulsion to obey its parents, so the ego submits to the categorical imperative of its superego."[103] The psychically healthy person accedes to his *principled subjection*, to the formative role of the father, tradition, and prevailing norms. An attempt of the child to resist this psychological maxim and maintain the initial integrity of mind is dangerous, resulting in a more sadistic superego. "The original severity of the super-ego does not . . .

represent the severity which one has experienced from it [the object, i.e., parent], or which one attributes to it." Rather, observes Freud, this severity represents "one's own aggressiveness"[104] toward the object. For psychoanalysis, then, accepting the presence of the introjected otherness in the mind and abiding by its rules is a *sine qua non* of normality.

The broader import of the Oedipus complex comes into view once we grasp its portrayal of a delicate balance between merging and distance in the relations of self to others. On the one hand, we must consort with others for the satisfaction of our sexual and emotional needs, and we are driven to establish bonds in the world as part of our natural psychic development. We are steered toward others by an internal force, and whether our attachments are a source of pleasure or pain, they inject substance into our lives. Without our attraction to and dependency on others, we would be impoverished creatures. Commencing with the father, the history of the self is the history of identifications, and it is "possible to suppose that the character of the ego is a precipitate of abandoned object cathexes and that it contains the history of those object-choices."[105] After the Oedipal stage, Freud claims, we no longer incorporate nipples or toys—we take in personalities. At times, we introject admired individuals because we wish to emulate them; at other times, we introject loved individuals because we have lost them. But whether we introject in order to become someone or to overcome our attachment to another, whether it is the future or the past with which we are coping, introjection and identification are essential for shaping our identities.[106] In contrast to Nietzsche, who presents the crafting of identity as a voluntary, assertive affair that should aspire to draw a circumference around the self, for the post-Oedipal self, others are always-already within us, influencing the way we speak and move, the things we designate as good and beautiful. Their involuntary presences—and the more global presence of tradition and culture—is the reason for our dialogical existence, for the emotionally excruciating, inner conversation that cannot and should not cease. To Freud, the self is a wholly porous being—and this characteristic is the foundation of its capacity for personal growth.

Freud nevertheless insists that our attachment to others typically involves disappointment and struggle, and he rejects any notion of consensual intersubjectivity, Marxian or otherwise. With the renunciation of his desire for the mother, the male child begins to accept the separate existence of objects and to recognize that these are governed by modes of interaction that escape his control. Even the object most dear to the self—the relation which could shape all other relations—must be acknowledged as ungovernable and as a source of pain. Each child begins, as it were, from an anthropocentric vision: the world is centered around him, obediently serving his needs for nourishment and care. "A child's demands for love are immoderate, they make exclusive claims and tolerate no sharing," writes Freud.[107] But with the Oedipus complex this vision terminates; the child experiences himself at the periphery of the environment he inhabits, an addendum to the family unit rather than its source and core. In contrast to the autoerotic oral and anal stages, the denial of primal wishes inaugurates a lasting consciousness that must learn to accommodate not only the happiness of union in relation to others, but also ire and fear, rivalry, and frustration. These sobering lessons endure, according to Freud, affecting the way the child acts and thinks throughout his life: "the little creature is often completed by the fourth or fifth year of life, and after that merely brings gradually to light what is already within him."[108]

To sum up, then, the Freudian account of psychosexual development delineates a self that differs in important respects from the selves envisioned by Nietzsche and Marx. In very different ways, both Nietzsche and Marx represent heightened aspirations for human autonomy, the former seeking an integrated and authentic identity, the latter a total remolding of social institutions in a rational and intersubjective way. But Freud calls into question the self's capacity to autonomously create and control the circumstances of its life, to profoundly shape its own identity or the identity of the surrounding culture, to achieve an inner or an external harmony. Freud, of course, was not alone in advancing such skepticism. We have seen that his contemporary, Weber, argued that the life-orders of modernity (such as capitalism and bureaucracy) are too complex and entrenched to be transformed by collective action, that rationalization careers through political and economic systems. But if Weber's sociological-institutional analysis calls into question our prospects of fleeing modernity, psychoanalysis calls into question the type of the self that longs for such flight. This theory castrates the modern, so to speak, implying that the Marxian and Nietzschean aspirations that dominated the late nineteenth century are merely delusions, ones that enshrine the narcissistic and megalomanic wishes of immature persons.

~ FREUD'S PORTRAYAL of the Oedipus complex suggests that this thinker views the self as a theater of contention and a site of conflictual relations with its environment. The fundamental experience of the self is one of *incessant* strife; the maturity of moderns consists in their capacity to accept this fact. This affirmation of friction and discontent (in both the inner and outer worlds) propels Freud to seek strategies for *coping* with our social-institutional circumstances, rather than for transcending them. In particular, the heroic coping of the self involves a struggle to integrate itself by recovering its fragmented and lost memories. Psychoanalysis, in fact, not only breaks with the prevailing nineteenth-century visions of the self, but also inaugurates a new path by which the modern self can mitigate its alienation and feelings of privation within existing social institutions. Along with other writers of the period, such as Bergson and Proust, Freud bids us to contemplate and cohere our temporal experience, and to celebrate the role of memory in healing the self. Overcoming neurosis is the immediate goal of recollection, the integration of personality its overarching one. Psychoanalysis emerged in an age when the contexts ensuring the activation of recollection were fading: migration took people away from familiar landscapes and streets, large families disintegrated and lost their collective stories, communal calendars and their unique organization of time became irrelevant. Memory is attracted to the specific: it requires familiar smells, objects, faces, or rituals in order to be activated, and these were losing their repetitive structure. Freud displaces these missing stimulators of memory by a dialogical method, the unsolicited flashes of memory by a structured setting where language is the chief key to recollection. Psychoanalysis, then, invented an artificial path to combat the socially induced fragmentation of modern life and regain the integrity of the self, a path that gathers the self through laborious introspection rather than through Weberian, ascetic engagement with the vocational world.

According to Freud, the art of healing should focus on our sexual history, on the most intimate domain of memory possible: by confronting events related to the denial of its early sexual wishes, the self can fathom its phobias, compulsive behaviors, bodily symptoms, anxiety, traumatic dreams, and other phenomena. Psychic illness is inherently connected to forgetfulness or repression. "Gaps appear in the patient's memory even while he narrates his case: actual occurrences are forgotten, the chronological order is confused or causal connections are broken, with unintelligible results. *No neurotic case history is without amnesia of some kind or other.*"[109] The task of the analyst is to assist the patient in reconstructing this jumbled experience into a meaningful narrative without distortion. "Psychoanalysis," as Michael Ruth notes, "is a *historical science* in that its fundamental theoretical tenet is that the individual—and by analogy the group—can act with a degree of freedom that is achieved through an understanding . . . of his past."[110]

But the past does not reveal itself easily. For psychoanalysis, the past is imbued with resistance, and "the patient brings out of the armory of the past the weapons with which he defends himself against the progress of the treatment—weapons that we must wrest from him one by one."[111] As the therapy advances gingerly and crucial moments within the past have been targeted, the patient may circumvent the impending remembrance by "acting out" his neurosis more forcefully than ever before. He compulsively repeats the behavior or symptoms by which he is tormented. The therapist should not become perplexed and discouraged by this, and "must allow the patient time to become more conversant with this resistance with which he has now become acquainted, to *work through it [Durcharbeitung]*".[112] Memory is work, because the self is invested in maintaining its present psychic organization, and would not easily question its own identity. The self's fear of uncovering the past is due not only to the painful truth that might be exhumed, but also to the disorientation that might ensue. To mitigate this fear, recollection of an event must be carefully narrated, turning the recovered memory into a part of one's life rather than a mere threat to it.

But how do individuals acquire *possession* of their memories? Freud argues that external remembrance is insufficient; the past must not only be cognitively grasped as one's own, but must also be relived. In therapy, memory is reexperienced through transference, wherein the patient is able to reactivate his early fears, sexual attractions, ambivalent feelings and so forth. The patient sees the analyst as "a reincarnation of some important figure out of his childhood or past, and consequently transfers on to him feelings and reactions which undoubtedly applied to this prototype."[113] These feelings and reactions may be of love, emulation, and attempts to please (positive transference), or of hate, fear, and mistrust (negative transference). The patient's relation to the analyst, in fact, *parallels the relation between the ego and the superego*, and by putting the analyst in place of his parents, the patient "is also giving him the power which his super-ego exercises over his ego, since his parents were . . . the origins of his super-ego" ("*. . . so räumt [er] ihm auch die Macht ein, die sein Über-Ich über sein Ich ausübt, denn diese Eltern sind [ja] der Ursprung des Über-Ichs gewesen*").[114]

The therapist is a mediator between self and civilization: through transference, the self is able to remold its relation to the superego, understanding and mitigating the fear of persecution that originated in early childhood and that later reasserts itself whenever a social norm is transgressed. The exposure of the emotional-sexual origins of anxiety and guilt empower the self to establish a necessary distance from the contents of the superego: they cease to monopolize the self's identity, becoming a part it can cope with or even alter. Therapy also renders the ideals and maxims of the superego less arbitrary, since it enables the individual to identify events that influenced her and the figures she unconsciously emulates; therapy transforms her character and personality from something contingent into an intelligible narrative. The combination of distance from and intelligibility of the superego does not, by any means, free the self from its psychic and social homelessness—yet it makes this predicament more bearable.

The same conciliatory and pragmatic approach could take place at the collective level, where therapy, of course, is impossible. Freud's semi-historical work on Moses, the founder of the Jewish faith, is an example of such a redefinition of our relation to the past and the cultural superego. By inquiring into the origins of the Jewish religion and the Egyptian who founded it, Jews could explain some of the fundamental characteristics of their religion, such as the notion of an abstract and single divinity, the unwavering obedience to the law, and the enduring feeling of guilt in believers. Once Jews have exposed the psychic-historic distortions in the self-narrative of their religion (particularly the murder of Moses) and traced the origins of their collective identity to repressed events, they could adopt some values and practices of their tradition while discarding others. They could even become, like Freud, "godless" Jews, active and critical agents in relation to the past rather than merely its passive bearers.[115]

The amelioration of our relation to the superego is possible only because psychoanalysis advances a new temporal vision. This vision ensures that healing be a perpetual possibility, since nothing in the past goes into oblivion and what may seem to have been dissolved is very much alive and assertive. "There is nothing in the id that corresponds to the idea of time . . . no alteration in its mental processes is produced by the passage of time."[116] Memory traces are whisked aimlessly and chaotically in the mind—until we narrate them in some meaningful way. The concept of time behind therapy joins this reassuring claim about the permanence of memories with the claim that personal (and collective) histories do not form a linear or dialectical totality. For Freud (as for Benjamin), time is not homogenous: it is composed of unique moments that define one's existence thereafter, moments from childhood that create cycles that may repeat indefinitely. Fear of being separated from one's mother shapes one's relationships with spouses; hostility and competitiveness toward the father later become an endless need to prove oneself. For psychoanalysis, the present is the setting where the drama of the past takes place.

This temporal vision is incompatible with the prevalent, teleological nineteenth-century conceptions of time. Psychoanalysis calls for a full reversal of Enlightenment and Post-Enlightenment convictions, inviting us to repossess the traumatic past instead of helplessly striving to realize a bright future. We should stop yearning for peace with the external world, for a distant day when we might feel that our deepest emotional and instinctual needs are being addressed by social institutions and norms; instead, we should attempt to salvage the past events that are constantly slipping away. "What we desire," Freud writes, "is that the ego, emboldened by the certainty of our help, shall dare to take the offensive in order to reconquer what has been lost."[117] Kant, the most eminent spokesman of the Enlightenment, could see the future as a time when the gulf between the empirical self and civilization on the one hand, and practical reason on the other, would subside; Freud believes that memory will explicate why mental doubleness and the agonism between individual and civilization are our inevitable destiny.

∾ 5

Michel Foucault: From the Prison-House of Language to the Silence of the Panopticon

"Maybe the target nowadays," writes Foucault, "is not to discover what we are, but to refuse what we are."[1] The present, according to Foucault, witnesses a unique sense of crisis: a distancing of the self from itself, a mistrust of existing subjectivities, a quest for new identities. The norms that have been governing our notions of responsible citizenship, of acceptable sexual identities, of what reason may mean, are no longer self-evident—while still being a part of us. From this perspective, the Foucauldian project is both a continuation of and a departure from Freud. Psychoanalysis, as we saw above, introduced the idea of a divided self, a conscious ego that recognizes itself as impelled and shaped both by the unconscious and by an internalized normalizing agency, the superego. The domination of this agency in particular establishes an inner experience of uncanniness and homelessness within our home, an encounter that is constitutive of modern subjectivity. Yet whereas Freud, who was fully aware of the malignant effects of the superego, believed a radical rebellion against this moral-regulative "garrison" within us would breed a disastrous anarchy where the instincts would reign, for Foucault it is precisely our growing aloofness from and awareness of certain internalized normalizing maxims that is a source of hope; our acknowledgement of their social, contingent, and coercive nature may lead us to finally reject and eject them. In this sense, the Foucauldian project begins where Freud urged us to halt.

Psychoanalysis identified the emerging rift within Western selves; Foucault wishes to insert his work within that rift. Freud viewed the domination of the superego as a precondition for the socially conscious conduct of the individual and for the survival of civilization; Foucault bids us to espouse an ethos of critical self-questioning in respect to the regulative truths that guide our actions and define our identity. Such questioning does not, he insists, pose a threat for the existence of society but on the contrary, is vital for its future. Foucault is neither a utopian like Marcuse nor a nostalgist like Heidegger: the restoration of a subjectivity that is at home within itself and the world is foreign to him; we are "always-already" within a network of power, combating its effects both from without and from within. Yet he believes that alleviation of the predicament of the modern self is both possible and desirable; his own writings should be seen as fostering the current "struggle against the forms of subjection—against the submission of subjectivity."[2]

To be sure, Foucault's critics have often questioned whether in engaging in struggles against subjection/subjectification Foucault succeeded in eliminating from his own work notions of subjectivity in general and Western ones in particular.[3] These critics correctly point to the normative concerns and ambiguous notions of selfhood that lurk behind the Foucauldian project; nevertheless, one should not overemphasize this background, since the *gist* of Foucault's work remains *negative*, more committed to questioning the present than to affirming an alternative. This signifies a reversal of the Weberian and Freudian conceptualization of entrapment. For these two writers, the modern self was snared because the external conditions of the present denied something essential to the self: the possibility of attaining a unified personality, in Weber's case, and a self that has less impaired instinctual satisfaction, a reduced sense of inner strife, and greater sublimation, in Freud's. For Foucault, in contrast, the modern self is trapped not because of specific needs and external conditions that the environment denies it, but rather because of the identity—any identity—that the social matrix imposes upon it from without and entices it to embrace from within. In fact, accounts of the self that are scientifically based (Freud) or that contain essentialist presuppositions and affirm the place of history in shaping the self (Weber) become, for Foucault, part of the modern malaise—and hence must be rebuffed by archaeological and genealogical means.

As I shall argue in this chapter, this negative and anti-essentialist character of the Foucauldian project is important: it contributes both to Foucault's extension and intensification of the entrapment perspective.

More specifically, this radicalization of entrapment occurs at three levels. First, once subjectivity—its specific contents and the notion itself—are viewed as a fabrication that needs to be contested and resisted, the critical enterprise inevitably unveils domain after domain, layer after layer, through which the self is constituted. Since there is no essence at the bottom of the self—one stemming, for example, from the body (instincts) or from disengaged reason—each exposition of the self's formation is but a momentary point of rest in an ongoing process of questioning. Second, the lack of anchor or Archimedean point propels Foucault to expand the problematic of entrapment to include new spheres, such as language and knowledge, as well as to elaborate a theory that views power as constitutive of social relations and practices as such. The sphere of language is particularly important in this context, since Foucault urges us to be suspicious of the words we use to describe, fathom, and even liberate ourselves, and he is especially suspicious of the scientific language of the human and social sciences that Weber and Freud so faithfully trusted. Third, Foucault intensifies the entrapment imagination by stressing the immanent position of the modern self: he claims that language and/or power always engulf this self, leaving it no exterior experience that escapes them; any degree of transgression or freedom we may acquire is always fragile and occurs within these spheres, and there is no moment of genuine transcendence and definite liberty. Now it is perhaps too early to say that with this radicalization of the Foucauldian project, the entire entrapment mode of thinking reached its zenith. Nevertheless, it seems that once we perceive our bodies, sexuality, language, and reason as profoundly shaped by modern social institutions, the entrapment critique has no more novel roads to explore. Indeed, the history of political thought since Foucault does not reveal any such paths.

The outline of this chapter is as follows. The first section explores Foucault's critique of both Freud and Weber, paying particular attention to their notions of subjectivity. I then distinguish between two snares that can be found in Foucault, both of which are conceptualized in terms of the imposition of identities and ways of life that they involve. I elaborate upon the first, archaeological-linguistic snare in the second section, which presents the emergence of post-Enlightenment notions of subjectivity as the upshot of structural transformations. According to Foucault, the modern epistemological arrangement (*episteme*) demands a sovereign, unified, and rational subject; it leads, moreover, to an unprecedented quest for producing the human sciences, bodies of knowledge through which we have come to understand

and define ourselves. Foucault sees the effects of this predicament as particularly evident in our language, which is progressively taken over by confining, scientific discourses. As I shall argue, the structural-epistemic snare is therefore essentially a linguistic one, and Foucault believes that it should be combated through language, especially avant-garde literature.

In the third section, I discuss Foucault's second snare: his theory of power. Foucault rebukes modernity since he thinks contemporary forms of power are omnipresent and highly productive; they concoct the self and render its practice of freedom—which in principle it is capable of—a rather strenuous task. But, as I shall demonstrate below, the dynamic between power and freedom in Foucault is far from clear and the distinction between them, in the absence of any presuppositions about the self, remains ambiguous. This difficulty, and the impalpability of power in general, suggests that the modern, disciplined self could recognize and exteriorize the imprints of power it bears only by espousing a new attitude: an unrelenting ethos of doubt toward itself and the truths that guide it. Before this ethos is elaborated on in the Conclusion, however, I will conduct a comparison between Foucault's and Weber's understandings of discipline that sheds new light on the former's work.

Historicizing the Psychoanalytic Subject, Dispersing the Personality: Foucault's Critique of Freud and Weber

Various theorists served as inspirational sources for Foucault: Nietzsche, Heidegger, Bataille, and Canguilhem come to mind, among others. Yet it is perhaps fair to say that, at least from a thematic point of view, the two theorists who influenced him most are Freud and Weber. Among other things, Foucault shared with Freud an intense interest in the study of sexuality, an interest evident in his first critical essays on modern literature during the early sixties, his study of bio-power in the seventies, and in his last project on the sexual ethics of the ancients. Like Weber, Foucault shared an equally intense interest in the study of modern institutions, their structure and rationalities, and especially their normalizing effects upon the self. Late in his life, Foucault even states: "[I]f Nietzsche interests me, this is only to the extent that Nietzsche for Weber was absolutely determining, even if in general it is not said."[4] Given this intellectual context of Foucault's work, it is important to examine his relations with Freud and Weber in more depth, and to study, in particular, his critique of these two theorists.

In the entrapment and proto-entrapment tradition, modernity is criticized on account of a specific vision of subjectivity: the agent of practical reason, the nonalienated worker, the overman, the personality, the neurosis-free self. The afflictions and ills of society are threatening because they deny a particular type of self its potentials, needs, and freedoms, however these may be defined. We have seen that for proto-entrapment writers notions of the self are also a vehicle for overcoming discontent, whereas for entrapment writers these notions do not have such a liberating function. For Foucault, however, the subject is but an instrumental invention, its construction a fiction motivated by a will to knowledge, a quest for philosophical certainty, an imperative for domination. Modernity is characterized by a growing urge to fix the substance of the self—to define its boundaries, interrogate its nature, establish it as the Other of other selves. In his archaeology, Foucault follows the French structuralism of the fifties and sixties, studying thought in terms of an underlying order and of rules that belie phenomenological notions such as will and consciousness. He continues to attack the notion of subjectivity in his genealogical phase. "Where the soul pretends unification or the self fabricates a coherent identity, the genealogist sets out to study the beginning—numberless beginnings whose faint traces and hints of color are readily seen by an historical eye. The analysis of descent permits the dissociation of the self, its recognition and displacement as an empty synthesis, in liberating a profusion of lost events."[5]

In *Madness and Civilization*, Foucault studies—without explicitly saying so—the "lost events" and the "exteriority of accidents"[6] that underlie the emergence of one aspect of the Freudian self. The superego appears in Foucault's interpretation less as an archaic ingredient of the psyche required by civilization as such, than as a product of very specific and recent discursive and institutional transformations. As in his other works, here Foucault points to a global metamorphosis in the Western understanding of the self by illuminating events at the social periphery and by juxtaposing different epochs; changing attitudes towards the mad are a case in point. The idea of impounding the madman and separating him from society is a relatively recent one, claims Foucault. From the middle of the seventeenth century, the madman was confined in the same space with the poor, the vagabond, the homeless, the criminal, and the unemployed. The goal of this unprecedented confinement was essentially negative: to inter the unproductive population that

threatened the emerging social order of the bourgeoisie, not to interrogate and reform this population. This intention, however, changed
with the introduction of the asylum during the early nineteenth century. For reformers of that time such as the Quaker Samuel Tuke and
the French humanist Scipion Pinel, the objective was the reintegration
of the madman into society. This was to be achieved by the inauguration of a new moral and social self-consciousness within the patient.
According to Foucault, the asylum, which separated the madman from
other categories of the confined, operated as a system of constant surveillance and observation whereby the patient was punished for any
abnormal and improper behavior. This semibehavioral regime of correction constructed a milieu of *fear*, whereby the madman was "kept in
perpetual anxiety, ceaselessly threatened by Law and Transgression."[7]
Yet the reformers realized that such fear—in order to be effective and
lasting—should be supported by means that transcended external sanctions. The madman, therefore, was trained to fear the insane and devi-
ant forces within himself, to objectify himself and to become both
conscious and responsible for his own abnormality.

> The madman . . . must feel morally responsible for everything
> within him that may disturb morality and society, and must hold
> no one but himself responsible for the punishment he receives.
> The assignation of guilt . . . becomes both the concrete form of
> coexistence of each madman with his keeper, and the form of
> awareness that the madman must have of his own madness.[8]

The asylum molded the patient into the perpetual warden of his own
transgression: he was trained to recognize his insanity as socially and
morally deplorable, to contain it through the exercise of self-distancing
and an identification with the critical gaze of the Other, and to punish
its eruptions by the self-afflictions of guilt; in Freudian terms, this
process amounts to an acquisition of a superego.[9] (Foucault himself
does not use this term, nor does he discuss Freud in this context.) The
Freudian depiction of a self divided between its ego and an acquired,
normalizing agency emerges in Foucault as a reflection of *a uniquely
post-Enlightenment historical development*: the asylum exhibits and accentuates the growing pressure in modernity to ensure the internalization
of and conformity to social norms of even the most marginal community members. As the evolving social and economic orders became
increasingly dependent upon an obedient and productive citizenry and
labor force, the asylum became a microcosm of this social universe; it

"reduces differences, represses vice, eliminates irregularities," and in general "denounces everything that opposes the essential virtues of society."[10]

Foucault performs a more explicit historicization of the Freudian subject and exposes it as an ensemble of contingent events in later works, especially in *The History of Sexuality*, vol. 1. As shown in the previous chapter, an essential claim of psychoanalysis is that the self is instinctual by nature and that the sexual drive in particular is its source of energy—a force that affects its desires, thoughts, dreams, speech, and conduct in unconscious ways. Not only is the sexual drive omnipresent in all of these life domains, but it also shapes humans from the outset: the specific and contingent path of a child's sexual ontogenesis is seen as constitutive of her adult life, affecting her character and being as a whole. According to Foucault, however, the pansexualism of Freudianism should be seen as the culmination of discursive developments that originated at the beginning of the nineteenth century. At that time, an increasing apprehension with regard to the reproductive capabilities and health of the social body gave rise to discourses on sex in fields such as medicine, pedagogy, and psychology. For these sciences—and primarily for the first—sex was a pivotal explanatory device.

> There was scarcely a malady or physical disturbance to which the nineteenth century did not impute at least some degree of sexual etiology. From the bad habits of children to the phthises of adults, the apoplexies of old people, nervous maladies and the degeneration of the race, the medicine of that era wove an entire network of sexual causality to explain them.[11]

From this perspective, the Freudian self is seen less as an innovation than as the fruition of discursive events germane to new social and political concerns. For Foucault, then, both the pansexualism of the self and the superego are artifacts fabricated by a cluster of institutions, practices, and discourses—not universal and unalterable features of the self as claimed by the proponents of psychoanalysis. (I return below to a discussion of Foucault's notion of bio-power.)

Despite his criticism of psychoanalysis, however, Foucault at the same time had cause to laud its concept of the self. Freud acknowledged the divided, conflictual nature of the self as well as its restlessness and compulsive quests for transgression; he allowed unreason to surface as a critical force in humans, depicting the self less as a master of its life than as a prisoner of its haphazard circumstances and history. In *The*

Order of Things, Foucault hails psychoanalysis as a "counter-science" with a subversive role in modern thought and culture. Psychoanalysis (as well as ethnology) has a privileged position, since it forms "a perpetual principle of dissatisfaction, of calling into question, of criticism and contestation of what may seem, in other respects, to be established" (*"un perpétuel principe d'inquiétude, de mise en question, de critique et de contestation de ce qui a pu sembler, par ailleurs, acquis"*).[12] Against the autonomous, unified, and rationally governed vision of the self, psychoanalysis poses a chaotic and fragmented void that induces bewilderment and a sense of powerlessness. To put it differently, psychoanalysis undermines the illusions that lurk behind what Foucault calls "humanistic" visions of the self, such as Weber's notion of the personality.

In contrast to his overall critical stance towards Freud, Foucault has much in common with Weber. As Foucault himself noted, they share an intellectual project that may be described as "an ontology of the present," one that asks, "What is the present field of possible experience?"[13] In their answers, Foucault and Weber concur upon two fundamental points. First, from a methodological point of view, they both hold that the self should be studied through an analysis of its empirical, external circumstances; life-orders or apparatuses *(dispositif)* such as the market, bureaucracy, the asylum, the prison, and the school are seen as constitutive of the self. To illustrate this point, they juxtapose the present circumstances of the self with past conditions and/or other cultures and the types of selves produced there. Second, Foucault and Weber arrive at somewhat similar conclusions regarding the predicament of the modern self: both see this self as disciplined and ruled by internalized norms that extinguish individuality; they see the social and economic orders of modernity as shaping productive and useful individuals suited to specific functional needs, a process that affects bodily conduct, habits of thought, gesture, and emotion. Finally, both agree that the modern self tends to relate to itself and others through self-objectification and myriad rationalizations.[14] In fact, Foucault seems to have followed Weber rather closely in his depiction of discipline, as we shall see in the third section.

But whereas Weber laments the difficulties of establishing a personality under contemporary social conditions, Foucault castigates notions of the self that resemble the personality. He sees these notions as an artificial attempt to avoid the imminent fragmentation and dispersion of life in general and in modernity in particular. Weber, as we saw above, posits the personality—with its quest for inner unity, a coherent narrative, self-imposed truths, and an ascetic existence—as a partial response to the increasing segmentation of domains of action and value and to the sense of meaninglessness this predicament generates. From Foucault's perspective, however, the personality longs for the enduring "sameness" of the self in a world that in numerous ways already begets such sameness: the structure of our knowledge and the working logic of our institutions establish precisely such a circumscription of subjectivity. Rather than resisting the detrimental effects of modernity—which Weber identified so well—the personality ends up supporting them. Hence Foucault adamantly rejects Weber's ascetic view and its quest for certainty.

> Max Weber posed the question: If one wants to behave rationally and regulate one's actions according to true principles, what part of one's self should one renounce? What is the ascetic price of reason? To what kind of asceticism should one submit? I posed the opposite question: How have certain kinds of interdictions required the price of certain kinds of knowledge about oneself? What must one know about oneself in order to be willing to renounce anything?[15]

The personality knows itself as a subject in need of guiding principles and a lasting identity; to construct itself as such, it espouses a normative "inner core" and the ascetic professionalism of modernity, systematically eschewing alternatives of action and value, as well as the threat of dispersion through self-expressivism. Weber still believed in the possibility of establishing a subjectivity on the basis of rational and conscious choices, thereby embracing a central aspect of humanism. This humanism is one of the principal targets of Foucault's criticism—especially as this school expresses itself in Husserlian phenomenology and in Sartre's *pour-soi*.

> One can say that all Western civilization has been subjugated, and philosophers have only certified the fact by referring all thought and all truth to consciousness, to the Self, to the Subject. In the rumbling that shakes us today, perhaps we have to recognize the birth of a world where the subject is not one but split, not sovereign but dependent, not an absolute origin but a function ceaselessly modified.
>
> *On peut dire que toute la civilisation occidentale a été assujettie, et les philosophes n'ont fait qu'en établir le constat, en référant toute pensée et toute vérité à la conscience, au Moi, au Sujet. Dans le grondement qui*

nous ébranle aujourd'hui, il faut peut-être reconnaître la naissance d'un monde où l'on saura que le sujet n'est pas un, mais scindé, non pas souverain, mais dépendant, non pas origine absolue, mais fonction sans cesse modifiable.[16]

For Foucault the self knows no transcendence: it is always embedded in or shaped by an episteme, a language, a matrix of power. It has no point of origin and no principle of truth, but is always in a state of flux and modification. "The self is not a substance; it is a form and this form is not above all always identical to itself."[17] Whereas modern theorists such as Weber view the dispersion of the self as an existential threat, Foucault, like other postmodern theorists celebrates it: unless a masking identity is forced upon the self by others or by itself, it reveals difference and heterogeneity, rapture and indeterminacy. Both Weber and Freud are guilty, in this view, of distorting these features of the self, the first by calling for an abiding set of ultimate values that perpetuate sameness, the second by presenting as given and inescapable a psychic structure of the self, while ignoring the particular historical configuration through which this self emerged. For Foucault and the notion of negative entrapment he advances, the task is to expose the manner by which our identities have been progressively impounded and concocted. A central reason for this process, for Foucault, has been the colonialization of modern thought by a will for knowledge, a will that has acquired a conspicuous force due to a unique epistemic arrangement.

Entrapment and Language

The Doubles of Modernity and Discursive Proliferation

Weber and Freud saw the human sciences as a valuable aid to the modern self: the cultural sciences allow one to understand present social circumstances and hence to develop a *Weltanschauung*, and psychology helps alleviate the various neuroses generated by contemporary life. With Foucault, in contrast, knowledge becomes part of the modern malaise: its underlying motivations are often suspect, and it is characterized by an expanding interrogation, categorization, and objectification of human beings. While in most of his works Foucault demonstrates this character of the human sciences by examining specific fields (psychiatry, medicine, the penal system, sexuality, and so forth), in *The Order of Things* he searches for the epistemological and archaeological grounds for this phenomenon. To facilitate his discussion, Foucault introduces the concept "episteme," by which he means the "historical a priori" of an age, the underlying structure of thought within which positive knowledge is formulated. The episteme is therefore a principle of intelligibility by virtue of which "ideas could appear, sciences be established, experiences be reflected in philosophies, [and] rationalities be formed" in a given era.[18] Foucault distinguishes between three epistemes: renaissance, classical, and modern. The latter, he argues, grapples with irreconcilable contradictions, which he demonstrates through an inquiry into three fields of knowledge: language, labor, and life.

The classical episteme, which extends roughly from Descartes to pre-Kantian thought, was characterized by the absence of a subject at the center of representations, avers Foucault. Signification was possible because language was seen as transparent, as providing an accurate representation of the world without calling for exercises of decipherment as in the renaissance. Because of the correspondence between words and a cosmos with a pregiven order, there was no need to problematize human nature from the point of view of its epistemic-constitutive and synthetic faculties. In the taxonomic table of knowledge characteristic of the classical age, humans occupy a place devoid of any particular distinction. "In [c]lassical thought," writes Foucault, "the personage for whom the representation exists, and who represents himself within it, recognizing himself therein as an image or reflection, he who ties together all the interlacing threads of the 'representation in the form of a picture of a table'—he is never to be found in that table himself. Before the end of the eighteenth century, man did not exist . . ."[19]

The modern episteme, in contrast, invented this new being, "man." Kantian philosophy introduced him both as an object among other objects and as a subject by virtue of which representation and knowledge are possible. Man is conceived of as finite: as an object, he is shaped by a mode of production, by a linguistic system, or by his place on the temporal-evolutionary scale; as a subject, he is unable to penetrate into "things in themselves." But Kant separated the two classes of finitude, and, moreover, posited finite subjectivity as a foundation for the forming of true representations of the world of objects and of man as part of it. This move, argues Foucault, established three intrinsic sets of doubles within modern thought, doubles that echo the Kantian double that was examined in the first chapter of this work.

The Empirical and the Transcendental. As empirical beings, humans find themselves immersed in and subjected to the laws and mechanisms of natural and social-historical realties. These realities define and shape humans, or in Foucault's words, establish "finite positivities." From this perspective, man is seen as "governed by labor, life, and language, his concrete existence finds its determination in them; it is possible to have access to him only through his words, his organism, the objects he makes."[20] Man's specific modes of existence can thus be captured by establishing sciences such as philology, biology, and economics. Kantian epistemology, however, also presented man as being consti-tuted by a "fundamental" nature. The transcendental subject is seen as providing the epistemic conditions that render all knowledge of expe-rience possible. This new role of the subject is explained by admitting that, while man's cognition must be finite and within the limits of space, time, and categories such as causality and substance, the universal and timeless quality of this *a priori*, transcendental framework guarantees the objectivity and communicability of knowledge. Kant viewed the prescribing cognitive apparatus as empty in itself, but as constitutive of sense-data, which it synthesizes to generate meaningful information about the phenomenal world.

As a corollary to the founding act of epistemic finitude, however, modern thought sought to base the empirical sciences that study man upon some "fundamental" features of his own finitude.

> The mode of being of life, and even that which determines the fact that life cannot exist without prescribing its forms for me, are given to me, fundamentally, by my body; the mode of being of production, the weight of its determinations upon my existence, are given to me by my desire; and the mode of being of language, the whole backwash of history to which words lend their glow at the instant they are pronounced . . . are given to me only along the slender chain of my speaking thought.[21]

In the modern episteme, then, knowledge about man is established by formulating essentialist presuppositions about the body and its mecha-nisms, about speech and its underlying structure, about desire and needs. (For example, since David Ricardo, modern economics does not explain production in terms of fluctuation in the exchange value of commodities—as did the analysis of wealth during the classical period—but on the grounds of lack and scarcity, both present and past, that characterizes the human experience. Today, rational-choice theory attempts to explain economic and social phenomena by presupposing the fundamentals of human self-interest and rationality.) Modern thought strives to divide the finite fundamental from the finite positivities, realizing that the former is its only basis for comprehending the fluctuations of the latter. "Our culture," writes Foucault, "crossed the threshold beyond which we recognize our modernity when finitude was conceived in an interminable cross-reference with itself."[22]

According to Foucault, however, the marriage of the empirical and the transcendental aspects of man establishes a paradoxical and unstable arrangement, since man becomes "an enslaved sovereign, [an] observed spectator" ("[un] *souverain soumis*, [un] *spectateur regardé*").[23] How can man—who is thoroughly shaped by a national language, by the needs bred by his economic system, by his evolutionary stage—be in possession of an insulated and fixed cognitive apparatus (and other fundamentals)? The transcendental is constantly under threat of being determined by unavoidable modifications in natural and historical empirical realities; in turn, these realities (and man as part of them) are in danger of being misrepresented and wrongly analyzed under the bias of a conditioned cognitive structure. Because of this reciprocal relation, modern thought is characterized by an oscillation between the fundamental and the positivities, by an intrinsic and compulsive search for defining their identity and difference, and by attempts to reduce the empirical to the transcendental—and *vice versa*. In an effort to resolve these tensions, post-Enlightenment philosophy approached man empirically through an exploration of his observed characteristics (for example, Comte's positivism) or through eschatology, where the subject is explained through true philosophical discourse and method (for example, Marx's historical materialism).

Cogito and the Unthought. Thought in the modern episteme, writes Foucault, discovers "both in itself and outside itself . . . an element of darkness, an apparently inert density in which it is embedded, an unthought which it contains entirely, yet in which it is also caught."[24] Since Descartes, the possibility of reflection is dependent upon the existence of a pure *cogito* or consciousness, one able to posit itself unconditionally against objectified social and natural surroundings. But the modern *cogito* must differ from the Cartesian one: now man recognizes that he may represent the world only because he possesses a body, a language, desires and needs—in short, because he is submerged in things whose origins and workings elude him. This spawns a sense of insecurity in the autonomy of *cogito*. Man recognizes, for example, that he is able to represent the world only because he is endowed from the outset with language, but he is never certain just how the words he employs affect his reflection, even his ability to conceptualize the notion of *cogito* itself; he is forced, therefore, into endless objectifications of language, into an effort to retrieve the "in itself" and transform it to "for itself." As Rabinow and Dreyfus observe, the dilemma is that "the background of taken-for-granted commitments and practices, precisely because it is unthought, makes thought and action possible, but it also puts their source and meaning out of our control."[25] Foucault views Freud's uncovering of the unconscious and the transcendental reductionism of Husserl's phenomenology as exemplifying the dichotomized nature of modern reflections on human consciousness.

The Retreat and the Return of the Origin. As an empirical being, man must understand himself as emerging through a chain of causality and within a time that is homogenous in nature, devoid of any distinctive "events." In this respect, he cannot have a fundamental, since his use of language, the nature of his needs, and the very evolution of his body only reveal a *gradual formation*. Nor, moreover, can his cognitive apparatus be free from this piecemeal generation. The multiplicity of developments does not disclose a moment at which man can witness his "birth," but rather deprives him of any discernible beginnings. The origin of man "is that which introduces into his experience contents and forms older than him, which he cannot master; it is that which, by binding him to multiple, intersecting, often mutually irreducible chronologies, scatters him through time . . ."[26]

In contrast to this endless retreat of his birth, however, man must also constantly renew the notion of an origin. The very construction of his history as an homogenous, temporal order to be understood within the framework of causality is possible only because there is already a subject that founds and enables this construction; ironically, the human subject as a distinct origin of cognition must be presupposed in order to reveal to the same subject that he has no clear origins and foundations. Thus, the paradoxical task of modern thought is that of "contesting the origin of things, but of contesting it in order to give it a foundation by rediscovering the mode upon which the possibility of time is constituted— that origin without origin or beginning, on the basis of which everything is able to come into being."[27] The preoccupation with the origin again steers modern thought into two opposing directions: while historicists such as Hegel, Marx, and Spengler see this return as involving a promised wholeness and plenitude, others such as Hölderlin, Nietzsche, and especially Heidegger, view it as leading to an escape from pregiven embeddedness and therefore to a void, a meaningless existence, an encounter with nihilistic thought.

The anthropocentric foundation of the modern episteme and the immanent contradictions it generates propels modern thought to augment its will for knowledge in new directions. As cognitive psychology strives to fathom man's generic capabilities for representation, social sciences such as sociology, political science, and cultural studies seek to unveil the social rules and cultural symbols by which man tacitly represents his environment and which enable him to function in it. None of these sciences, contends Foucault, has been able to develop a convincing methodology and conceptual system of its own: each remains, in fact, dependent on models of the natural sciences (especially biology), as well as of economics and philology. This methodological confusion and dependency only deepens their profusion. Moreover, the mistrust in the purity and autonomy of cogito calls for repeated efforts to retrieve the unthought, as psychoanalysis does, and the recovery of the origin engenders studies that extend from ethnology to evolutionary theories.

The proliferative trend that the modern epistemic arrangement introduced into the human sciences also affects other domains of knowledge that are central for Foucault, although he does not make the connection explicit. Once representations of the world are seen as dependent on man's reason alone, unreason becomes something deeply threatening that needs to be closely examined and eliminated, if possible. Once man's proper functioning in the social environment has been conceived of in terms of his ability to unconsciously represent for himself the norms and rules of society, it becomes necessary to examine and correct those who, like the delinquent, fail to abide by such representations. Once the impact of the body on the transcendental subject has been established as suspect, it becomes imperative to understand how the body's dark mechanisms, especially its sexuality, could influence the being and consciousness of man. Thus, while epistemic events cannot by themselves explain the developments in the history of madness, criminality, and sexuality, they fostered changes that occurred at the genealogical level.

Language as a Battlefield: Discourse and Transgression

The global effect of the modern episteme, then, is the ubiquity of the will to knowledge and truth, a will that "daily grows in strength, in depth, and implacability."[28] The hold of this will is especially manifest in the modifications of our language: it becomes saturated with a scientific discourse that objectifies the world and relates to things through true and false statements, that makes the norm (with the aid of statistics) into a governing principle and invents endless categories to designate human beings. But if, on the one hand, language in modernity becomes a sphere through which human experience and self-understanding are shaped and confined, then on the other, language (or writing, *écriture*) also becomes the domain through which the modern self asserts its freedom and expands its existential horizons.[29] Apollonian discourse and Dionysian literature pull language in opposite directions, both intensifying their hold upon it simultaneously.[30] In Foucault's view, the dualistic nature of our language (and our preoccupation with words in general) is a unique characteristic of the modern episteme.

For the classical episteme, as noted above, language was a transparent medium, the assumption being that words correspond to what they signify in an unproblematic fashion; representation, then, "was a matter of dividing nature up by means of a constant table of identities and differences for which language provided a primary, approximative and rectifiable *grid*."[31] The vision of harmony induced by a preexisting Divine order extends to the natural association of signified and signifier, and thus "language was a form of knowing and knowing was automatically discourse."[32] According to Foucault, the breakdown of this declared self-evident association in the late eighteenth century prompted the collapse of the classical episteme as a whole. "The threshold between Classicism and modernity . . . had been definitively crossed when words ceased to intersect with representations and to provide a spontaneous grid for the knowledge of things" (*"Le seuil du classicisme à la modernité . . . a été définitivement franchi lorsque les mots ont cessé de s'entrecroiser avec les représentations et de quadriller spontanément la connaissance des choses"*).[33]

In the wake of this breakdown, language came to be seen as an autonomous and potent domain; it began to "acquire its own particular density, to deploy a history and objectivity, and laws of its own."[34] In modernity, language has an ambiguous position: if it is recognized as the form through which any thought must express itself, it is also distrusted for molding and distorting this thought.

Having become a dense and consistent historical reality, language forms the locus of tradition, of the unspoken habits of thought, of what lies hidden in people's minds; it accumulates an ineluctable memory which does not even know itself as memory. Expressing their thoughts in words of which they are not the masters, enclosing them in verbal forms whose historical dimensions they are unaware of, *men believe that their speech is their servant and do not realize that they are submitting themselves to its demands.*[35]

Since the nineteenth century, language as a time-bounded reality has become the principal terrain of entrapment, according to Foucault. As moderns, we live with the consciousness that "we are already, before the very least of our words, governed and paralyzed by language" *("nous sommes, avant la moindre de nos paroles, déjà dominés et transis par le langage");*[36] thought is conditioned by the *a priori* and inescapable grammatical structure of language, its national and idiomatic characteristics, its historical vicissitudes, its multiple meanings, ambiguities, and context-dependent quality. Language is seen as one of the historical-empirical spheres in which man is enmeshed and as posing to him a very profound challenge, since only by employing words may he acquire knowledge about the world and himself. The sense of entrapment within language could arise, however, only because modern philosophy depicted man as a sovereign, transcendental subject, and as an independent moral agent by virtue of his free will and consciousness. Both of these interrelated claims may be questioned once we recognize the possible imprints of language: can it be, contra Kant, that our notions of time, space, and causality are conditioned by the language we employ? Or that the universality and law-like inclinations of Western moral theories are related to the abstractness that has been inflicted by our words? Once man understands himself as being mired in language, his sense of finitude and of groundless existence is accentuated. As Rajchman suggests, Foucault views modernity as an age where "[a]ll scientific, aesthetic, and moral problems are reduced to problems of language, and languages have no warrant of foundation beyond themselves."[37] Yet modern thought has been unwilling to accept the arbitrary boundaries imposed by a language unfettered by reality; it seeks, therefore, "to destroy syntax, to shatter tyrannical modes of speech, [and] to turn words around in order to perceive all that is being said through them and despite them."[38] More specifically, Foucault argues, the assay to overcome the obstacles that language poses to knowledge has assumed two paths.

First, positivists like Russell sought to purge language of all unique, accidental, and imprecise elements and thus to achieve the ultimate formalization of language. Boole and others had an even more ambitious project in mind, striving to develop a symbolic logic that would dispense with everyday language altogether. The goal of both of these exercises was to reconstruct or develop a new language that reflects preverbal thought in its inviolate transparency. Second, writers such as Marx, Nietzsche, and Freud embraced the historical and multilayered composition of language. They engaged in works of exegesis, convinced that an understanding of the meaning buried within words would illuminate our economic, moral-cultural, and psychic realities. In general, many of our endeavors to transform our identities and to regain the ability to freely define them focus on examining and criticizing the words with which we relate to others and describe ourselves.

Now Foucault can be seen as sharing the post-Enlightenment trepidation at the reign of language in general and the reign of scientific discourse in particular. (From this perspective, Foucault situates himself in the midst of the modern episteme, his augury of its coming demise notwithstanding.) Foucault's early works advance "the illusion of autonomous discourse,"[39] the archeologist's conviction that the production of knowledge and its effects on human experience should be explained by studying discourses and the rules that govern their formation—rather than by the genealogical analysis of how the human sciences interact with complex sets of power struggles, political strategies, and contemporary institutions and practices. Even in Foucault's studies of power during the 1970s, the central role he ascribes to discourse is not diminished, and at times he seems to perceive power struggles as "taking place within discourse itself."[40] In any event, it is clear that Foucault (especially in books such as *The Order of Things, The Archeology of Knowledge,* and *The History of Sexuality,* vol. 1) attributes a critical role in the self's formation to language that is permeated by bodies of knowledge *(savoirs)* and, more generally, by *any socially structured, orderly speech* (which is what Foucault means by discourse). He clearly expresses his position in *L'ordre du discours.*

"There is undoubtedly in our society," writes Foucault, "a profound logophobia, a sort of dumb fear . . . of everything that could possibly be violent, discontinuous, querulous, disordered even and perilous in it, of the incessant, disorderly buzzing of discourse."[41] This fear of what could be termed centrifugal speech breeds numerous means of controlling and circumscribing discourse. To begin with, the sayable and thinkable are subject to external constraints or "a system of exclusion." The most important of these is based on the separation of true and false statements, a separation introduced by Platonism. Since then, "the highest truth no longer resided in what discourse *was,* nor in what it *did:* it lay in what was *said.*"[42] In the Western tradition, argues Foucault, words have generally been divorced from deeds, measured by the truth they contain rather than by the action and awe they demand. Foucault emphasizes that the dichotomization of discourse into true and false statements, and the will to truth that supports this dichotomy, have undergone numerous historical transformations, and have always been dependent upon institutional support. In modernity, however, discourses of knowledge have penetrated into an increasing number of institutions, governing areas such as the formation of economic policies or the operation of the penal system. (A related rule of exclusion, present in Western discourse since the seventeenth century, is the designation of the madman's speech as either meaningless or as the Other of reason.)

In addition to these external restrictions on discourse, there are internal ones that foster its coherence and continuity. First there is the principle of commentary, according to which some works are rated as basic, classic, and essential, and thus serve as the foundation for endless criticism and interpretation. This introduces a hierarchy into discourse and leads to the formation of tradition. Commentary thus "limit[s] the hazards of discourse through the action of an *identity* taking the form of *repetition* and *sameness;*" a second principle, authorship, "limits this same chance element through the action of an *identity* whose form is that of *individuality* and the *I.*"[43] The concept of the author, argues Foucault, fabricates a sense of unity among works, of a common purpose and consciousness behind them, and of an essential relation between these works and the individual's biography and times. A third internal factor is the segmentation into disciplines. Scientific propositions are meaningful—and can be assigned a true or false status—only if they relate to a defined set of objects, employ acceptable methods, embrace a certain theoretical field. "Disciplines," writes Foucault, "constitute a system of control in the production of discourse, fixing its limits through the action of an identity taking the form of a permanent reactivation of the rules."[44]

Discourse fictionalizes order and regularity; we should therefore conceive of it "as a violence that we do to things, or at all events, as a practice we impose upon them" *("comme une violence que nous faisons aux choses, en tout cas comme une pratique que nous leur imposons").*[45] Unable or unwilling to cope with the open and chaotic elements in our experience, we neutralize discourse, trying to "avert its powers and its dangers, to

cope with chance events, to evade its ponderous, awesome materiality."[46] The logic of discourse, therefore, has something in common with
the logic behind both the disciplining, bureaucratic machine and the
sociability-fostering superego: it posits the singularity of phenomena as
a dangerous disruption, advancing predictability as the main tenet of its
creed. According to Foucault, the orderliness, containment, and hence
the imposed violence of discourse have intensified in modernity. Since
our thought lacks any foundation—beyond language itself—upon
which to make judgments, we must circumscribe our language and
extend the applicability of scientific discourse. For example, "[i]t is as
though the very words of the law had no authority in our society, except
insofar as they are derived from true discourse" ("*comme si la parole
même de la loi ne pouvait plus être autorisée, dans notre société, que par un
discours de vérité*").[47] This apollonialization of discourse and thought,
however, is precisely what is eschewed by modernist art and the new,
transgressive counter-discourse: literature.

> Thus, as Klossowski's language recasts itself, projects back over
> what it has just said in the helix of a new narrative . . . the speaking
> subject scatters into voices that prompt one another, suggest
> one another, extinguish one another, replace one another—
> dispersing the act of writing and the writer into the distance of the
> simulacrum where it loses itself, breathes, and lives . . . Literature's
> being concerns neither men, nor signs but this space of the
> double . . . Distance and proximity of the Same, where we others
> now find our only language.
>
> ~Foucault, "The Prose of Actaeon"

Foucault's extensive writings on literature during the sixties should be
seen in the context of Barthes' *nouvelle critique* and the *Tel Quel* journal.
This intellectual milieu followed Robbe-Grillet's anti-humanism,
emphasized the liberating role of avant-garde literature, and saw modernist writings (and art) as constituting an autonomous sphere where it
engages in self-reflective activity. Foucault shared these beliefs, and
commented on some of the writers whose works interested the *nouvelle
critique:* Flaubert, Roussel, Artaud, Blanchot, Klossowski, Bataille, and
others. His main contribution to literary theory, however, is located not

so much in these individual essays (or book, in the case of Roussel) as in his ability to place the problematic of contemporary literature in the context of the modern episteme.

Modern literature, argues Foucault, does not escape the consciousness of finitude that is immanent to post-Enlightenment thought. Yet, whereas for the human sciences finitude demarcates the limits of human experience and knowledge, for literature finitude must be explored—and violated. Literature dwells "in that region where death prowls, where thought is extinguished, where the promise of the origin interminably recedes."[48] The quest of avant-garde writings is to leap beyond the confines of representation—to probe into cruelty and excess, the loss of boundaries and intermingling between self and other, the upset of narrativity and coherence, angst and uncanniness, unconscious images and desires, sexuality and death—it is about "limit experiences."[49] During the classical period, literature was subordinated to the representative task of language; it therefore enhanced the sense of an orderly and pleasant world governed by universal moral and aesthetic values. Modern literature, however, "becomes detached from all the values that were able to keep it in general circulation during the classical age (taste, pleasure, naturalness, truth), and creates within its own space everything that will ensure a lucid denial of them (the scandalous, the ugly, the impossible)."[50]

Finitude and the transgressive ethos of contemporary literature, then, are fundamentally interrelated, in Foucault's view. Finitude means that whatever limits are imposed on human beings—limits primarily delineated by language—they cannot be justified by a natural, eternally ordered world. As a consequence (and as was discussed in the first chapter of this study), these boundaries are always suspect, blurred, and open to question through the mode of writing. The death of God established a new understanding that "nothing may again announce the exteriority of being" *("rien ne peut plus annoncer l'extériorité de l'être").*[51] Since nothing that is designated stands outside and against us, our experience thus becomes both "interior" and undefinable, calling for bounds beyond its arbitrary circumscription. "Toward what," asks Foucault, "is transgression unleashed in its movement of pure violence, if not that which imprisons it, toward the limit and those elements it contains?"[52] Yet transgression is purely negative: "no content can bind it, since, by definition, no limit can possibly restrict it."[53] Transgression is a movement that breaks existing forms; it does not affirm new ones. Needless to say, the limit—of experience, of reason, of identity—cannot be eliminated, and thus contestation has the character of repeated, infinite, and non-totalizing leaps. These leaps, Foucault seems to argue, bring about a dual revelation: on the one hand, they unveil uncharted terrains of thought and life; on the other, they often discover that what resides beyond the limit is not an Other separated by an unbridgeable Difference, but is rather Identity and the Same (as exemplified by the false gulf between madness and reason).

Now, since the perimeter of finitude is principally linguistic, modernist literature is propelled to ponder the question of language or, more specifically, it *reflects upon itself* as a constitutive part of language. Free from the classical task of representing the world, the word become its own subject. Literature thus appears as "a silent, cautious deposition of the word upon the whiteness of a piece of paper, where it can possess neither sound nor interlocutor, where it has nothing to say but itself, nothing to do but shine in the brightness of its being."[54] This new insulation of the word from the world, however, goes hand in hand with the work being woven into a matrix of words and works that preceded it: writing involves allusion to other texts, references to the traditions they have established, contemplation of the medium and its various forms, and a questioning of the meaning of writing itself. This self-referential activity forms the "library" of modernist literature, of which Flaubert is the founder, avers Foucault. In writing *The Temptation*, Flaubert "produced the first literary work whose exclusive domain is that of books." Following him, "Mallarme is able to write *Le Livre* and modern literature is activated—Joyce, Roussel, Kafka, Pound, Borges. The library is on fire."[55]

As the works of this library are becoming unfettered by the task of realistically representing their times, they also rebut the fiction of the "author" and the presupposition of a common purpose and meaning behind an oeuvre. According to Foucault, a text is singular and independent, referring to other texts in the library rather than to texts by the same author; writing is about the beings and possibilities of words, not about the life of the author, who remains external and secondary. This propensity of modernist literature to detach the work from the author is correlated with the dissolution of the narrator *within* the work. Sade's work, for example, "does not have an absolute subject," and thus "never discovers the one who ultimately speaks."[56] The anonymity of the narrator and the multiplication of speaking voices have major consequences, according to Foucault. Literature confronts the Kantian legacy, accelerating "the breakdown of philosophical subjectivity and its dispersion in a language that dispossesses it while multiplying it within the space created by its absence," a development which is "probably one of the fundamental structures of contemporary thought."[57] Indeed, writing is not a way to forge a self, to reflect a biography, to search for the coherence of a life story, or to acquire immortality through the preservation of one's name. Rather, "[w]here the work had the duty of creating immortality," writes Foucault, "it now attains the right to kill, to become the murderer of its author."[58] Foucault even suggests that some of those who have been most sensitive to this disintegration of the subject in writing—Hölderlin, Nietzsche, Artaud, Roussel—have internalized this predicament to an extent that forced them to succumb to madness.

This depiction of modernist literature manifests its role as a mirror image of discourse in Foucault's work during the sixties. If discourse is an attempt to establish a positive, durable knowledge about man, transgressive literature is an attempt to call into question any accepted truth, definition, norm. If discourse relates to the world through a dichotomy between true and false statements, literature seeks an aestheticization of life and valorizes *any* act and thought as long as it is rebellious, lurid, and new. If discourse introduces through commentary a hierarchy among works, the library is a matrix of references where the text that alludes often becomes more important than the text alluded to. If discourse promotes the idea of a subject that weaves various works together—emphasizing the indispensability of the author's psychology, biography, and intentions for grasping these works' import—literature introduces a cacophony of voices that resist reduction. If discourse regards the speech of folly as meaningless or as an Other, literature recognizes that this speech may come from those who have fathomed some of the fundamental truths of our culture. If, in sum, discourse is the centripetal mode of our language, literature is the centrifugal one.

The Order of Things ends on an optimistic note. The epistemic trap may have a loophole after all: the subversiveness and self-reflection of post-Enlightenment literature may bring about the downfall of the modern episteme, suggests Foucault. "Man," he argues, "is in the process of perishing as the being of language continues to shine ever brighter upon our horizon" *("L'homme est en train de périr à mesure que brille plus fort à notre horizon l'être du langage").*[59] Yet this faith did not last for long. After the events of 1968, Foucault ceases to conceptualize a global and total change, and adopts a more overtly political stand that advances local and limited struggles. Thus, during the seventies he supplants the epistemic trap with a theory of power, advancing the doublet power-freedom instead of the doublet discourse-literature. (Discourse and the will to knowledge remain critical, but they are now studied in connection with power.) As we shall see, Foucault's theory of power rebuffs the idea that a historical situation exists that could be described as "free" and purged from discontent; concurrently, this theory does not recognize any sphere of life or language as immune to the effects of power. In fact, Foucault's later writings portray literature itself less as a vehicle for liberation than as a symptom of a specific configuration of power.[60] This reversal is epitomized by his change of views regarding sexuality.

From Daring Transgression to the Banality of Confession

In Foucault's early works, sexuality is the ultimate designation of human limits, and writing about sexuality the expression of transgressive thought *par excellence*. The emergence of sexuality as definitive of our finitude is *structural*, an event "tied to the death of God and to the ontological void which his death fixed at the limit of our thought."[61] Following Bataille, Foucault asserts that in the absence of God, sexuality is the primal, natural boundary; it "marks the limit within us and designates us as a limit."[62] The scandalous language of writings about sexuality profanes our world, breaks our most sacred taboos, challenges what we believed to predate any social organization, and even uncovers what lies in the depth of a mind we thought to be pure consciousness. As sexual conversation proliferates, it brings about a new type of being. "Sexuality," writes Foucault "is only decisive for our culture as spoken, and to the degree that it is spoken." And since we are compelled to speak about it incessantly, its appearance as a "fundamental problem marks the transformation of a philosophy of man as worker to a philosophy based on a being who speaks."[63] In other words, for a modern self who transcends and transfigures itself through language, sexuality is a critical feature of identity and existence.

In *La Volenté de Savoir* Foucault turns this position on its head. The ingredients remain the same: modernity, language, sexuality, and the formation of the self are still integrally related, but instead of being a transgressive/liberating act, the infusion of our speech with sexuality now becomes the manifestation of a power at work. Let us examine this reversal. According to Foucault's new view, the modern preoccupation with sex originates in pastoral practices of the seventeenth century, and even more so with the eighteenth-century perception of the human body as a biological entity of insurmountable importance for the state. In the competition among European nation-states, the well-being and vigor of the social body were vital. The state therefore had to encourage the study and regulation of health and disease, mortality rates and life expectancy, diets from infancy to adulthood, birth rates and hygiene. "Western man," writes Foucault, "was gradually learning what it meant to . . . have a body, conditions of existence, probabilities of life, an individual and collective welfare, forces that could be modified, and a space in which they could be distributed in an optimal manner."[64] The state became an administrator of living beings, manipulating the population as a whole and the life of each individual separately in an attempt to match reproduction to the needs of production or warfare. Henceforth, the power and vigor of the state demanded overseeing its people as complex biological creatures—not simply as legal entities.

For this politics, which Foucault calls "bio-power," sex obviously became a major object of analysis. Sex was no longer "only a matter of sensation and pleasure, of law and taboo, but also of *truth and falsehood.*"[65] Particularly during the early nineteenth century, the discourse on sex spread into diverse disciplines: demography, biology, medicine, psychiatry, psychology, criminology, and pedagogy. In each of these fields, argues Foucault, human sexual behavior was investigated and converted into an object upon which propositions can be constructed. New categories and names were invented and then portrayed as capturing some essential truth about the character, moral worth, appearance, and mental abilities of a person. Each new category—the hysteric or frigid woman, the hypermasturbating child, the pervert—became in time a human "type." Indeed, if in the preceding centuries "the sodomite had been a temporary aberration," with the discourses on sexuality the homosexual was turned into "a species."[66]

The elaboration of these discourses or bodies of knowledge has been dependent upon the appropriation of the confessional practice from its religious context by the clinic, school, hospital, or home. "The transformation of sex into discourse, . . . the dissemination and reinforcement of heterogeneous sexualities," elucidates Foucault, "are perhaps two elements of the same deployment: they are linked together with the help of the central element of a confession that compels individuals to articulate their sexual peculiarity—no matter how extreme."[67] The confession, of course, does not leave a person neutral: it demands a certain relation to oneself, an introspection and monitoring of behavior and thought, a fostering of dependence upon an expert who interprets the truth within oneself, an acceptance of the underlying assumptions and terminology of the discourse—even a deepening and magnification of the very notion of interiority. Since the Romantic period, we see this interiority as the domain most secure from power, as the one containing the gist of our singularity and bounded identity. It is a vast container of individual feelings, images, memories, and thoughts, the truthful expression and formation of which is vital for authenticity and freedom. Foucault finds these convictions—and the hermeneutical exercises they call for—ironic, especially as they manifest themselves in the confessional disposition of the modern self.

> The obligation to confess . . . is so deeply ingrained in us, that we no longer perceive it as the effect of a power that constrains us; on the contrary, it seems to us that truth "demands" only to surface . . . Confession frees, but power reduces one to silence; truth does not belong to the order of power, but shares an original affinity with freedom.[68]

Power, it seems, *can even produce our notion of freedom itself.* (As we shall see, this Foucauldian argument makes distinguishing between genuine freedom and a produced one a rather baffling project.) This possibility of false notions of freedom sheds new light on the meaning of sexual literature since the late eighteenth century. Rather than epitomizing defiance, these writings could be seen as exemplifying the successful masking of power; their minute recollection and confession of sexual acts and fantasies is not a demonstration of courage, but of a certain banality. Sade and the anonymous Englishman who diligently described his sexual adventures in *My Secret Life* illustrate the operation of power in our subjectification, the latter author being only "the most direct and in a way the most naive representative of a plurisecular injunction to talk about sex."[69] But the idea that sex contains the key to our liberty misled not only these writers, in Foucault's view, but also more contemporary theorists such as Reich and Marcuse, who advanced the "repressive hypothesis" associating the ills inflicted by capitalism and bourgeois life with repressed sexuality.

In Foucault's writings during the 1970s, then, literature is no longer the force that counters discourse, but a by-product of both discourse and bio-power; the marriage between language and sexuality does not breed transgression, but rather covert submission. These transformations in Foucault's position reveal something vital to his thought as a whole: *They demonstrate that a theory of entrapment that lacks a subject or presuppositions about the self must adopt an ethos of suspicion, that it can find no point of rest, since any time it finds an anchor from which to transgress or resist an extant order, it ends up questioning this anchor itself.* This dynamic is constitutive of Foucault's notions of power and freedom, to which I now turn.

Entrapment and Power

Power and Freedom

"I believe," writes Foucault, "one's point of reference should not be to the great model of language *(langue)* and signs, but to that of war and battle. The history which bears and determines us has the form of war rather than that of language: relations of power, not relations of meaning."[70] This attack on the centrality of language in social critique is aimed at semiotics, as well as at Foucault's own early thought. Modernist literature, he now seems to be claiming, is impotent as a vehicle for transformation, and discourses, moreover, do not originate out of epistemic structures but because of ever-changing, undetermined power struggles. By envisioning such a battle, Foucault radicalizes the terms through which entrapment theorists describe the relation between the self and its social environment. Before I examine this radicalization, however, a brief explication of his concepts of power and freedom is called for.

Foucault views power in operative terms, defining it as "a way in which certain actions modify others," or as a "total structure of actions brought to bear upon possible actions."[71] Power is exercised by individuals and groups upon others, or, more precisely, upon their potential endeavors; it does not aspire to subdue or destroy individuals (which would be pure violence), but to govern their conduct and their relationship to themselves by structuring "the possible field of action."[72] This structuring enables as it limits, fostering certain outcomes while eliminating the option of others. To achieve its specific goals, power may have to narrow the field of possibilities to a minimum, yet it must leave a certain element of choice in order to be effective. Power is "exercised only over free subjects and only insofar as they are free,"[73] since only then does the individual have the necessary conditions to govern herself. But this space for action may also breed resistance, and, in point of fact, "faced with a relationship of power, a whole field of responses, reactions, results, and possible invention may open up."[74]

For Foucault, then, ontological or metaphysical inquiries into the nature of power are misguided. "Something called Power," he writes, "with or without a capital letter, which is assumed to exist universally in a concentrated or a diffused form, does not exist. Power exists only when it is put into action . . ."[75] In Foucault's nominalist and descriptive approach, power cannot be a substance or a commodity such as wealth, knowledge, or influence, although it may be related to these in various ways. Power is operative within a field of relations; it is not a resource to be accumulated in virtue of these relations. Foucault is also critical, therefore, of the liberal depiction of power as something that can be legitimately "transferred" from the governed to the governor. This view, which is based on the monarchical model, portrays power as centered in the hands of a ruler; the danger, accordingly, is that power is susceptible to overflows, to crossing its agreed-upon boundaries by infringing upon the rights of citizens and oppressing them. For Foucault, then, liberals are guilty not only of reifying power, but also of misrepresenting it as negative in nature. We should understand, he argues, that "power produces; it produces reality; it produces domains of objects and rituals of truth. The individual and the knowledge that may be gained of him belong to this production" ("le pouvoir produit; il produit du réel; il produit des domaines d'objets et des rituels de vérité. L'individu et la connaissance qu'on peut en prendre relèvent de cette production").[76]

Foucault's critique of liberal notions of freedom follows a parallel line. For liberals of the Hobbesian tradition, freedom is something to be possessed by constructing a cluster of rights around a private sphere; freedom, in other words, can be understood as a "state." For Foucault, in contrast, freedom (like power) exists only in action: "liberty is a practice;"[77] it should be understood in terms of verbs, not nouns, in the plural and not in the singular. "Rather than speaking of an essential freedom, it would be better to speak of an 'agonism' . . . less face-to-face confrontation [between the individual and power] which paralyzes both sides than a permanent provocation."[78] Agonism rather than possession: a person is free only to the extent that she unveils, questions, and refuses a certain configuration of power—and to the extent that she invents, experiments, and elaborates an alternative and self-determined mode of life and selfhood. This elaboration, however, does not presuppose—as do Kantian, Hegelian, and Marxian theories—a pre-given human nature or end that needs to be revealed and nourished. Rather than thinking in terms of a final "liberation," Foucault argues, we should view the construction of subjectivity as an ongoing and open project.[79] As Rajchman eloquently puts it, Foucault understands freedom as an "experience of fragility of a kind of identification taken for granted. Who we are would not be the image or source of this freedom, but just what is constantly freed or opened to question by it."[80]

In conceptualizing this notion of freedom, Foucault continues to employ an opposition between Dionysian and Apollonian elements. Even before articulating the concept of freedom explicitly, Foucault spoke of "something in the social body" that opposes power, a "plebeian quality or aspect" that can be seen as "a centrifugal movement, an inverse energy, a discharge" *("mouvement centrifuge, l'énergie inverse, l'échappée").*[81] If power, like discourse, is characterized by the predictable cast it imposes upon things, then freedom and the "plebeian quality" are transgression-like, questioning the forms induced by power and maintaining a certain dynamism in the constitution of identities; moreover, like the opposition between literature and discourse, the one between freedom and power offers no final victories, but rather demands ongoing, incessant struggle. Freedom thus becomes the foundation of Foucault's critique of modern power: he denounces modernity for limiting the self's capacity to shape itself through practice without the interference of scientific categories and naming, without the infiltration of norms into everything from sexual conduct to performance at work, without the surveillance that inheres in the architecture of public spaces, and more. In this respect, freedom assumes in Foucault's thought an equivalent role to that of the desire for meaning in Weber's, or to that of instinctual satisfaction in Freud's. (Foucault would not have said, however, that we have a basic, natural *need* for freedom.)[82] We have seen how Weber and Freud present their elastic presuppositions about the self in a way that eliminates the possibility of programmatic politics. Similarly, Foucault's quest for more individual distinctiveness and autonomy in self-formation guides his critique, yet is not translated into a comprehensive political vision: this quest remains a critical, not a regulative, principle. Bearing this principle in mind could help us clarify why Foucault sees modern power as particularly insidious.

The Web of Power

"Power," writes Foucault, "is tolerable only on condition that it masks a substantial part of itself. Its success is proportional to its ability to hide its own mechanisms."[83] The normalizing forms of power successfully traverse modern society because they remain invisible and unconscious. Foucault demonstrates these characteristics of power in *Discipline and*

Punish, where he examines its disciplinary/objectifying aspects and contrasts it with the monarchical modality of power. If the latter was
symbolized by the king's body and required recurring public spectacles
to manifest his might, disciplinary power deepens its penetration and
increases its efficiency the more it succeeds in establishing a machine of
surveillance wherein individuals are constantly perceivable, while the
corporeality of power is reduced to an instrumental fiction. Thus
Bentham's Panopticon, which serves Foucault as a metaphor for contemporary forms of social organization, "is a machine for dissociating
the see/being seen dyad: in the peripheric ring, one is totally seen,
without ever seeing; in the central tower, one sees everything without
ever being seen."[84] "Visibility" is therefore "a trap"[85]—and a silent
one, too.

Instead of attracting attention to its own actuality, modern power
pushes a person back on himself. The "perfection of power should tend
to render its actual exercise unnecessary . . . the inmates should be
caught up in a power situation of which they are themselves the bearers."[86] Power is optimized when the gaze, the words, and the norms of
the other—whether warden, psychiatrist, therapist, or teacher—are
internalized and integrated into one's identity. As long as power successfully divides and individualizes human beings, this process can be
presented as one of self-formation rather than of imposition, and as
long as it classifies them within a matrix of categories and subcategories,
it fabricates a sense of difference and uniqueness while a global uniformity of identities progressively reigns.

Given this intangible and deceiving nature of power, Foucault comes
to valorize philosophy and critical thought, regarding them as vital for
the unmasking of power and the practice of freedom. "Philosophy is
precisely the challenging of all phenomena of domination at whatever
level or under whatever form they present themselves," Foucault
writes.[87] Since "man is a thinking being,"[88] he is able to expose as
historically conditioned the categories with which we describe ourselves and the norms that govern our lives. Thus, the kind of philosophy
Foucault has in mind is Nietzschean and skeptical: it strives to do away
with the notion of Truth. As we have seen above, the will to truth
already appears as endemic to modern society in Foucault's early writings; now, however, its sources are presented in light of their close
affinity with quests for domination.

[Power relations] cannot by themselves be established, consoli-
dated, nor implemented without the production, accumulation,

circulation, and functioning of discourse. There can be no possible exercise of power without a certain economy of discourses of truth which operate through and on the basis of this association. We are subjected to the production of truth through power and we cannot exercise power except through the production of truth.[89]

As Foucault has convincingly shown throughout his work, new institutions and practices—such as the asylum, the hospital, the prison, or the plurisecular confession—provide the necessary settings for observation, documentation, and experimentation, and hence for the accumulation of bodies of knowledge such as psychiatry, clinical medicine, criminology, and psychoanalysis. These bodies of knowledge, in turn, shoulder the necessary justification and organizing principles for the relevant institution or practices. The emergence of social sciences such as demography, statistics, and public health studies is also intertwined with the regulative imperatives of bio-power. Foucault's general point is that the human sciences require disciplining, subjectifying, and administrative-supervising techniques, and that this underlying context is constitutive of these sciences. Not only are the human sciences therefore methodologically flawed, as argued in *The Order of Things*, but they are imbued with a pursuit of domination.

Foucault is thus skeptical of views such as Habermas's in *Knowledge and Human Interest*, which perceive the human sciences as serving the interests of society and as being potentially emancipatory.[90] Foucault questions our ability to oversee the production of knowledge and its uses, presenting it as yet another sphere of modern life—similar to the market, bureaucracy, sexual morality—that is out of collective control. Rather than advancing enlightenment or transparent communication, this production brings about the subjection of modern selves: it fosters the fib of inherent truths that are definitive of identities, objectifies and helps utilize bodies, and increasingly entrusts the regulation of society to experts, who are themselves entangled in the institutional matrix they inhabit. Confronting power is an intricate project, since we should not enlist the aid of science in criticizing present social conditions, certainly not in the name of a repressed human nature or impaired psyche; science, moreover, should not be our instrument for gauging the probable consequences of changes we may introduce into our educational system, health and mental health practices, penitentiary institutions, and so forth. Exercising our freedom means combating the entrenched role of the human sciences in our culture and the ways of thought they have ingrained. "It is not a matter of emancipating truth from every system of power (which would be a chimera, for truth is already power) but of detaching the *power of truth* from the forms of hegemony, social, economic, and cultural, within which it operates at the present time."[91]

This struggle against the hegemonic forms of power/knowledge in modern society is an endless one: Foucault rejects as illusory the notion of a situation that—both from spatial and temporal perspectives—is struggle-free. From the spatial point of view, Foucault understands power as intrinsic to any type of human relation. "Power is everywhere; not because it embraces everything, but because it comes from everywhere" (*"Le pouvoir est partout; ce n'est pas qu'il englobe tout, c'est qu'il vient de partout"*) writes Foucault.[92] He displaces his early assertion that, with the death of God, man's experience is necessarily interior, with the presentation of the individual as enmeshed within a web of power that has no exterior; instead of discontinuous instances and circumscribed domains in which power is exercised we should think of it as "capillary," as involving a "microphysics" that pertains even to minute details in everyday life. In postulating such a ubiquity of power, Foucault animates the social universe, depicting it as swarmed with constantly operative, agile forces. Any passivity should be eliminated in understanding this universe: an individual is not simply shaped—like an after effect—through her "circumstances" in a benign or detrimental fashion; rather, she is subject to deliberate campaigns that strive to overcome her resistance. This characterization of the relation between the self and its surroundings leaves little credence for notions such as communitarian "shared understandings," Habermasian "ideal speech situations," or even liberal *modus vivendi*.

From a temporal point of view, Foucault's theory does not contain a future or past state in which the operation of power could be or could have been arrested; he posits neither a time of a primal horde and of blissful narcissism nor a dim hope for a charismatic leader who could change the course of history. Although even his own early theory allowed for a total metamorphosis because of the discontinuities among epistemes, Foucault now views progress (in the sense of a coherent whole) as a mirage: we may dismantle some contemporary practices, replace hegemonic discourses with subjugated ones, even exercise our freedom in aesthetic transfiguration—but the fact remains that one snare will only be displaced by another, that no future situation exists in which the mutual warfare could be dissolved. In other words, while Foucault is an apostle of a radically transformed society (in his work, "the present as such is brought under attack"),[93] he also mitigates the aspirations associated with such a transformation by presenting the entrapment within a condition of mutual warfare as an ahistorical and trans-spatial constant.

It is impossible to transcend power, furthermore, not only because of its "everywhereness," but also because of its centerless and disconnected nature. Foucault insists that while certain affinities may exist among apparatuses *(dispositifs)*, they should be seen as emerging and functioning independently, without a coherent plan or core behind them. Foucault warns us that there are no "headquarters that preside over its [power's] rationality; neither the caste which governs, nor the groups which control the state apparatus, nor those who make the most important economic decisions . . ."[94] Power does not call for a deductive methodology that presupposes a tangible nucleus, an omnipotent group or individual. Instead, we should conduct "an ascending analysis of power, starting, that is, from its infinitesimal mechanisms, which each have their own history, their own trajectory, their own techniques, and tactics . . ."[95] Foucault concedes that there are "global strategies" of power, and that certain institutions and classes—especially the state and the bourgeoisie—are capable of colonializing and utilizing the micro-exercises of power for their own advantage. Yet the rationality and effects of power in one apparatus do not necessarily correspond to those of another, and the defeat of one (or of the global strategy itself) would not loosen the grip of the others. Agonism demands the acceptance of this fragmentary nature of power, as well as the lack of easy, nameable targets.

Instead of such targets, Foucault calls us to accept the anonymity of power, its being "both intentional and nonsubjective."[96] At the operational level, the "machinery" of power is operated by people who act consciously and intentionally. Yet the advantage of the machinery is that it dictates the rules, techniques, rationale, and objectives of power without regard for autonomous subjectivities and individualities. As Foucault dramatically demonstrates in his discussion of the Panopticon, the architectonic structure itself prescribes the functions and conduct of each person. But the anonymity of power also pertains to its origins, especially at the microlevel: while we can isolate certain individuals and groups (for instance, Pinel, Bentham, La Salle, and the Quakers) as those who invented certain institutions and techniques of power, this identification does not explain why the latter have mushroomed within the whole social body. Moreover, Foucault follows Mandeville, Smith, Kant, Marx, Freud, and Weber in depicting the extant social order as a fruition of (in his case, injurious) unintended consequences, so that even if a mastermind had been behind the introduction of power, it would have been pointless to study this mind's intentions. (For example, the police of the seventeenth century may have wanted to strengthen the monarchy, but by developing techniques for controlling the population they established a new matrix of power that rendered the monarch anachronistic and superfluous; modern prisons were intended to reform the criminal, but instead they perpetuate criminal behavior.) We must relinquish all remnants of a God-based thinking: our social world is completely fathomable in terms of its working logic, but there is no agent behind it, just a series of more or less contingent events in whose aftermaths we are mired. (The realization that the world lacks explication in terms of human purpose and human will poses a challenge for the modern self, since this self can be certain neither about the efficacy of its own acts of resistance, nor that these acts would not generate an even more detrimental social universe, especially as it moves from a negative critique to a positive affirmation of alternatives.)

But perhaps by insisting upon the anonymity of power Foucault seeks to convey another idea: that power is in me as well as in you, that it is internal as well as external, that I am responsible for its operation as well as you are. One can say that Foucault is both a Rousseauist and the ultimate foe to the Rousseauist dream: both theorists depict a horizontal society in which each member is simultaneously dominating and being dominated; yet whereas for Rousseau this predicament presents the only hope for true freedom, for Foucault it breeds unprecedented enslavement. "We are much less Greeks than we believe. We are neither in the amphitheater, nor on the stage, but in the Panoptic machine, invested by its effects of power, which we bring to ourselves since we are part of its mechanism" ("*Nous sommes bien moins grecs que nous ne le croyons. Nous ne sommes ni sur les grandins ni sur la scène, mais dans la machine panoptique, investis par ses effects de pouvoir que nous reconduisons nous-mêmes puisque nous en somme un rouage*").[97] To annihilate this self-generated machine, we will have to counteract external forces and to call into question some of our deepest emotions, bodily movements, beliefs, motivations, habits of thought. Practicing our freedom would demand a struggle within a landscape where the lines between the external and the internal are continuously blurred; it would demand erecting walls that have long crumbled. Before I conclude this discussion by examining how Foucault envisioned such a project, his views on discipline should be mentioned. The study of discipline is essential to Foucault's critique of modernity and has become one of his enduring legacies; it is especially pertinent for this study, moreover, given the uncanny and little-addressed similarities between Foucault and Weber in this matter.

Discipline: A Comparison

In his attempt to divulge the degree to which the modern self is fabricated and the depth of its normalization, Foucault studied the emergence of disciplinary techniques and their modes of operation. This work reveals some striking resemblances between Foucault and Weber, although Foucault's writings on discipline are far more complex and elaborate, and break new ground in critical respects. Noting some of the similarities and differences between the two theorists will allow us to clarify the recent history of commentary on discipline. To begin with, both Weber and Foucault emphasize that the imperatives behind the inauguration of disciplined modes of conduct include needs for greater predictability, utility, efficiency, speed, and control. The disciplines regard the body and mind as clay from which desired capabilities and aptitudes could be extracted. This objectified perspective on the human body, both agree, originated in the armies of early modern Europe and spread from there to the whole social body: schools, hospitals, factories, prisons, bureaucracy, and more.

Discipline demands that the body should be habituated in precise, judgment-free fashion. "The content of discipline," writes Weber, "is nothing but the consistently rationalized, methodically trained and exact execution of the received order, in which all personal criticism is unconditionally suspended and the actor is unswervingly and exclusively set for carrying out the command. In addition, this conduct under orders is uniform."[98] Similarly, Foucault notes that in discipline "it is a question not of understanding the injunction, but of perceiving the signal and reacting to it immediately according to a more or less artificial, prearranged code."[99] This Pavlovian-like habituation and the other features of discipline are achieved by "indefinitely progressive forms of training" and exercises, which ensure both that "automatic docility"[100] is obtained, and that the elements (that is, bodies) shall be "interchangeable."[101]

In the process of disciplinary training, the human body is taken as a material to be reconstituted according to specific needs. As Foucault observes, in the Classical age "the human body was entering a machin-ery of power that explores it, breaks it down and rearranges it."[102] For Weber this process is particularly evident in the industrial plant, where with the "mechanization of discipline . . . the psycho-physical apparatus of man is completely adjusted to the demands of the outer world, the tools, the machines—in short to an individual 'function.' The individual is shorn of his natural rhythm as determined by the structure of his organism; his psycho-physical apparatus is attuned to a new rhythm through a methodical specialization of separately functioning muscles . . ."[103] Foucault argues that with discipline time is redistrib-uted and reconstituted as "an obligatory rhythm [that is] imposed from the outside"; with this imposition, "a sort of anatomo-chronological schema of behavior is defined. The act is broken down into its ele-ments," and to each movement, "is assigned a direction, an aptitude, a duration." As a consequence of this analysis of time, objects, and organs, power is able to constitute "a body-weapon, body-tool, body-machine complex" *("un complexe corps-arme, corps-instrument, corps-machine")*.[104]

The disciplines thus allow the formation of impersonal human machines that are composed of predictable individuals who function in full synchronization with each other and from which any distinctive, disruptive characteristics have been eliminated. Weber notes that in the modern army, like any bureaucratic organization, "[i]n place of indi-vidual hero-ecstasy or piety, of spirited enthusiasm or devotion to a leader as a person, of the cult of 'honor,' or the exercise of personal ability as an 'art'—discipline substitutes habituation . . ."[105] Foucault makes the same point, arguing that with discipline "the individual body becomes an element that may be placed, moved, articulated on oth-ers. Its bravery or its strength are no longer the principal variables that define it; but the place it occupies, the interval it covers, the regularity . . . The soldier is above all a fragment of mobile space, before he is courage or honor" *("Le corps singulier devient un élément qu'on peut placer, mouvoir, articuler sur d'autres. Sa vaillance ou sa force ne sont plus les variables principales qui le définissent; mais la place qu'il occupe, l'intervalle qu'il couvre, la régularité . . . L'homme de troupe est avant tout un fragment d'espace mobile, avant d'être un courage ou un honneur")*.[106]

There are, of course significant differences between Weber and Fou-cault. The latter observes, for example, that discipline often involves a certain ordering of space and the invention of architectonic formations that ensure control by their very structure. Foucault also argues that while discipline imposes radical uniformity, it introduces at the same time an infinite number of categories, subcategories, ranks, and so forth, that constitute a scale by which individuals are constantly differentiated and separated from one another. But Foucault's most consequential departure from Weber lies in his argument that the disciplines are the birth place of the human sciences. The two meanings of the word "discipline" are in fact related: according to Foucault, the system of supervision at the school, hospital, factory, prison, and other institutions provides convenient circumstances for observing human behavior and reactions to different conditions and requirements. This system also permits the formation of individual files and documentation in archives, and an elaboration of statistical knowledge based on this stored information. The "small techniques of notation, of registration, of constituting files, of arranging facts in columns and tables that are so familiar to us now, were of decisive importance in the epistemological 'thaw' of the sciences of the individual."[107] Foucault sees the ritual of the examination as exemplifying the marriage between discipline and knowledge, since it is both a (compulsory) way to train and assess individuals, as well as a method of transmitting knowledge to them and gaining knowledge of them. From Foucault's perspective, then, in developing the discipline of sociology, which is based on the accumulation of data and the formation of rules of expected conduct, Weber was relying on the practices and modes of social organization that he adamantly criticized. As in many other areas of his work, Foucault encourages us to be vigilant precisely where other critics of modernity believed they were on solid, unblemished ground.

Conclusion

Despite the substantial differences between Foucault's early work on language and his late theory of power and discipline, the same ethical passion sustains both: the exigency of denormalizing our existence in its entirety, of breaking through the current fields of experience. Predictability and functionality form the creed that sustains not only our notions of citizenship, rationality, and sexuality, but our language too. Loosening the grip of normalizing society would demand, then, a new language free from notions such as universal truth, from norms determined by the social sciences, and from deep meanings to be uncovered by hermeneutics. This loosening, however, would also demand new practices of everyday life wherein the range of free actions is expanded in a concrete (rather than merely juridical) way. In searching for new ways to form our selfhood, Foucault examined the Greeks' and Romans' "art of existence," and "care for the self," suggesting that there is a notable affinity between the Hellenic period and our own. Similarly to the Greek ethical outlook, which was not governed by universal precepts, "the idea of morality as obedience to a code of rules is now disappearing, has already disappeared. And to this absence of morality corresponds, must correspond, the search for an aesthetics of existence."[108]

Foucault, in other words, continues the individually-based responses to entrapment advanced by Weber and Freud, sharing with his predecessors a sense of political pessimism, realism, and ambivalence regarding collective action. While he attaches importance to personal measures, local movements, and revolutions in resisting contemporary forms of domination, exclusion, categorization, surveillance and so on, he is also skeptical of them. "People do revolt, that is a fact. And that is how subjectivity . . . is brought into history, breathing life into it. A convict risks his life to protest unjust punishments; a madman can no longer bear being confined and humiliated; a people refuses the regime that oppresses it. That does not make the first innocent, does not cure the second, and does not ensure for the third the tomorrow it was promised . . . No one is obliged to find that these confused voices sing better than the others and speak the truth itself."[109] Indeed, rather than suggesting novel options for collective action, Foucault's main response to entrapment (and the response to which he devoted most of his attention during his last years) was based on exploring new/ancient ways to form our individuality, ways that significantly differ from the solutions advanced by Weber and Freud.

According to Foucault, the ancients followed an ethical way of life that was also an aesthetic one, wherein an individual gave a distinct shape to his conduct. More precisely, this type of conduct began where the imperative of following moral conventions ended; Foucault does not seem to be arguing that we can live without such conventions entirely, but that the space accorded to them varies historically in a considerable way. For the Greeks, he believes, the aesthetic way of life involved continuous work on the self by itself, a deliberate setting of limits and distribution of pleasures.[110] Through these exercises, the ancients elaborated a style that was personal and singular without presupposing that they were uncovering this singularity from the depth of the self; rather, they created it by exercising their freedom. According to Foucault, the subject can be constituted in an "autonomous way, through practices of liberation . . . as in Antiquity, on the basis of course, of a number of rules, styles, inventions to be found in the cultural environment."[111] While the communal setting is indispensable—both as a source of models and as a context for practice—the critical aspect of the aesthetic cultivation of the self is that the "work on the self with its attendant austerity is not imposed on the individual . . . *but is a choice about existence made by the individual.*"[112]

The notions of individuality, choice, and agency involved in Foucault's account are inspired by Hippocratic medicine;[113] in order to fully fathom his vision of the self, we should recapture some tenets of this medicine. In particular, Hippocratic (as well as Galenic) medicine presupposes that each human being has a unique constitution based on a particular combination *(crasis)* of the four humours (phlegm, blood, yellow bile, and black bile); while there are certain basic personality types (for example, the phlegmatic or melancholic) corresponding to the predominance of one humour or another, these categories are merely rough approximations in portraying each individual's physiological composition. Furthermore, this theory of medicine suggests that health hinges upon the preservation of our original constitution of humours throughout life, a preservation demanding an *ongoing* regime of diet, sex, exercise, sleep, and so on; this regime is specific to each individual, and attuned to changing circumstances of the body, age, season, and place. As noted by Hippocrates, "it appears to me necessary to every Physician to be skilled in nature, and strive to know . . . what man is in relation to the articles of food and drink, and to his other occupations, and what are the effects of each of them to *every one*" (*Common Cultural Heritage*, emphasis added). The individuality of this type of medicine entails that there are no universal solutions to the same disease, that human beings cannot conduct themselves according to norms in matter of health, and that the preservation of health is an incessant endeavor throughout life, not limited to times of emergency. Hippocratic medicine demands, then, not only considerable range of options in our daily practices, but also a profound awareness and responsibility of the self toward its own well-being. Acting virtuously in this context means shaping the substance of life throughout the day, every day, and in continuous manner from day to day.

Foucault views this medical care as being the foundation of a more general vista. The Greek citizen assumed responsibility not only over his health, but also over the molding of his character and conduct. For example, in moderating his sexual activities in terms of intensity, as well as type and number of partners, the Greek was acting not merely out of medical considerations, but also out of the need to demonstrate for himself and others his ability to shape himself into an ethical being—one capable of moderation in all human (not only sexual) intercourse. More specifically, Foucault suggests that this citizen was concerned with two, interrelated attributes: first, he was committed to being active and to shunning passivity and dependency; second, he valorized self-control *(enkrateia)* over his desires and natural hunger for pleasure (without suppressing his pursuit of pleasure or trying to decipher its deep meanings). These points could also be stated otherwise: the activity, virility, and manliness of the citizen expressed themselves in his ability to deliberately tame his deportment according to criteria that he set for himself even though he often had the opportunity to act without such restrictions. Foucault argues, furthermore, that the ethical dimension of this molding of character is not exhausted in the relation of the self to itself: the voluntary act of imposing limits on our sexual conduct has a political and public dimension, since the ability to display moderation in the public domain and in matters of state hinges in part on our ability to exercise restraint in private matters. Hence "the individual fulfilled himself as an ethical subject by shaping a precisely measured conduct that was plainly visible to all and deserving to be long remembered."[114]

What is worthy of remembrance is not only the ethical fabric of the self, but also its aesthetics. To lead an ethical way of life is also to lead a beautiful way of life; for the Greeks, the two are inseparable. In Foucault's interpretation, one can distinguish two different senses in which a way of life can be beautiful, and these two paths are counterpoised to one another. On the one hand, the life of the individual may acquire a style, a certain characteristic form, since there is a wide range of human conduct free from social conventions. Which action to rein and which to approve, on which occasions, with regard to whom, and with which accompanying attitudes and bearing—all these and other decisions allow the self to develop a particular style that runs like a recurrent theme through the various spheres of its life. On the other hand, Foucault suggests that the aesthetics of existence, at least since Plato, also spring from a certain harmonic relation between the order of the soul and the ontological order of the world. "Through the *logos*, through reason and the relation to truth that governed it, such a life [that is, the aesthetics of existence] was committed to the maintenance and reproduction of an ontological order, moreover, it took on the brilliance of a beauty that was revealed to those able to behold it or keep its memory present in mind."[115] While Foucault did not have the chance to develop the implications of his studies of the ancients for contemporary life, it is the former sense of aesthetics that he seems to find attractive to the modern self. The aesthetic existence of the self would involve individual style that is free from convention and requires deliberate choice, enabling one to take responsibility over one's life and realize life's full potential; this existence, moreover, would involve immersion in practices of everyday life that engulf everything from sex and friendship to work and thought, and would thereby bridge private and public conduct.

At this point the Foucauldian vision of the self intersects with liberal visions on the one hand and with Romantic-expressivist vistas on the other; one may even surmise, in fact, that Foucault's stupendous popularity is due in part to his earnest call for the reinvigoration of these two sources of selfhood. Foucault shares with liberals the demand that an individual's life be unaffected by others, but (as noted) he does not suggest that the individual's choices should adhere to either universal, moral imperatives or to rationally determined beliefs and life plans. Instead, the choices Foucault has in mind pertain to questions of how the self could express its distinctiveness (which is not pregiven) through its mode of conduct in a self-constituted range of experiences. To be sure, it is doubtful that, given the homogenizing and domineering practices of modern capitalism and production mechanisms, the aesthetic exploration of singular style and identity could be a viable option for most working people; this aesthetic served a small elite in antiquity and is likely to serve only such an elite in the future. In any event, if the early Foucault championed difference and rapture within the self, a yearning for the unity of life now seems to infuse his vision. In this focus on the experience of the individual, Foucault, the harsh critic of modernity, apparently embraces what Simmel thought most characterizes modern culture, where "life itself becomes the purpose of life."

In positing this model as an answer to a profoundly disciplined society, Foucault was inevitably inviting a new kind of ethos, one that may be termed an "ethos of suspicion." Since "it is already one of the prime effects of power that certain bodies, certain gestures, certain desires, come to be identified and constituted as individuals,"[116] if the self wishes to reclaim its distinctiveness a calling into question of all these aspects of its identity is imperative. This journey of critical reflection could be halted at any point, but in principle it has no end: since there is nothing pregiven or natural about the self, any of its characteristics might be divulged as another—yet uncovered—fabrication of power. For negative entrapment, the dilemma of whether it is really the self that makes the choices is not a meaningless one—only open ended.

Furthermore, because power could also produce the self's notions of freedom (as demonstrated by the practice of the confession), one must be circumspect in case the adversary of power might really be the same as power and the act of defiance in truth an act of reaffirmation.[117] Thus, because normalizing power permeates all aspects of our being—including our motivations and tools for confronting it—the more inclusive we wish our liberty to be (and Foucault's aesthetic of existence certainly urges such inclusivity), the more doubtful we have to become about our present selves.

Seen from this perspective, one wonders whether the late Foucault was confronting an early Foucauldian problematic: The ethos of hyper-suspicion and its aftermath resembles the quandary of cogito and the unthought. As Foucault explains in *The Order of Things* (see the "Entrapment and Language" section above), contemporary critical thought (cogito) is always vulnerable, fearful of being under the sway of forces which it is unaware of or misunderstands; in Foucault's genealogical stage, this unthought is not desire or language, but an omnipresent and intangible power. To foster the freedom of the self, Foucauldian philosophy strives to uncover how the mind and body have been silently and thoroughly shaped; similarly to other post-Enlightenment intellectual projects, this thought seems to be "imbued with the necessity of thinking the unthought—or reflecting the contents of the *In-itself* in the form of the *For itself*" (*"traversée par la loi de penser l'impensé—de réfléchir dans la forme du Pour-soi les contenus de l'En-soi"*).[118] However, by fully fathoming the forces that have shaped it, by retrieving them and placing them under the light of critical thought, the self might reveal that it is nothing but an artifact of power—even when it believed it had successfully resisted this power. The disciplined, modern self gradually learns that the mechanisms that have forged it predate it and escape its control. Some may perceive a danger in this endless project of clarification and articulation: its possible *fulfillment* could result in an agent that is divorced from the sources of selfhood that render its life worthwhile, an agent that has lost its adherence to externally imposed fundamental values, motivations, notions of freedom—in short, everything that endows its life with meaning. From this point of view, the more the self is able to achieve lucidity about its predicament by unveiling the imprints of power, the more it grapples with the prospect of groundless, nihilistic existence; the more assured it becomes of the independent origins of its choices and conduct, the more it must wonder whose choices these are anyway. But Foucault does not flinch in the face of such a prospect. On the contrary, for him the path that leads to genuine freedom—a path that involves a dynamic self-formation, a following of the Socratic dictum "know [and question] yourself," and a valorization of contingency—passes through the place where we encounter the void in the midst of our selves.

∼ Conclusion

I N MODERNITY, A SINGULAR RIFT has developed in the relation between the self and our collective life-orders. These orders constitute a "cloned social space" that seems to reflect our energies back against us, turning us into prisoners of the violent creativity and intelligence we have projected in constructing our social worlds. This work was concerned mainly with the second phase of response to this rift: with twentieth-century political thought. We have seen that in that century a distinct historical imagination—shared by some of the most prominent social and political thinkers of the time—pictures the self as trapped in the life-orders of modernity. Since Weber, Freud, and Foucault helped both to reflect and to shape the twentieth century's intellectual and cultural scenes, exploring affinities among them offers us a unique opportunity to understand the predicament of the modern self. To be sure, each of these writers advances a distinct type of entrapment: for Weber, the evaporation of meaning and lack of self-determination in a disciplinary, "use"-oriented society; for Freud, the inhibition of instincts and psychic and social homelessness; and for Foucault, the ascendance of centripetal language and productive configurations of power/knowledge. Each of these visions highlights a certain aspect of the relation between self and society, bears a different set of presuppositions (or lack thereof) about the self, and offers a particular response to the present. But their differences render the similarities among them all the more startling and telling. If such dissimilar writers exhibit shared convictions about the plight of the modern self, perhaps they convey as a group a truth that transcends diverse theoretical frameworks and disciplines; perhaps, indeed, they constitute a loose "school" of their own. What follows is an attempt to synthesize the main themes of the entrapment imagination and its bearing upon the self.

To begin with, the distinctiveness of this imagination is demonstrated in a central question: What is the self's position in and possible response to history? As we have seen, entrapment theorists believe the self exists "within" history, not at its apex, nor at the dawn of a new, emancipated era. Weber, Freud, and Foucault reject the belief that human beings are the authors of history, able to stand above current events, rationally deliberating about their aims and needs and steering the future in desirable directions. In the entrapment vista, history is a train careening out of control, and we can neither willfully divert it to a new track nor simply pull the emergency brake and step off. Instead of piloting history, the best we can do is to cope with its dehumanizing effects, mostly through individual projects.

These convictions are not necessarily embraced by other critical theorists of modernity, not even by those, such as Walter Benjamin and Hannah Arendt, who share the concerns of entrapment writers. Entrapment writers adamantly reject the foundations for redemption and hope professed by the above two theorists: in contrast to Benjamin, entrapment writers refuse to await catastrophe and the ensuing messianic metamorphosis of the human predicament; in contrast to Arendt, they refuse to believe that moderns can introduce a break in history and enliven the public sphere to make it effective and meaningful. Although Benjamin and Arendt display a deep-seated pessimism that distinguishes them from proto-entrapment theorists, they allow for modes of intervention in historical time and thus for the possible alleviation of the modern's overall predicament. Let me then briefly sketch the responses of Benjamin and Arendt to the present in order to highlight the distinguishing characteristics of the entrapment imagination, particularly the refusal of this imagination to embrace hopefulness—an optimism stemming either from the transcendence of worldly existence or the revival of the political.

Entrapment writers, as we have seen, are leery of the notion of progress, at least if taken as a concept that pertains to all departments of life and presupposes an interrelation among these departments. Benjamin is one of the most outspoken and articulate critics of this modern fixation with the future as a horizon of limitless improvement. "The concept of progress should be grounded in the idea of catastrophe," he writes. "That things 'just keep on going' *is* the catastrophe."[1] This gloomy picture of history assumes many forms in Benjamin, but two directions seem paramount. First, he suggests that while progress in the forms of capitalism and technology promises the accelerated satisfaction of needs and of profane happiness, this satiety involves the powerlessness, inner impoverishment, and especially the isolation of individuals. The malaise of capitalism, for Benjamin, is less about the inability of individuals to express themselves through work and more about the collapse of community—of purpose and meaning that stem from a shared human world. Benjamin even suggests that capitalism is a new type of religion, one whose creed is the nihilism and despair of the secluded individual. "Capitalism is entirely without precedent," he writes, "in that it is a religion which offers not the reform of existence but its complete destruction."[2]

Second, Benjamin believes that the concept of perpetual progress instills a dangerous philosophy of temporal existence. Progress presupposes constant renewal and thus the nonidentity of one moment with the next. While Benjamin believes that the notion of time in modernity is flat and homogenous, he suggests that time in this epoch is conceived of as a linear chain, whereby with each passing minute the difference between the present and the past is continually established, and the distance from yesterday is affirmed by the constantly renewed novelty of material existence. When applied to the sphere of human identity, this temporal vista generates *forgetfulness*, which in Benjamin's view is the gist of the modern catastrophe. Without an integrated memory, both individual and community life are doomed to repeat the same cycles of violence, exploitation, and injustice that are conspicuous throughout human history. (Benjamin designated this cycle as "mythic.") Memory and tradition have an ethical import, since they teach us about hopes that have been dashed, benevolent plans that have turned into horror—in short, the failures of grand human action. With the contemporary emphasis on individuation and our technological orientation toward the world, Benjamin contends, our "remembered world *[Merkwelt]* breaks up more quickly," and "the mythic in it surfaces more quickly and crudely."[3]

But in contrast to entrapment theorists, Benjamin believes that (profane) history is about to be eclipsed, that modernity secretes the possibility of a break in time—precisely by virtue of its mythic character. The destructiveness of capitalism can induce spiritual transformation: Benjamin suggests that capitalism "is the expansion of despair, until despair becomes a religious state of the world in the hope that this will lead to salvation."[4] The total bleakness of the human predicament in modernity completes history by manifesting the latter's total futility and senselessness; concomitantly, this manifestation makes the moment ripe for messianic intervention. The intoxication with material plenitude (or happiness) assists the "coming of the messianic kingdom . . . for in happiness all that is earthly seeks its downfall." For Benjamin, historical time is the time of the body and its incessant needs, needs that moderns have made it their disastrous mission to address; the nearing messianic time, in contrast, is a time of justice and expiation, attentive to spiritual needs that allow for genuine fulfillment. This state of completion and redemption depends on the messiah (whose appearance and actions we cannot command or prophesize), but it must be launched by human efforts so that past human experience will be integrated into "a completely remembered world"[5] that preserves the ethical lessons of those who preceded us. Despite the lethe of the happiness-seeking self, Benjamin believes that forgetfulness can be defeated and oblivion can be transformed into a redemptive recovery of memories. While each generation has been endowed with "a weak messianic power," moderns may prove to have been particularly bequeathed with the task of assisting the messiah in this project, both because of their despair (which intensifies their holiness and their possession of redemptive powers) and because of their distinct historical-critical consciousness (which releases them from the distortions of inherited ideologies and could goad them to read history anew). Echoing Freud, Benjamin suggests that remembrance heals the self and the community, and that the past is accessible through semicyclical temporality and the union of distant moments in nowtime *(Jetztzeit)*. But whereas for Freud memory allows us to make peace with our homelessness and discontent, for Benjamin memory is potentially explosive, opening the way for our ultimate deliverance from the bleak present. More generally, Benjamin takes the gloominess that infuses Weber, Freud, and Foucault and turns it on its head: he reminds us of the transcendental—as well as the human—capacity to generate spiritual and existential metamorphosis in conditions that may seem to be most hopelessly and irrevocably entrenched, most immune to radical change.

A second alternative to the historic imagination of entrapment theorists is suggested by Arendt. Arendt advocates a *political response* to modernity, one centered on the restoration of the ancients' notion of the public sphere and on a transformation of the bureaucratic nation-state. In fact, while Freud, Foucault, and even Weber can be seen as

skeptical of politics, questioning its efficacy for transforming the predicament of the modern self, Arendt claims that the distinctive human
capacity for political action is the sole remedy for the self's dehumanizing plight. These different estimations of politics are surprising, since
Arendt agrees with the essence of the entrapment critique. She vehe-
mently rebukes modern society for bridling the expression of individual
distinctiveness, for expecting "from each of its members a certain kind
of behavior, imposing innumerable and various rules, all of which tend
to 'normalize' its members, to make them behave, to exclude spontaneous action or outstanding achievement."[6]

Arendt suggests (in an analysis that bears striking resemblances to
Foucault's notions of bio- and pastoral-powers) that the contemporary
imposition of sameness can take place only with the emergence of
"society," an entity composed of a large, anonymous population whose
chief concern is the preservation of life as a bare biological process and
the satisfaction of material needs springing from this process. "Society"
is a relatively new sphere of human existence, one that since the early
modern period has increasingly inserted itself between the private and
public spheres. Society thus represents the total collapse of the classical
Greek vision of a dividing line between the private and public spheres,
and for us the distinction between them is "entirely blurred, because we
see the body of peoples and political communities in the image of a
family whose everyday affairs have to be taken care of by a gigantic,
nation-wide administration of housekeeping."[7]

The emergence of society introduced destructive notions of temporality. According to Arendt, for the ancients the private sphere was
characterized by the inevitable and continuous cyclical movement of
life, the evanescence of bodies coming into existence and withering
away; the political sphere alone escaped this cyclicality,[8] and the
ancients perceived it as "rectilinear," since it housed an evolving tradition and stories composed of words and deeds performed by individuals seeking immortality in collective memory. But in modernity, a
collective organism, "society," has been invented; *the necessity formerly
associated with the reproduction of biological existence in the private sphere
alone has now begun to dominate the public sphere as well.* Arendt suggests
that the individual's body has ceased to be bound within personal cycles
of decay and growth, becoming instead part of a larger entity whose
existence within rectilinear time has become the main goal of politics.
The preservation of this entity has turned politics into the bureaucratic
art of cultivating, manipulating, supervising, and measuring popula-
tions in order to secure their prolonged existence and vitality. This

politics, in other words, has wedded a rectilinear notion of historical time with the continuous and inevitable movement of biological life, thereby giving birth to the notion of teleology.[9] History, the realm of freedom, of the grand and the unexpected, has been thereby vanquished by a temporal vista that sees politics as driven by the imperative of promoting the mere biological preservation of the community, class, nation, or race.

But despite her strong affinities with entrapment writers, Arendt departs from them in her response to modernity and insists on the virtue of reviving the political sphere and with it humans' capacity for action. A line can be redrawn, she suggests, between the realm of production and that of unconditioned performance, between the facet of identity enmeshed in the cyclicality of preservation and decay and the facet articulating individuality in a linear, public story. Entrapment writers picture identity as formed in the labyrinth of the social nexus, almost regardless of political regimes and ideologies; Arendt views the political sphere as the true theater of identity and character formation, and she spurns the notion of wholly situated selves. She contends that humans are political beings characterized by an almost ineradicable desire for positive freedom; they yearn for a shared public sphere in which to express their distinctiveness. This valorization of the political depends upon the prospect of a break in teleological time. In concord with Benjamin, Arendt seeks the interruption of this time and the breakdown of the determinism that rules a society enthralled with fulfilling material-biological needs; in contrast to Benjamin, however, she finds solace in the display of purely secular interruptions.

According to Arendt, the emergence of society and of the false belief in the inevitable and mechanistic movement of a large body in time have not been able to arrest the occasional revivals of public space that seem to erupt from nowhere. Arendt discovers in modern revolutions the proof that history can still be interloped and redirected, as well as the continuous longing for freedom. For example, she maintains that "it was nothing more or less than [the] hope for a transformation of the state, for a new form of government that would permit every member of the modern egalitarian society to become a 'participator' in public affairs, that was buried in the disasters of the twentieth-century revolutions."[10] This very same hope was expressed in the spontaneous founding of councils (in one form or another) in almost every revolution since the late eighteenth century, although Arendt believes that only the American Revolution was able to establish enduring political institutions that preserved public spaces and freedom within their bounds.[11] In grappling with a response to "the social," Arendt therefore turns to the experience of modern revolutions, suggesting that the councils can still become an enduring part of government and that citizens may still become independent and responsible actors. The councils, proclaims Arendt, are "the best instruments . . . for breaking up the modern mass society, with its dangerous tendency toward the formation of pseudopolitical mass movements, or rather, the best, the most natural way for intercepting it at the grass roots."[12] For Arendt, then, entrapment theorists failed to perceive these persistent manifestations of humans' capacity to bring about something new, these reassertions of human dignity; they overlooked the capacity of moderns to reinvent the political *despite* being atomized, normalized, and materially fixated.

Entrapment writers advance visions that eschew theology and even meaning in history; hence they refuse to shape human existence in anticipation of a catastrophic, redemptive explosion. In addition, none of these theorists suggests that under contemporary conditions politics could be a theater where individuals freely form their identities: the entrapment critique implies that neorepublicanism is hardly an answer to the pervasive normalization taking hold of everyday life. Rather, the entrapment position means that the Benjaminian and Arendtian ways of confronting modernity are improbable since they demand a "grand" change; seeing little grounds for hope on the collective level, entrapment writers insist on placing more weight on individual paths of reclaiming the self. These writers profess that if our collective destiny holds no clear promise of freeing ourselves from the dehumanizing effects of social institutions, then the best we can do is devise personal ways of *coping*. Coping, not rescue; strategies for surviving with dignity, rather than for consummating emancipation and closure. Coping, not anticipation; a disillusionment with the past and future, rather than an attempt to (re)enact an idealized vision of them. Coping means facing our embeddedness in the dehumanizing circumstances of modernity with a new type of heroism, an ongoing and incomplete assay to recover, integrate, and assert the self.

This normative position signifies that coping, as entrapment writers understand it, entails breaking away from the Enlightenment tradition (the impact of which is still evident in Habermas).[13] Writers who believed in the teleological direction of history, such as Kant, summoned individuals to embrace hope as a fundamental guide for conduct, suggesting that contributing to the betterment of mankind would redeem their lives from meaninglessness: they had only to behold the expected promise of the future before deciding upon the right course for present action. But entrapment writers entreat us to disengage ourselves from all utopianism. Weber writes that "we must not and cannot promise a fool's paradise and an easy street, neither in the here and now nor in the beyond, neither in thought nor in action, and it is the stigma of our human dignity that the peace of our souls cannot be as great as the peace of one who dreams of such paradise."[14] Their deep-seated disagreements on other topics notwithstanding, the new ethos of coping advanced by these writers requires disillusionment and realism. One must be courageous in facing the present, and this means relinquishing unqualified aspirations for well-being and autonomy, for a conflict-free and benign social order. Quests for self-determination that do not take into consideration objective conditions (Weber) or that are motivated by the mere search for uninhibited, pleasurable satisfaction (Freud), are presented as either a blind failure to act responsibly or as a form of semipsychotic breakdown. Hence Weber's personality accepts "the demand of the day," and Freud's psychoanalytic self acknowledges the "reality principle." Foucauldian resistance never contemplates an unblemished social predicament as its goal, never pictures a world devoid of power relations and mutual subjection. Resistance, in Foucault's view, takes the form of local confrontations that achieve limited ends and set the stage for the subsequent struggles. If for Kant, then, the maturity of moderns involves their ability to transform their circumstances through *selbstdenken*, this maturity, according to entrapment theorists, implies their ability to exhibit truthfulness about their marred present and wariness concerning their ability to shape the future. This notion of coping emerges from entrapment theorists' shared analysis of the self's plight, and it seems fitting to conclude the present discussion by synthesizing and summarizing this analysis.

Entrapment theories, to begin with, are distinguished by their depiction of the self as both a theater of contention and a site of conflictual relations with its environment; in both of these domains, the substance of strife is identity-related. Entrapment theories displace the Judeo-Christian discourse of an internal conflict between the good will and the evil will with one that concerns the ability of the self to form and express itself vis-à-vis institutions, rules, expectations. Yet this vision manifests itself differently in each writer. The Weberian personality seeks to assert itself against a world governed by functional necessities and instrumental rationality, while being perpetually torn between incommensurable value spheres (or polytheistic gods, to use Weber's

metaphor). Freud sees the individual's life as composed of two interrelated struggles: one within the mind, where psychic agencies ceaselessly
undermine each other, and another between the self and a restricting,
consuming civilization. Foucault goes as far as to present human relations as war-like—with the embattled territory being one's body, conduct, or self-understanding—and the self as unable to determine the
boundaries of its own authenticity. Differences among these pictures
notwithstanding, they all consider the fundamental experience of the
modern self to be one of *irresolvable* strife. The inner conflict cannot be
resolved because it is interwoven with the external one, because conflicts between different aspects of identity echo and reenact conflicts
between the self and the life-orders of modernity (and among these
life-orders themselves). Under entrapment, the most intimate dilemmas are also the most global and impersonal; *the internal and the external
are hopelessly intertwined.* Yet it is worth noting that the search for the
harmonious integration of human faculties, activities, or values—a
theme shared by Western philosophers from Plato to Schiller and
beyond—is not wholly relinquished by Weber, Freud, or Foucault. The
personality, the psychoanalytic patient, the self engaged in the art of
existence—all hunger for greater inner coherence, for a self-forged
narration. But the theories of conflict advanced by the three writers
suggest definite limits to these types of projects, limits that are
historically constituted, rather than ontologically inevitable.

The inability to resolve internal and external contention testifies that
the self cannot be depicted as a sovereign "Man." But the three writers
also undermine the notions of human supremacy by presenting
moderns as inadequate political beings unable to handle their new
social realities. None of the political systems and ideologies that have
emerged in modernity can significantly alter contemporary life-orders
(capitalism, bureaucracy, reformative institutions, science, *kultur* in
general), and overcome the threats they pose for the self. Entrapment
writers go out of their way to demonstrate that changes in the political
sphere—whether in the form of mass democracy, communism, fascism,
or other—do not necessarily affect what happens elsewhere. Even
Weber, who cherished the engagement in politics and did not take
its effects lightly, emphasizes that the *fachman* is as likely to dominate communist societies as democratic ones—that meaninglessness,
instrumentalism of reason, shallowness of selfhood, and other diseases
of modernity are unlikely to be addressed by politics. The same, of
course, holds for the subjugating superego and the psychic mechanism
of normalization, as well as for bio-power, methods of governability,

discipline, and other Foucauldian phenomena (some of which emerged in monarchies and later became entrenched both in mass democracies and in totalitarian regimes).

Such is the entrapment writers' notion of the modern self in the political arena. But entrapment signifies the questioning of the human position not only as a sovereign political being, but also as a reflective and thinking entity. In a limited sense, this assault on the critical spirit of the Enlightenment begins with Weber, who presents reason as neutral and incapable of establishing justifiable rules for personal and collective conduct. Freud goes further, presenting the self as the playground of uncontrollable psychic forces, its thoughts and very being determined by unconscious desires stemming from somatic sources, or by inherited maxims espoused uncritically because of infantile psychological needs. And for Foucault, the self is a feeble epistemological anchor, the human sciences a testament to the history of strategic power games, rather than to progress in truth-finding methods. Taken together, these three skeptical views of reason present a formidable labyrinth: we moderns seem to lack an uncontestable and shared ground for choosing between ways of life and values; we cannot be certain of our own (unconscious) motivations for embracing one course of action rather than another; and even the knowledge and language we employ to formulate our dilemmas may be entirely skewed. This being the case, entrapment means that existential, psychological, and linguistic bafflements cannot be resolved by reason. Moreover, the powerlessness of humans as political beings and as reflective beings are interdependent. If our self-knowledge is indeed deeply distorted, limited in perspective and context-dependent, or even epistemologically impossible, how can we possibly steer toward a new economic structure or rationale for collective institutions? *The death of radical politics may be inherently intertwined with the decline of cognitive man.*

The skepticism of entrapment writers toward the notion of radical, all-encompassing change may stem in part from their recognition that the social world lacks a determinant. In the nineteenth century, theorists tended to assume the interconnectedness of various spheres of human life, a theme shared, for example, by Rousseau's republicanism, Comte's positivism, Hegel's idealism, and Marx's materialism; in practice, this conviction propelled the great revolutions of the modern era, especially the French and Russian revolutions. Weber and Foucault reverse this presupposition, the former in his theory of value spheres, the latter in his depictions of loosely related *dispositifs*. Once social institutions are no longer viewed as comprising a totality, the motivation to revolutionize one sphere of human life—whether it be economic, political, erotic, or other—is greatly diminished, because such action cannot revolutionize human existence as a whole: the nuclear family is unrelated to the state; specialization is independent of capitalism. Furthermore, far from believing that the social world rests on an underlying unity and a final cause, entrapment writers reject the notion of an agent or addressee responsible for this world. In Kafka's novel *The Trial*, when K. asks an expert how to gain an acquittal, he learns that "that power is reserved to the highest court of all, which is quite inaccessible to you, to me, and to all of us. What the prospects are up there we do not know."[15] Like Kafka, entrapment theorists conceive of modernity as a peculiar hybrid in which the intensification of prescriptive human behavior goes hand in hand with the evaporation of the tangible foundations for these prescriptions. Obedience to a transcendental entity or even to corporeal ones (the feudal lord, the father in the primal horde, the monarch) has been displaced by obedience to commands whose origins are subjectless (the bureaucratic machine, the superego, the Panopticon). For Weber, Freud, and Foucault, we have become the bearers, the containers of prescriptive anonymity; coping with the domination of the no one in quasi-independent spheres of life has become a debilitating psychological and political challenge.

Entrapment writers combine this notion of anonymous domination with a view of modern selves as existentially separate and emotionally bereft; the absence of any agent responsible for normalization is echoed by the absence of the human bonds necessary to confront normalizing pressures. Psychoanalytic theory gives a central place to the painful experience of individuation during the Oedipal stage, suggesting that separation and loss are preconditions for a productive, civilized personhood. But Weber and Foucault take a less benign view. The former argues that isolation begins with the destruction of semifeudal modes of production: in capitalism, human relations are impersonal, motivated by self-interest, and dictated by economic need; in the office, each person is trained to become a specialized "cog," with loyalty to the organization rather than to actual people. Foucault examines these processes via the post-Enlightenment practices of imprisonment and the clinical confession, suggesting that individuation is a mechanism for controlling both a group in a given space and each person's invented inwardness. The results of this movement toward aloneness, which can be extrapolated from the writings of Weber and Foucault, are twofold: atomized individuals find it difficult to assemble the knowledge and develop the cognitive understanding needed to truly and comprehensively fathom their predicament; moreover, even if such an understanding could be attained, detached individuals lack the mutual trust and social practices necessary for ameliorative collective action.

This constructed separateness poses a serious threat for entrapment writers, because they conceive of identity as context-bound, formed through active engagement with given rules, relations, practices, and institutions. Entrapment writers bear an affinity with Wittgenstein on this point. "When philosophers use words—'knowledge,' 'being,' 'object,' 'I' . . .—and try to grasp the *essence* of the thing, one must always ask oneself: is a word ever actually used in this way in the language-game which is its original home? What *we* do is to bring words back from their metaphysical to their everyday use."[16] Similarly, entrapment writers refuse to speak about abstract individuals and constitutive attributes of humans (including their alleged communal nature). These writers examine the self in its "everyday use," in the "existential-games" in which it dwells. Weber, Freud, and Foucault believe that in modernity these games impose predetermined endpoints for human character and identity, and offer little openness and playfulness. However, in the absence of an "underlying" self, entrapment writers cannot conceptualize an alternative vision of society: their rejection of a metaphysical foundation of the self leads them to skepticism regarding any proposed escape from modernity, since in their view the self is too elastic to suggest a clear path for such an escape.

But while this elastic view of the self promotes apprehension, it also serves Weber, Freud, and Foucault by democratizing our moral language. This democratization becomes possible since none of them *defines* a human being by her basic need to produce, live in a community, conduct herself rationally, belong to the race, possess political liberty, or explore herself aesthetically. Hence, in spite of his essentialist presuppositions, Weber does not suggest a superior, metaphysically-based model of selfhood. The personality is no higher than the mystic, the nationalist no better than the pacifist. Similarly, Freud emphasizes (despite the biological presuppositions underlying his delineation of the psyche) that the moralist patient consumed by a demanding ego-ideal is neither preferable to nor substantially different from the socially aloof psychotic, and the same lack of supremacy and essentialism applies to the relation between the heterosexual and the homosexual. Foucault's negative notion of entrapment deliberately aims at questioning any hierarchy and discourse of truth that is constitutive of identities. Of course, one may argue that the validity of these writers' expressions of discontent is undermined by their disquiet with ontological discourse, and that their depiction of human beings as clay-like leaves little ground for critique. But this objection is misplaced, since entrapment theories rebuke modernity in the name of myriad *denied capacities* and oppose the dominance of normalized and disciplined human conduct in a world where a multiplicity of meanings, sexualities, or languages could have existed; this is one of their most significant contributions. The critical theories advanced by Weber, Freud, and Foucault do not champion a particular vision of the self, only general paths of self-formation. They point (in different degrees) to the possible richness of human identities and modes of being, affirming the exploration and cultivation of this richness by individuals within a hospitable social and political environment.

Weber, Freud, and Foucault profess that in the recent history of the West this richness has been progressively receding, and that we must therefore strip history of any vestiges of a benign narrative. As noted above, for these writers time no longer promises a morally improved or whole individual, as it did in the eyes of many theorists during and after the Enlightenment, such as Helvétius and Marx, Fichte, and Spencer. The latter, for example, believed in social progress and growing individual perfection, and developed one of the most renowned theories of human adaptability in the nineteenth century. Spencer writes that "as surely as a clerk acquires rapidity in writing and calculation . . . so surely must the human faculties be molded into complete fitness for the social state; so surely must evil and immorality disappear; so surely must man become perfect."[17] This Lamarckian vision rests on the premise that a rightly conceived social order, one that incorporates modern gains in knowledge and productive capacities, creates the external conditions that induce perfection in the human character. In this view, humans are malleable and inclined to internalize the principles guiding their social organizations—to inhale the goodness of their institutional environments, as it were. While entrapment writers indeed share Spencer's belief in the self's malleability, they reverse the relation between transformations in the spheres of knowledge, production, and organizations on the one hand and identity on the other. For entrapment theorists, time promises, if anything, to create increasingly narrow specialists, disturbed neurotics, minutely produced bodies. It is precisely the unlimited ability of the self to be crafted according to functional necessities that underlies these writers' fear of modernity and of history's current course.

Yet remarkably, hand in hand with their discontent with the present and their even greater mistrust of the future, entrapment writers are almost devoid of nostalgia: with them, time has been demythologized in both directions. The temporal consciousness of entrapment writers seems to reflect and reinforce the growing "homogenization" (to use Benjamin's term) of time and its gradual uncoupling from spiritual, communal, or political meanings. Not long ago, time was still open to political crafting. This was famously epitomized by the Jacobin regime and its attempt to introduce a new calendar: 1793 was year II, the week was abolished and replaced by ten-days units, the cyclicality provided by the seven days of the Georgian calendar was replaced by the allocation of distinct names to the days of the year, the name of each day celebrating either a natural or agricultural motif. The new "empire of images" (as Fabre d'Eglantine called it)[18] thus reflected the Jacobins' conviction that through politics moderns could consciously and freely shape their temporal experience, as well as intensify the import imbued in this experience and enrich their daily existence. The total collapse of these convictions—and their underlying hope of rescuing modern time from the uniformity that has taken hold in other spheres of life—became evident in 1884. Under the pressure of economic groups such as the railroad barons, the International Prime Meridian Conference in Washington, D.C., established Greenwich as the zero meridian, divided the Earth into 24 equal time zones, and defined a universal day that "is to begin for all the world at the moment of mean midnight of the initial meridian." This decision turned the day into an almost mathematical concept, identical worldwide regardless of geographical location or season; time became interchangeable, divided into equal units that repeat themselves endlessly. The domination of the clock in modern life has therefore made hopes for a qualitatively new day (or era) seem unlikely, a view that is evident in the entrapment imagination. This imagination reflects the understanding that *time has been neutralized, depoliticized, turned into a uniform and universal domain devoid of hope or longing.* One may even argue that the strategies of coping suggested by entrapment writers emerge when the collective is no longer oriented—as a collective—toward historical time and when the self is forced to accommodate itself to social reality on its own.

The coping strategies that were embraced by entrapment theorists point us in divergent directions. The Weberian path presents work as the main theater of coping. In this vision, modernity is paradoxical: while this epoch has generated unparalleled forms of discipline and normalization in the workplace, it has also established new vocations and myriad opportunities for the development and assertion of person-hood. The threats of meaninglessness and fragmentation can be miti-gated by work—through its consistency, the opportunities it offers for personal growth, the human bonds it establishes, the social recognition it affords. But work, in the Weberian vista, posits two major challenges to the self. First, the self must perform an imaginative leap, picturing a large cause and embracing vocations that foster its embeddedness in projects whose horizons transcend its own. Weber suggests that a self's sense of worth depends on its awareness that its efforts and actions are enduring and echo in the community; it must overcome a consciousness of the distance between, say, a writer and her unseen readers, or between the politician and her anonymous audience and followers. The second challenge to the self is the imperative to choose values without a metaphysical ground or communal authority, and to hold steadfast to these individually-based positions. Weber submits a challenging inter-action between these strongly held moral positions and limiting, objec-tive conditions of a given vocation. (This interaction seems to hold for more vocations than Weber considered, including journalism, educa-tion, social work, medicine and nursing, environmental activism, and more.) The Weberian way of coping with modernity is grounded in two tenets: that the larger community still exists (despite the growing atomization of individuals), and that meaning can be gained from self-assertion within its institutional bounds. For Weber, then, meaning and integration are predicated upon our ability to master a clear, individual voice that is oriented outward, toward the values and needs of the collective.

Freud does not belittle the communal-cultural world that Weber held dear, but the sort of coping suggested by psychoanalysis leads else-where. Freud's theory recommends that moderns face their unhappi-ness, fragmentation, and paralysis by taking interiority as their critical domain of engagement. In this vision, coping means confrontation with unexplained phobias and obsessions, compulsions and infantile desires, traumas and somatic symptoms, guilt and shame—it means a quest to free ourselves from inhibiting emotional dispositions. Each of us is handed (by means of collective and individual conditions that escape our control) a personality with one type of neurosis or another, as well as with specific experience of homelessness; our distinctiveness as moderns consists not only in the intensity of these neuroses and in the novelty of homelessness, but also in our capacity to deliberately con-front these phenomena. We now have the scientific tools and reflective

cultural context for unlocking our interiority. In making such an assertion, psychoanalysis suggests a complete transformation of our evalua-
tion of the self. With this theory, *psychic self-knowledge* becomes a
constitutive element of personal fulfillment and maturity; it is a cherished possession, a nonmaterial and even spiritual achievement that
neither withers away nor hinges upon a shared world of practices and
projects for its realization. To grow as a person, one should narrate one's
own history in the therapist's chambers and have faith in the healing
potency of private words; one should become, in other words, less
dependent upon the sort of public deeds recommended by Weber. The
contrast between Freud and Weber is in fact even greater, since the
Freudian strategy for coping implies that the modern self is not flat,
as Weber argued, but rather contains an abundance of meanings,
almost too many to bear. The modern, according to this Freudian vista,
comprehends that—as the world engulfing her becomes more vast,
impersonal, and repressive—her inwardness offers an enchanting
engagement that is easily at her disposal.

Finally, the Foucauldian strategy of coping opposes uniformity with
aestheticism, normalization with the freedom of self-formation. The
disciplinary practices and scientific discourses of modernity have
proven that the self is almost entirely plastic; but we can celebrate this
malleability and accept few predetermined limits in shaping our identities. As our metaphysical accounts of the self collapse one by one, we
are in a unique position to question our underlying conventions and
beliefs, to free our imaginations, and to envision new modes of human
existence; we have the responsibility of choosing and even rechoosing
the ethos that will guide our lives. This choice is concerned less with
moral rules than with beauty, originality, and style. Life in its entirety is
potentially a field where the self could shape itself, since an aesthetic
dimension can be found in the way the self relates to and interacts with
others, in the way it cares for its body and diet, in the way it casts its
habitat and appearance. The distinctive style that the individual forms
in these diverse departments of life allows her to achieve integration,
both internally and in her conduct in the world. In the Foucauldian
vision, this integration is not architectonic but democratic and poetic; it
is founded on creative resonances and affinities rather than on a fixed
hierarchy of goods. Indeed, the aim of integration is not to overcome meaninglessness (or repression and psychic homelessness), but
rather to infuse the self's entire existence with an erotic dimension and
to generate *pleasure* in the various facets of its existence. Ultimately,
Foucault celebrates the desires for both beauty and distinctiveness not

only for their own sake, but first and foremost because he recognizes that without them the self would not be able to savor life in a deep and enduring way.

The contemporary persistence of these three modes of coping, on the one hand, and the pervasive influences of the logic inherent in our life-orders, on the other, imply that the experience of entrapment may linger in the foreseeable future. The problematic of entrapment first evolved in the late eighteenth century, due to an inherent tension between the novel aspirations of moderns to author their own identities and the new normalizing social institutions. This rift between the self and its environment seems to have intensified in the course of modernity: on the one hand, we witness the globalization of markets, production, culture, science, legal norms, political structures, and more.[19] This may lead to greater normalization and uniformity of identities. On the other hand, contemporary culture is characterized by a growing deliberation over the nature of our identities and the forces that shape them. As Anthony Giddens writes, "In the post-traditional order of modernity . . . self-identity becomes a reflectively organized endeavor." We continuously revise and actively intervene in shaping our selfhood, seeing reflexivity as a continuous and pervasive project. "At each moment . . . the individual is asked to conduct a self-interrogation in terms of what is happening, to take control over his or her experience."[20]

Because of this paradoxical predicament whereby modernity seems to move in two diverging directions, social critique can find no resting point: it is likely to search instead for new fields in which the self is trapped, unknowingly shaped by its social environment. Of course, these new domains may be less revealing than those exposed hitherto by entrapment writers, and with Foucault's negative notion of entrapment this school may have reached its theoretical apex. But what Gadamer observes in respect to tradition may hold true in a more inclusive sense. Gadamer writes that there is an inescapable horizon that always eludes our cognitive grasp. Self-understanding, therefore, cannot "be integrally related to a complete self-transparency in the sense of full presence of ourselves to ourselves. Self-understanding is always on-the-way; it is on a path whose completion is a clear impossibility."[21] Whether one believes that the horizon of identity is essentially shaped by tradition and its benign language or by social institutions, the attempt to fully expose this horizon is both never-ending and uncertain. The reflective self strives to stand outside the words it uses, the productive functions it inhabits, the cultural practices it performs, or the emotional fabric it reproduces while consorting with others—in short, to objectify and fathom the forces that engulf it and to establish its autonomy through an act of critical distancing. Yet whenever the self attempts to pull away, it finds itself thoroughly embedded and cannot free its thought in an absolute and definite way: it is destined to oscillate between thought and unthought, self-authorship and unseen forces that mold it. This tenuous place of the self was, in fact, also recognized by Foucault, who late in his life noted that his object was not to think "from the outside" of some "naïve positivity" as the foundation of critique, but "to learn to what extent the effort to think one's own history can free thought from what it silently thinks, and so enable it to think differently."[22] If Gadamer and Foucault are correct about the nature of thought (even if they disagree about the motivation for and goal of reflection) then political theory is likely to continue to dwell in the maze it has established since Kant and the age of the emerging doubles, alternating between the expanding and ever-more penetrating social institutions of modernity on the one hand and the growing demands of the self to fully author its identity on the other. If we are to extricate ourselves from this maze, either our institutions or our notions of identity will require significant transformation.

Abbreviations

Foucault

AME   Michel Foucault, *Aesthetics, Method, and Epistemology, Essential Works of Foucault*, vol. 2, ed. James Faubion (New York: The New Press, 1998).

ARK   Michel Foucault, *The Archaeology of Knowledge*, trans. A. Sheridan (New York: Pantheon Books, 1972).

DE   Michel Foucault, *Dits et écrits*, vols. 1–4 (Paris: Gallimard, 1994).

DP   Michel Foucault, *Discipline and Punish: The Birth of the Modern Prison*, trans. A. Sheridan (New York: Vintage Books, 1979).

EST   Michel Foucault, *Ethics: Subjectivity and Truth, Essential Works of Foucault*, vol. 1, ed. Paul Rabinow (New York: The New Press, 1997).

HDLS   Michel Foucault, *Histoire de la sexualité*, vol. 1 (Paris: Gallimard, 1976).

HS   Michel Foucault, *History of Sexuality*, vol. 1, trans. Robert Hurley (New York: Vintage Books, 1980).

LCP   Michel Foucault, *Language, Counter-memory, Practice: Selected Essays and Interviews by Michel Foucault*, ed. Donald F. Bouchard (New York: Cornell University Press, 1977).

MC   Michel Foucault, *Madness and Civilization*, trans. Richard Howard (New York: Vintage Books, 1988).

MELC   Michel Foucault, *Les mots et les choses* (Paris: Gallimard, 1996).

OD   Michel Foucault, *L'ordre du discours* (Paris: Gallimard, 1971).

OT   Michel Foucault, *The Order of Things* (New York: Vintage Books, 1973).

PK   Michel Foucault, *Power/Knowledge: Selected Interviews & Other Writings, 1972–1977*, ed. Colin Gordon (New York: Pantheon Books, 1980).

PO   Michel Foucault, *Power, Essential Works of Foucault*, vol. 3, ed. James Faubion (New York: The Free Press, 2000).

PPC   Michel Foucault, *Politics, Philosophy, Culture: Interviews and Other Writings 1977–1984*, ed. Lawrence Kritzman (New York: Routledge, 1990).

SP   Michel Foucault, "The Subject and Power," in H. Dreyfus and Paul Rabinow, *Michel Foucault: Beyond Structuralism and Hermeneutics* (Chicago: University of Chicago Press, 1983), pp. 208–228.

SPNP   Michel Foucault, *Surveiller et punir: Naissance de la prison* (Paris: Gallimard, 1975).

Freud

SE   Sigmund Freud, *The Standard Edition of the Complete Psychological Works of Sigmund Freud*, vols. I–XXIV, eds. J. Strachey and A. Freud (London: Hogarth Press, 1953–74).

Kant

AK   *Kant's Gesammelte Schriften*, ed. Royal Prussian Academy of Sciences and its successors (Berlin: Georg Reimer, 1900ff).

Marx

MEW	Karl Marx and Friedrich Engels, *Marx-Engels Werke*, vols. suppl. 1–39 (Berlin: Dietz Verlag, 1958–68).

Nietzsche

NW	Friedrich Nietzsche, *Nietzsche Werke*, vols. I–X (Berlin: Walter de Gruyter, 1967–74).
WM	Friedrich Nietzsche, *Der Wille zur Macht* (Tübingen: Alfred Kröner Verlag, 1952).

Weber

ES	*Economy and Society*, eds. G. Roth and C. Wittich (Berkeley: University of California Press, 1978).
FMW	*From Max Weber: Essays in Sociology*, eds. H. Gerth and C. Mills (New York: Oxford University Press, 1946).
GAR	Max Weber, *Gesammelte Aufsätze zur Religionssoziologie*, vols.1–3 (Tübingen: J. C. B. Mohr, 1920–21).
GARS	*Gesammelte Aufsätze zur Religionssoziologie*, 3 vols., ed. J. Winckelmann (Tübingen: J. C. B. Mohr, 1924).
GASS	Max Weber, *Gesammelte Aufsätze zur Soziologie und Sozialpolitik*, (Tübingen: J. C. B. Mohr, 1924).
GAW	Max Weber, *Gesammelte Aufsätze zur Wissenschaftslehre* (Tübingen: J. C. B. Mohr, 1922).
GPS	*Gesammelte politische Schriften*, 2d edition, ed. J. Winckelmann (Tübingen: J. C. B. Mohr, 1958).
MSS	*The Methodology of the Social Sciences*, eds. E. Shils and H. Finch (New York: Free Press, 1949).
MWST	*Max Weber: Selections in Translation*, ed. W. G. Runciman (Cambridge: Cambridge University Press, 1978).
RK	*Roscher and Knies: The Logical Problems of Historical Economics* (New York: The Free Press, 1975).
WG	*Wirtschaft und Gesellschaft*, 4th edition, ed. J. Winckelmann (Tübingen: J. C. B. Mohr, 1976).

Notes

Introduction

1. Ian Wilmut's team needed 277 cloned embryos to produce Dolly, and at this point the technology of cloning seems unsafe.

2. For example, many cases of male infertility could be resolved by intra-cytoplasmic sperm injection. In this method, a single sperm (or the progenitor of a sperm cell) is inserted into a recipient egg. Stem cells could be produced from the developing gonads of aborted embryos or from embryos created by *in vitro* fertilization, but ultimately not used.

3. For criticism of human cloning on the grounds that it might endanger the identity of individuals, see, for example, George Annas, "Why We Should Ban Human Cloning," *The New England Journal of Medicine*, vol. 339, no. 2 (July 1998): 122–125; and Arthur Caplan, "Testimony and Prepared Statement," The Committee on Energy and Commerce, Subcommittee on Oversight and Investigations, United States House of Representatives, March 28, 2001, at http://energy commerce.house.gov.

4. "Technology is . . . no mere means. Technology is a way of revealing. If we give heed to this, then another whole realm for the essence of technology will open itself up to us. It is the realm of revealing, i.e., of truth." See Martin Heidegger, "The Question Concerning Technology," in *Basic Writings*, ed. D. F. Krell (New York: Harper & Row, 1977), p. 294.

5. Karl Marx, "Economic-philosophical Manuscripts," in *The Portable Marx*, ed. Eugene Kamenka (New York: Penguin Books, 1983), p. 140.

6. For discussions of the self in the liberal-communitarian debate see: John Rawls, *A Theory of Justice* (Oxford: Oxford University Press, 1971); Michael Sandel, *Liberalism and the Limits of Justice* (Cambridge: Cambridge University Press, 1982); and Alasdair MacIntyre, *After Virtue* (Notre Dame: University of Notre Dame Press, 1984).

7. A number of studies have examined two of the three writers in question

(for example, Weber and Foucault, or Freud and Weber), but there seems to be no systematic study of the three thinkers as a group sharing a common theme. Some of the comparative studies are mentioned in the relevant chapters below.

8. See Reinhart Koselleck, "Neuzeit: Remarks on the Semantics of the Modern Concepts of Movement," in *Futures Past* (Cambridge, MA: MIT Press, 1985), p. 246.

1. Modernity: Hyper-Order and Doubleness

1. Condorcet was a firm believer in reason. Elaborating a view that originates with Descartes and Bacon, he proclaims that "[t]he time will . . . come when the sun will shine only on free men who know no other master but their reason." See Antoine-Nicolas De Condorcet, *Sketch for a Historical Picture of the Progress of the Human Mind*, trans. June Barraclough (London: Weidenfield & Nicolson, 1955), p. 179. Condorcet cites some evidence for the progressive realization of this prophecy: the revolution in the arts and sciences, technological innovations, the dissemination of knowledge, the ethos of critical thought, and the use of statistics and the related improvement in predictability. Condorcet's faith in reason is hence different from Kant's. He thought that control over human destiny would be achieved through the use of statistics and the deliberate regulation of human life in light of them (i.e., la *science morale*, which incorporates statistics, probability, rational choice theory, and more). One can learn, he suggested, solid facts about society (such as the rate of population growth, the functioning of the legal-jury system, and the level of education), which renders public decision-making optimal for society's benefit. Condorcet in fact predicted that the moral sciences created in his own days, sciences whose object is man himself and "the direct goal of which is the happiness of man," will eventually "enjoy a progress no lesser than that of the physical sciences." See Ian Hacking, *The Taming of Chance* (Cambridge: Cambridge University Press, 1990), p. 38. This objectification of human beings advocated by Condorcet continues the materialism of theorists such as Holbach, Bentham, and Helvétius; it is part of a rich tradition in modern thought that attempts to cope with the challenge of human order by invoking the material and statistical laws humans must obey. I discuss the Kantian vision of reason-based order in the second part of this chapter.

2. The word "normal," in the double sense of a mean and a desired state, initially appeared in the first half of the nineteenth century. Originally, in the writings of Broussais, it appeared in a medical context, referring to the condition of an organ; charted along a continuum, this condition was considered pathological at either extreme. Comte was among the first to use the word in a social and political context. According to him, one of the rules at work in the history of civilization is that "man's activity is continually given fresh ascendancy to the normal state over the different modifications of it." See Auguste Comte, *System of Positive Polity*, vol. 2 (London: Longmans & Green, 1875), p. 377. See also G. Canguilhem, *On the Normal and the Pathological*, trans. C. R. Fawcett (Dordrecht, 1978), and Ian Hacking, *The Taming of Chance*, Ch. 19. In what follows, I refer to texts written prior to this usage of the word.

3. Adam Smith, *The Wealth of Nations*, V, i. f. 50 (my emphasis). For a

discussion of the differences between books I and V, see E. G. West, "Adam Smith and Alienation," in *Essays on Adam Smith*, eds. A. Skinner and T. Wilson (Oxford: Clarendon Press, 1975), pp. 540–552. See also R. L. Heilbroner, "Decline and Decay in The Wealth of Nations," *Ibid.*, pp. 524–539.

4. For the development of discipline in this context, see E. P. Thompson, "Time, Work-Discipline and Industrial Capitalism," *Past and Present*, 38 (Dec. 1967): 56–97.

5. As Marc Raeff demonstrates, the seventeenth and eighteenth centuries witnessed an avalanche of ordinances that promoted discipline in German society. An essential aim of these ordinances, at least in the social realm, "was to undermine, constrict, and eventually to eliminate what may be called traditional (premodern) patterns of social behavior." See Marc Raeff, *The Well-Ordered Police State* (New Haven, CT: Yale University Press, 1983), p. 85. For a discussion of the German state's intervention in economic life, particularly in the planning of forestry, see James Scott, *Seeing like a State: How Certain Schemes to Improve the Human Condition Have Failed* (New Haven: Yale University Press, 1998), Ch. 1.

6. J. G. Herder, *J. G. Herder on Social and Political Culture*, ed. F. M. Bernard (Cambridge, UK: Cambridge University Press, 1969), p. 310.

7. J. J. Rousseau, *Emile*, trans. Barbara Fox (London: Dent, 1969), p. 10. For a discussion of the close relation between Rousseau's and Herder's critiques of modernity, see F. M. Bernard, *Self-Direction and Political Legitimacy* (Oxford: Oxford University Press, 1988). I use masculine pronouns alone in the next few sections in order to maintain consistency with the language of Rousseau. While these pronouns are used by most authors under discussion, their use in Rousseau has special meaning, since it is unclear to what extent women were in fact included in his critical discourse. This question, while an important one, is beyond the scope of this work. As a general rule, I employ masculine language and the concept of "man" wherever it seems particularly pertinent to the intentions or underlying convictions of the author.

8. J. J. Rousseau, "Discourse on the Origin of Inequality," in *The Basic Political Writings*, trans. D. A. Gress (Indianapolis: Hackett, 1987), p. 59.

9. Rousseau, "Discourse on the Origin of Inequality," p. 81.

10. Rousseau, "Discourse on the Origin of Inequality," p. 106, note 15 (translation altered).

11. Rousseau, "Discourse on the Sciences and the Arts," in *The Basic Political Writings*, p. 4.

12. J. J. Rousseau, *Politics and the Arts: Letter to M. D' Alembert on the Theater*, trans. Allan Bloom (Ithaca, NY: Cornell University Press, 1960), p. 67. A. Ferrara argues that the tragic fate of Rousseau's Julie demonstrates this point. According to this interpretation, Rousseau presents Julie as a person who denies her feelings and authentic needs for the sake of following social conventions and expectations. She conceives her life as a collection of roles (wife, mother, daughter) to be optimally fulfilled—and this ethic leads to her destruction. On *Julie, or The New Heloise* in this context, see A. Ferrara, *Modernity and Authenticity: A Study of the Social and Ethical Thought of Jean-Jacques Rousseau* (Albany: State University of New York, 1993), Ch. 5.

13. Rousseau scorns the conviction that any law exists in nature, or at least that such a law could be found and agreed upon through reasoned reflection. See "Discourse on the Sciences and the Arts," p. 35.

14. See James Tully, *An Approach to Political Philosophy: Locke in Context* (Cambridge, UK: Cambridge University Press, 1993), p. 282 (my emphasis). For a general discussion of natural law in the seventeenth century in authors such as Grotius, Pufendorf, Cumberland, and Locke, see Knud Haakonssen, *Natural Law and Moral Philosophy* (Cambridge, UK: Cambridge University Press, 1996), especially Ch. 1.

15. John Locke, *Second Treatise of Government* (Indianapolis: Hackett Publishing Company, 1980), p. 71.

16. Alexander Pope, *An Essay on Man*, IV, 332–340, 394–396, 336–338. On Pope's *Essay on Man*, see Maynard Mack, *Alexander Pope: A Life* (New York: Norton & Yale University Press, 1985), pp. 522–546; on Deism and its social import, see Charles Taylor, *Sources of the Self* (Cambridge, MA: Harvard University Press, 1989), Ch. 16.

17. Alexander Pope, *An Essay on Man*, I, 130.

18. Isaiah Berlin, *The Roots of Romanticism* (Princeton, NJ: Princeton University Press, 1999), p. 23. In this context, see Louis Dupré's inclusive study of Western attempts to establish a synthesis of human beings and cosmos, and a related synthesis of God and nature; according to Dupré, the gradual breakdown of these attempts since Ockham marks the emergence of modernity. See his *Passage to Modernity: An Essay in the Hermeneutics of Nature and Culture* (New Haven: Yale University Press, 1993). In the same vein, Pierre Manent suggests that the malaise of the modern self is intertwined with its self-understanding as an historical, undefined being rather than as possessing any constitutive nature in general and a moral one in particular. See Pierre Manent, *The City of Man*, trans. Marc LePain (Princeton: Princeton University Press, 1998).

19. Kant, "Universal History," *Perpetual Peace*, p. 31; *AK*, VIII, p. 20.

20. M. Shelley, *Frankenstein, or The Modern Prometheus* (New York: New American Library and Penguin, 1965 [1831]), p. 200.

21. See Susan Shell, "Commerce and Community in Kant's Early Thought," in *Kant and Political Philosophy: The Contemporary Legacy*, eds. R. Beiner and W. J. Booth (New Haven, CT: Yale University Press, 1993), pp. 124–125. See also Shell's book, *The Embodiment of Reason* (Chicago: University of Chicago Press, 1996).

22. For Kant, the concept of *Kultur* has two main components, personal-internal and collective-external. On the latter level, he mentions developments such as mankind's increasingly sophisticated interaction with nature, technological innovations, progress in the arts and sciences, the establishment of constitutional and republican regimes, and the league of peace. On the internal and individual level, he notes the process whereby people learn to sublimate their brute desires, to discipline themselves, and to give more room to their intellectual needs. See Immanuel Kant, *Critique of Judgment*, trans. J. H. Bernard (New York: Hafner, 1965), no. 83; *AK*, V, no. 83.

23. Immanuel Kant, *Critique of Pure Reason*, trans. N. K. Smith (New York: St. Martin Press, 1929), A 127–128, B 164. For discussions of the Kantian notion of

the self, see David Kelmm and Günter Zöller (eds.), *Figuring the Self: Subject, Absolute, and Others in Classical German Philosophy* (Albany, NY: State University of New York Press, 1997), part I.

24. Immanuel Kant, *What Real Progress Has Metaphysics Made in Germany Since the Time of Leibniz and Wolff?* trans. Ted Humphrey (New York: Abaris Books, 1983), p. 73; *AK*, XX, p. 270.

25. Immanuel Kant, *Groundwork for the Metaphysics of Morals*, trans. H. Paton (New York: Harper & Row, 1964), p. 120.

26. Kant, *Critique of Judgment*, no. 83; *AK*, V, no. 83. Kant harnessed to his historical account of civilization a vision of the self that had already been advanced by Hobbes. According to the latter, felicity is nothing but "a continual progress of desire, from one object to another; the attaining of the former being still but the way to the latter." See Thomas Hobbes, *Leviathan* (New York: Penguin, 1968), p. 160.

27. More specifically, the Kantian imperatives read as follows. (1) "Act as if the maxim of your action were to become through your will a universal law of nature," and (2) "Act in such a way that you always treat humanity, whether in your person or in the person of any other, never simply as a means, but always at the same time as an end." *Groundwork for the Metaphysics of Morals*, p. 89, 96.

28. Immanuel Kant, *Observations on the Feeling of the Beautiful and the Sublime*, trans. J. T. Goldthwaite (Berkeley: University of California Press, 1965), p. 81; *AK*, XX, p. 93.

29. Immanuel Kant, *Anthropology from a Pragmatic Point of View* (The Hague: Martinus Nijhoff Press, 1974), p. 101, p. 103; *AK*, VII, p. 233, p. 235 (my emphasis). Another strategy of nature is the imagination: it [nature] "very wisely and beneficially dazzles the man who is naturally lazy by presenting objects of imagination to him as real ends." The imagination steers people to think that their happiness depends on achieving—through hard, socially useful work—this very one, particular object of consumption (see *Anthropology*, p. 141; *Ak*, VII, p. 275). Kant's account of the role of imagination in the burgeoning of civilization is not very original. In *Theory of Moral Sentiment*, for example, Smith observes that human beings in general, and in commercial society in particular are hungry for fame, influence, and a type of aesthetic enjoyment that comes from the acquisition of objects (or to use his language, "baubles and trinkets"). The contentment associated with the accomplishment of these ends is a mirage, but one that is an essential fuel to the economy. "It is well that nature imposes upon us in this manner," writes Smith. "It is this deception which rouses and keeps in continual motion the industry of mankind. It is this which first prompted them to cultivate the ground, to build houses, to found cities and commonwealths, and to invent and improve all the sciences and arts, which ennoble and embellish human life." See Adam Smith, *Theory of Moral Sentiment*, eds. D. Raphael and A. Macfie (Oxford: Oxford University Press, 1976), p. 183. See in this context the commentary by I. Hont and M. Ignatieff in their "Needs and Justice in *The Wealth of Nations:* an Introductory Essay," in *Wealth and Virtue: The Shaping of Political Economy in the Scottish Enlightenment* (Cambridge, UK: Cambridge University Press, 1983), pp. 8–13.

30. Immanuel Kant, "*Religion within the Boundaries of Mere Reason,*" in *Religion and Rational Theology*, trans. George di Giovanni (Cambridge: Cambridge

University Press, 1996), p. 75; *AK*, VI, p. 27. In his account of self-love, Kant is clearly following Rousseau; in contrast to the latter, however, Kant sees self-love as beneficial, and suggests that it exists prior to social life, rather than emerging as the artificial byproduct of this life.

31. Kant continues: "Man has a propensity for *living in society*, for in that state he feels himself to be more than a man, i.e., feels himself to be more than the development of his natural capacities. He also has, however, a great tendency to isolate himself, for he finds in himself the unsocial characteristic of wanting everything to go according to his own desires, and he therefore anticipates resistance everywhere . . . Now this resistance awakens all of man's powers, brings him to overcome his tendency towards laziness, and driven by his desire for honor, power, or property to secure status among his fellows . . . Without [these] characteristics of unsociability . . . man would live as an Arcadian shepherd, in perfect concord, contentment, and mutual love, and all talents would lie eternally dormant in their seed." See Immanuel Kant, "Universal History," in *Perpetual Peace and Other Essays* (Indianapolis: Hacket, 1985), pp. 31–32; *AK*, VIII, p. 21.

32. Kant, "Universal History," pp. 31–32; *AK*, VIII, p. 21.

33. Kant, moreover, is famous for suggesting that even war—the epitome of human competitiveness as well as barbarity—has an essential role in the creation of culture because it develops talents and technology. "In spite of the dreadful afflictions with which [war] visits the human race," writes Kant, it is nevertheless an occasion "for developing all the talents serviceable to culture to the highest possible pitCh." See Kant, *Critique of Judgment*, no. 83; *AK*, V, no. 83.

34. Immanuel Kant, "The Metaphysics of Morals," in *Practical Philosophy*, trans. Mary Gregor (Cambridge, UK: Cambridge University Press, 1996), p. 565; *AK*, VI, p. 445.

35. Kant, "Perpetual Peace," in *Perpetual Peace and Other Essays*, p. 124; *AK*, VIII, p. 366.

36. As Albert Hirschman shows, theorists as different as Spinoza, Pascal, Mandeville, Montesquieu, Hume, and Smith believed that the stability of civil society and capitalist markets are dependent upon a useful inner dynamic of human predispositions. These writers, each in his own way, posited one set of inclinations called "passions" (such as envy, violence, revenge, sexual lust, and craving for pleasure) as being opposed to and checked by another set of inclinations called "interests" (such as gain, good name, and status). Hence Montesquieu, for example, writes that "it is fortunate for men to be in a situation in which, though their passions may prompt them to be wicked, they have nevertheless an interest in not doing so." (See A. Hirschman, *The Passions and the Interests* [Princeton: Princeton University Press, 1977], p. 73.) According to Montesquieu, the virtues that are cultivated through engagement in commercial relations are also beneficial in the political sphere. Moderation and sound judgment, for example, are needed for political, republican life as much as for successful economic activity. Despite the wealth that capitalism creates and the possible corruption of character that may come with abundance, this economic order may be seen as actually having a positive effect upon the character of the individual and hence upon the quality of the polity, he holds.

37. Kant, "Idea for a Universal History," in *Perpetual Peace*, p. 33, 38;

AK, VIII, p. 22, 27, 28. Kant clarifies his conception of transnational political bodies in his later essay, "Perpetual Peace." On the contemporary relevancy of his arguments and suggestions, see the collection *Perpetual Peace: Essays on Kant's Cosmopolitan Ideal*, eds. J. Bohman and M. Lutz-Bachmann (Cambridge, MA: MIT Press, 1997), especially J. Habermas, "Kant's Idea of Perpetual Peace, with the Benefit of Two Hundred Years' Insight," pp. 155–178, and K. Baynes, "Communitarian and Cosmopolitan Challenges to Kant's Conception of World Peace," pp. 219–234.

38. Kant, *Critique of Judgment*, no. 83; *AK*, V, no. 83. On Kant's vision of human betterment, see Eyal Chowers, "The Marriage of Time and Identity: Kant, Benjamin, and the Nation-State," *Philosophy and Social Criticism*, vol. 25 (3): 57–80.

39. According to Kant, "Reason does not . . . follow the order of things as they present themselves in appearance, but frames for itself with perfect spontaneity an order of its own according to ideas [of pure reason] to which it adapts the empirical conditions, and according to which it declares actions to be [practically] necessary." See *Critique of Pure Reason* [A548/B576]. Indeed, despite his naturalistic explanation of social order, Kant does not suggest that peace among nations—the ultimate embodiment of "external" order—could be perpetuated without a moral transformation of individuals. On this point, see Paul Guyer, *Kant on Freedom, Law, and Happiness* (Cambridge: Cambridge University Press, 2000), Ch. 12.

40. Immanuel Kant, *"Religion Within the Boundaries of Mere Reason,"* p. 131; *AK*, VI, p. 96 (translation altered).

41. Kant, "Idea for a Universal History," in *Perpetual Peace*, p. 38; *AK*, VIII, p. 28 (translation altered). In contrast to the Kantian vision articulated above, Reinhart Koselleck argued that the attempt of Enlightenment writers to turn the absolutist, political realm into one that is compatible with and subject to bourgeois morality had catastrophic consequences—the French Revolution. See his *Critique and Crisis* (Cambridge, MA: MIT Press, 1988).

42. Kant, *Critique of Judgment*, p. 122; *AK*, V, p. 453.

43. Kant, *What Real Progress Has Metaphysics Made in Germany Since the Time of Leibniz and Wolff*, p. 141; *AK*, XX, p. 307 (my emphasis). For a discussion of Kant's notion of the highest good, see Allen Wood, *Kant's Ethical Thought* (Cambridge: Cambridge University Press, 1999), pp. 311–313.

44. Kant, *Critique of Judgment*, no. 85; *AK*, V, no. 85. Kant's glorification of man as a moral being is also expressed in his notion of the sublime. As Ronald Beiner suggests, Kant believes that "to regard objects of nature as supremely sublime is a kind of insult to our own nature as rational beings . . . Kant's solution to this problem was to construe sublime objects of nature as mere projections of a sublimity actually located within ourselves as moral beings." See Ronald Beiner, "Kant, the Sublime, and Nature," in *Kant and Political Philosophy*, p. 281.

45. Yirmiahu Yovel, *Kant and the Philosophy of History* (Princeton: Princeton University Press, 1980), p. 180.

46. Kant, "Theory and Practice," in *Perpetual Peace*, pp. 64–65 (note); *AK*, VIII, p. 280.

47. Jean Paul Richter, *Horn of Oberon: Jean Paul Richter's School of Aesthetics*, trans. M. Hale (Detroit: Wayne State University Press, 1973), p. 15, 16. I am

indebted here to M. Gillespie. See his *Nihilism Before Nietzsche* (Chicago: University of Chicago Press, 1995), pp. 64–65. Jacobi also advanced a well-known critique of Kantian nihilism, a predicament that springs from the notion of things-in-themselves and the self's inability to escape its own representation. For a discussion of these critiques of Kant, see Frederick Beiser, *The Fate of Reason: German Philosophy from Kant to Fichte* (Cambridge, MA: Harvard University Press, 1987). Jean Paul's and Jacobi's critiques are still echoed in contemporary discussions of the self. Adam Seligman, for example, suggests that modernity involves a quest of the self for absolute authority over itself and for independence from any transcendent order; this condition, he believes, is dangerous since it leads to nihilism, lack of direction, and meaninglessness. See Adam Seligman, *Modernity's Wager* (Princeton: Princeton University Press, 2001).

48. This work is concerned, for the most part, with intellectual transformations in the Continent. Yet it seems pertinent to discuss Mary Shelley's work here, since the themes she so imaginatively expresses are also shared by contemporary German writers, as exemplified by Jean Paul Richter. It should be noted, however, that there is no agreement in the literature about Mary Shelley's intent. *Frankenstei*n has been viewed, for example, as the first science fiction work that probes the dangers of technology, as a modern reworking of a Gothic myth, as a critique of Christianity and an affirmation of materialism, as an example of the distorted patterns of masculinity and femininity in Romanticism, as a case study in psychotic breakdown, as a symbolic expression of class struggle and of the old aristocracy's fears of the barbaric masses, and more. It seems to me, however, that it would be more illuminating to embrace a historical-philosophical reading of the novel.

49. For a discussion of these writers, see John Pizer, *Ego-Alter Ego: Double and/as Other in the Age of German Poetic Realism* (Chapel Hill, North Carolina: University of North Carolina Press, 1998). Needless to say, the theme of the double was not confined to Germany or Britain; perhaps the most renowned work employing this motif was Fyodor Dostoyevsky's *The Double* (1846).

50. Masao Miyoshi, *The Divided Self* (New York: New York University Press, 1969), p. ix. For other studies of the theme of the double, ego and alter-ego, and *Doppelgänger* in literature, see Paul Coates, *The Double and the Other: Identity as Ideology in Post-Romantic Fiction* (New York: St. Martin Press, 1988); Karl Miller, *Doubles: Studies in Literary History* (London: Oxford University Press, 1985); and Carl Francis Keppler, *The Literature of the Second Self* (Tucson: University of Arizona Press, 1972). For studies focused on the psychological dimension of this theme, see Robert Rogers, *A Psychoanalytic Study of the Double in Literature* (Detroit: Wayne State University Press, 1970) and Otto Rank, *The Double*, trans. H. Tucker (Chapel Hill: University of North Carolina Press, 1971).

51. Paul Cantor, *Creator and Created* (Cambridge: Cambridge University Press, 1984), p. xii. In another study, M. H. Abrams suggests that the first to develop the notion of humanity's Promethean role was Shaftesbury, who in this context glorified the imaginative poet. The same theme appears in the works of German writers such as Lessing, Goethe, and Herder. See: M. H. Abrams, *The Mirror and the Lamp* (New York: Norton, 1958), pp. 272–285.

52. In contrast to its use in popular culture, in the novel Frankenstein is the name of the scientist and not of his creation.

53. Mary Shelley, *Frankenstein*, p. 74 (my emphasis). It should be noted that Shelley's vision of creating a human being is not new. The idea that human beings can create other, semi-human beings appears in ancient myths, including Arab and Greek ones. In Jewish tradition, the creature termed *golem* is very familiar, especially since the thirteenth century. Nonetheless, the differences between Shelley's monster and the golem are striking. According to Jewish tradition, especially the Kabbala, the golem is conceived by mastering the mystic and magical aspect of religion; it is proof of a great devotion to and an understanding of God, not a Promethean rebellion against the divine. Moreover, the golem is created by mastering the mystic power of Hebrew words, not through scientific knowledge of chemistry, biology, and anatomy. Finally, in contrast to the modern monster, the golem lacks the capacity of speech and is perceived as a mere tool without any intrinsic worth. On the idea of the golem in Jewish tradition, see Moshe Idel, *Golem* (New Haven: Yale University Press, 1990).

54. M. Shelley, *Frankenstein*, p. 46.

55. *M. Shelley, Frankenstein*, p. 52.

56. *M. Shelley, Frankenstein*, p. 53.

57. See Muriel Spark, *Mary Shelley* (New York: Dutton, 1987), p. 164. Spark observes that "we may visualize Frankenstein's *Doppelgänger* or Monster . . . as representing reason in isolation, since he is the creature of an obsessional rational effort" (p. 164).

58. M. Shelley, *Frankenstein*, p. 116.

59. *M. Shelley, Frankenstein*, p. 207.

60. *M. Shelley, Frankenstein*, p. 209.

61. *M. Shelley, Frankenstein*, p. 125. On this point, see Harold Bloom, "Afterword," in *Frankenstein*, pp. 212–223.

62. M. Shelley, *Frankenstein*, p. 138.

63. *M. Shelley, Frankenstein*, p. 192.

64. *M. Shelley, Frankenstein*, p. 160.

65. *M. Shelley, Frankenstein*, p. 195.

2. Proto-Entrapment Theories

1. The yearning for inner wholeness, as opposed to Kantian dualism, is indeed articulated by writers such as Herder, Humboldt, Schiller, and Nietzsche. These writers urge us to generate harmony between reason and feelings, desires and will, imagination and perception, body and soul. For example, Humboldt writes that "the true end of man is the highest and most harmonious development of his powers to a complete and consistent whole." See Wilhelm von Humboldt, *The Limits of State Action*, ed. J. W. Burrow (Cambridge: Cambridge University Press, 1969), p. 16. Mill quotes these same words in *On Liberty*.

2. Friedrich Nietzsche, "On the Uses and Disadvantages of History for

Life," in *Untimely Meditations*, trans. R. J. Hollingdale (Cambridge: Cambridge University Press, 1985), p. 63; "Vom Nutzen und Nachteil der Historie für das Leben," *NW*, vol. III1, p. 247. Nietzsche reiterates this idea, which is fundamental to his thought, in numerous cases. For example, in the same work he insists that "all living things require an atmosphere around them, a mysterious misty vapor; if they are deprived of this envelope, if a religion, an art, a genius is condemned to revolve as a star without atmosphere, we should no longer be surprised if they quickly wither and grow hard and unfruitful . . . every human being [and nation] that wants to become *mature* requires a similar enveloping illusion, a similar protective and veiling cloud; nowadays, however, maturity as such is hated because history is held in greater honor than life" (p. 97); *NW*, vol. III1, p. 294. Elsewhere Nietzsche states that self-defense means "not to see many things, not to hear many things, not to permit many things to come close—first imperative of prudence, first proof that one is no mere accident but a necessity." These insights about the imperative of distance for selfhood seem to reflect his own experience: "At an absurdly early age, at seven, I already knew that no human word would ever reach me: has anyone ever seen me saddened on that account?" See Friedrich Nietzsche, "Why I am so clever," "Ecce Homo," in *On the Genealogy of Morals and Ecce Homo*, trans. Walter Kaufmann (New York: Vintage Books, 1969), nos. 8 and 10; "Warum ich so klug bin," "Ecce homo," *NW*, vol. VI3, nos. 8 and 10.

3. Nietzsche, "On the Uses and Disadvantages of History for Life," p. 78, p. 79; *NW*, vol. III1, p. 268, 270.

4. Nietzsche, "On the Uses and Disadvantages of History for Life," p. 84; *NW*, vol. III1, p. 277.

5. Nietzsche, "On the Uses and Disadvantages of History for Life," p. 85; *NW*, vol. III1, p. 278. Even those who could have reflected critically on this predicament remain silent. "Are there still human beings," asks Nietzsche of his fellow philosophers, "or perhaps only thinking, writing, and speaking-machines?" *(Ibid.)*

6. Nietzsche, *On the Genealogy of Morals and Ecce Homo*, Part 1, no. 12; *NW*, vol. VI2, p. 292.

7. Friedrich Nietzsche, *The Gay Science*, trans. Walter Kaufmann (New York: Vintage Books, 1974), no. 1; "Die fröhliche Wissenschaft," *NW*, vol. V2, no. 1. The impoverishment of meaning is interwoven with the impoverishment of truth and the will to truth—a development Nietzsche celebrates. While truth may offer comfort, it is also dangerous: life is becoming, change, formlessness, renewal; hence the desire for truth could be seen as a "concealed will to death" (Nietzsche, *The Gay Science*, no. 344; *NW*, vol. V2, p. 258). Nietzsche believes that the decline of the will to truth is embedded in the dynamic of this will itself, which fabricates truth only to question it at a later stage. In modernity, indeed, "we no longer believe that truth remains truth when the veils are withdrawn" (*The Gay Science*, no. 4; *NW*, vol. V2, p. 20).

8. For a discussion of this point, see Michel Haar, "Nietzsche and Metaphysical Language," in *The New Nietzsche*, ed. D. Allison (Cambridge, MA: MIT Press, 1985), p. 13.

9. Nietzsche, *The Gay Science*, no. 125; *NW*, vol. V2, p. 159.

10. Lionel Trilling, *Sincerity and Authenticity* (London: Oxford University Press, 1972), p. 99.

11. Herder, *Herder on Social and Political Culture*, p. 292.

12. Herder, *Herder on Social and Political Culture*, p. 293. Herder agrees with Rousseau that contentment and well-being should be formed by a certain relation to oneself and not through multiple layers of external dependency. "If happiness is to be found on this earth, it has to be looked for within every sentient being. Every man has the standard of happiness within himself. He carries it within the form in which he has been fashioned and it is only within this sphere that he can be happy . . ." (p. 311).

13. Charles Taylor, *Hegel* (Cambridge: Cambridge University Press, 1975), p. 15.

14. Nietzsche, "On the Uses and Disadvantages of History for Life," p. 123; *NW*, vol. III1, p. 329.

15. Nietzsche, "Schopenhauer as Educator," in *Untimely Meditations*, p. 127; "Schopenhauer als Erzieher," *NW*, vol. III1, p. 334.

16. Nietzsche, *The Will to Power*, trans. W. Kaufmann and R. Hollingdale (New York: Random House, 1967), no. 767 (translation altered); *WM*, p. 512.

17. Nietzsche, *The Will to Power*, no. 941; *WM*, p. 630. In my discussion of Nietzsche's concept of authenticity, I am indebted to Jacob Golomb. See his "Nietzsche on Authenticity," *Philosophy Today*, no. 34 (1990): 243–258.

18. Nietzsche, "On the Uses and Disadvantages of History for Life," p. 111; *NW*, vol. III1, p. 313.

19. Nietzsche, "Schopenhauer as Educator," p. 129; *NW*, vol. III1, pp. 336–337.

20. For a discussion of the relation between art and chaos in Nietzsche, see Jean Granier, "Nietzsche's Conception of Chaos," in *The New Nietzsche*, pp. 135–141. Schiller is probably the first to theorize the aesthetic cultivation of identity that later inspired Nietzsche. He avers that our humanity is expressed in a *Spieltrieb* (play drive) that allows our faculties of form and contemplation on the one hand, and of perception and feeling on the other, to coalesce. "In the enjoyment of beauty, or aesthetic unity, an actual union and interchange between matter and form, passivity and activity, momentarily takes place" [Friedrich Schiller, *On the Aesthetic Education of Man*, eds. E. Wilkinson and L. A. Willoughby (Oxford: Oxford University Press, 1967), p. 189.] At these moments, the active, imposing form itself invokes the experience of enjoyment, and hence feelings stop being a mere reaction to sensory data. This healing event in which our separate faculties are conjoined is seen by Schiller as morally neutral, yet as necessary for harmonious existence, and hence also for the proper use of the rational will. "There is no other way of making sensuous man rational," he writes, "except by first making him aesthetic" (p. 161).

21. Nietzsche, *The Gay Science*, no. 335; *NW*, vol. V2, p. 243.

22. Nietzsche's attitude to collective institutions is demonstrated by the following statement: "State is the name of the coldest of all cold monsters. Everything about it is false; it bites with stolen teeth, and bites easily . . . All-too-many

are born: for the superfluous the state was invented . . . Only where the state ends, there begins the human being who is not superfluous: there begins the song of necessity, the unique and inimitable tune." See Friedrich Nietzsche, "Thus Spoke Zarathustra," in *The Viking Portable Nietzsche*, trans. W. Kaufmann (London: Chatto & Windus, 1971), Part One, "On the New Idol"; "Also sprach Zarathustra," *NW,* vol. VI1, pp. 57–59. As Peter Berkowitz suggests, Nietzsche sees a profound contradiction between the good life and the political life, between living according to the laws of oneself and living according to convention and imposed public law. See his *Nietzsche: The Ethics of an Immoralist* (Cambridge: Harvard University Press, 1995), pp. 165–169. For a different view, see Peter R. Sedgwick, "Introduction: Nietzsche's Institutions," in *Nietzsche: A Critical Reader*, ed. P. Sedgwick (Oxford: Blackwell, 1995), pp. 1–12.

23. Karl Marx, "Economic and Philosophical Manuscripts," in *Early Writings*, trans. R. Livingstone and G. Benton (New York: Penguin Books, 1992), p. 359; "Ökonomisch-philosophische Manuskripte," *MEW,* suppl. 1, p. 548.

24. Karl Marx, *Capital: A Critique of Political Economy*, vol. 1, trans. Ben Fowkes (New York: Penguin Books, 1990), p. 549; "Das Kapital: Kritik der politischen Ökonomie," *MEW,* vol. 23, pp. 446–447.

25. Marx, *Capital*, vol. 1, p. 283; *MEW,* vol. 23, p. 192. There is an extensive discussion in Marxist theory about whether Marx held a vision of human nature that is valid in all places and times, whether such a vision is necessary for communism and for the introduction of social change, and whether such a vision could be compatible with the specificity and variety of humans' practical circumstances as presented by historical materialism. While Marx does not offer a consistent stance in this matter, he seems to be suggesting that there are essential human potentials and needs (especially sociability and self-realization through labor) whose specific form changes in the course of history; human nature, in other words, is at the same time both fixed and open-ended. An inclusive attempt to explore Marx's concept of human nature can be found in Daniel Brudney's *Marx's Attempt to Leave Philosophy* (Cambridge: Harvard University Press, 1998).

26. Marx, *Capital*, vol. 1, p. 284; *MEW,* vol. 23, p. 193.

27. Marx, "Economic and Philosophical Manuscripts," p. 324; *MEW,* suppl. 1, p. 512.

28. Karl Marx, "Excerpts from James Mill's Elements of Political Economy," in *Early Writings*, p. 266; "Auszüge aus Mills '*Éléments d'économie politique* '," *MEW,* suppl. 1, p. 451.

29. Marx, "Excerpts from James Mill's Elements of Political Economy," p. 260 (translation altered); *MEW,* suppl. 1, p. 445.

30. Karl Marx, "The German Ideology," in *The Portable Marx*, trans. E. Kamenka (New York: Penguin, 1983), p. 197; "Die deutsche Ideologie," *MEW,* vol. 3, p. 75.

31. Karl Marx, *Capital: A Critique of Political Economy*, vol. 3, trans. David Fernbach (New York: Penguin Books, 1991), pp. 359–368; "Das Kapital: Kritik der politischen Ökonomie," *MEW,* vol. 25, pp. 261–270. See also Richard W. Miller, "Social and Political Theory: Class, State, Revolution," in *The Cambridge*

Companion to Marx, ed. Terrell Carver (Cambridge: Cambridge University Press, 1991), pp. 55–105.

32. "The German Ideology," p. 193 (translation altered); *MEW,* vol. 3, p. 75. In the context of the self-civilization relation, Marx often uses terms such as enslavement, submission, and control. For example, he says that "this crystallization of social activity, this consolidation of what we ourselves produce into an objective power above us, growing out of our control, thwarting our expectations, bringing to naught our calculations, is one of the chief factors in historical development up till now" (Karl Marx, "The German Ideology," p. 177). The same idea is omnipresent in his later works: "Freedom in this sphere [production], can consist only in this, that socialized man, the associated producers, govern the human metabolism with nature in a rational way, bringing it under their collective control instead of being dominated by it as a blind power" (Karl Marx, *Capital,* vol. 3, p. 959). With Marx, outward collective control becomes a prerequisite for self-realization, the consummation of humans' social nature, material well-being, freedom, and self-respect.

33. Rousseau, "On the Social Contract," in *The Basic Political Writings,* p. 151.

34. The notion of autonomy and the view of the self associated with it has no doubt galvanized many calls for radical social change, or for "total revolution" *(Totale Umwälzung),* as Bernard Yack puts it. Yack thinks that the positive valuation of this human potential allowed little patience with obstacles to its realization. He therefore sees the Rousseauian-Kantian conceptual invention—together with the view of social institutions as interdependent and composing a cohesive totality—as constitutive of the critical mode of thinkers as diverse as Schiller and Marx, Nietzsche and Rousseau: "The Rousseauian-Kantian understanding of human freedom introduces a new way of viewing the failings of social institutions: institutions that do not in some way embody our freedom to define our own ends strip us of our humanity. And the failure of social institutions to recognize and embody our humanity is seen as the obstacle to a human life only when all social phenomena are viewed as part of an interdependent whole. If the same spirit of social interaction informs all institutions and individual action there will be no "human" sphere of society into which we can escape to develop our humanity." See Bernard Yack, *The Longing for Total Revolution* (Berkeley: University of California Press, 1992), p. 24.

Yack's illuminating study seems to agree with Isaiah Berlin's argument concerning the role of positive liberty in political theories since the late eighteenth century. Berlin has suggested that writers such as Rousseau, Kant, and Marx started by dividing the self into lower and higher components and continued by contending that only the attainment of the higher, moral self would allow us to be truly human and to realize our essence. This opened the way for revolutionary and totalitarian theories that purported to have found the proper social and political configuration to ensure the attainment of the desired self. See Isaiah Berlin, "Two Concepts of Liberty," in his *Four Essays on Liberty* (Oxford: Oxford University Press, 1969). Finally, Reinhart Koselleck makes a similar argument: during the Enlightenment, the progressive bourgeoisie came to believe that the morality of society is endangered by monarchical political institutions, and that society must externalize its judgments if it aspires to be free. Toward the end of the eighteenth century, then, "The critical disjunction between the realm of natural goodness and a polity (which this division had turned into a realm of sheer power) became intensified . . . Society, to save itself, not only appointed itself a moral judge, but feels compelled to ensure its existence, to carry out its verdict." See Reinhart Koselleck, *Critique and Crisis: Enlightenment and the Pathogenesis of Modern Society* (Cambridge, MA: MIT Press, 1988), p. 171.

What I have been suggesting above, however, is that one can also reverse the argument of Yack, Berlin, and Koselleck. The conceptualization of the self's humanity as conditioned upon the exercise of autonomy *might be a solution* to the discontent with modernity no less than its cause; collective autonomy permitted modern theorists to envision a response to the more fundamental challenge of doubleness. If, as I argue in Chapter 1, moderns have been primarily preoccupied with a struggle against the uncontrollable civilization they have brought about, and with an existential gulf between them and their creation, then autonomy and positive liberty may have originally been part of a conceptual scheme whose aim was to resolve this agonism. These concepts allowed the redefinition of relations between the members of a society and their economy, political institutions, and shared public spaces, and the envisioning of an orchestrated subjection of the double to human needs and potentials. (In Rousseau, liberty as autonomy is conceptualized in the same work in which he suggests the social contract, and by then his critique of modernity was well established.) Once freedom is understood as autonomy and is postulated as a shared human capacity, identity can be expanded outward: it becomes reflected in the makeup of social institutions, engulfing what has been a distant Otherness. Rather than imposing upon us an oppressive hyper-order, then, the social world could closely echo and affirm our humanity.

35. Marx, "The German Ideology," p. 193; *MEW,* vol. 3, p. 74.

36. Marx, "The German Ideology," p. 194; *MEW,* vol. 3, p. 77.

37. Karl Marx, "On the Jewish Question," in *Early Writings,* p. 220; "Zur Judenfrage," *MEW,* vol. 1, p. 355. Hegel's search for a unity between self and social institutions is epitomized in the state. As he writes, "It is only as one of its [the state's] members that the individual has objectivity, genuine individuality, and ethical life. Unification pure and simple is the true content and aim of the individual, and the individual's destiny is the living of the universal life." See George Wilhelm Friedrich Hegel, *The Philosophy of Right,* trans. T. M. Knox (London: Oxford University Press, 1952), no. 258. On Hegel's attempt to overcome the division within the self in general, and in the context of Kant's philosophy in particular, see Steven Smith, *Hegel's Critique of Liberalism* (Chicago: University of Chicago Press, 1989), pp. 17–31.

38. Karl Marx, "Critique of Hegel's 'Philosophy of Right,'" in *Marx-Engels Collected Works,* vol. 3 (New York: International Publishers, 1975), p. 48; *MEW,* vol. 1, p. 250.

39. Marx, "Critique of Hegel's 'Philosophy of Right,'" p. 234; *MEW,* vol. 3, p. 370 (my emphasis).

40. Marx, "Excerpts from James Mill's Elements of Political Economy,"

p. 278, p. 265; *MEW,* suppl. 1, p. 451, p. 462. On this matter, see also Brudney, *Marx's Attempt to Leave Philosophy,* p. 177.

41. Marx, "Excerpts from James Mill's Elements of Political Economy," p. 278; *MEW,* suppl. 1, p. 463.

42. Marx, "Economic and Philosophical Manuscripts," p. 348; *MEW,* suppl. 1, p. 536.

43. Marx, "The German Ideology," p. 189; *MEW,* vol. 3, pp. 70–71 (my emphasis).

44. For the primacy of the productive forces in Marx, see G. A. Cohen's convincing interpretation, *Karl Marx's Theory of History: A Defence* (Princeton: Princeton University Press, 1978), especially Ch. 6. It should be noted that despite this primacy, even Cohen believes that this rule should be qualified. See, for example, his discussion of how the relations of production can steer the development of the forces of production (p. 165).

45. Karl Marx, "The Communist Manifesto," in *The Portable Marx,* p. 207; "Manifest der Kommunistischen Partei," *MEW,* vol. 4, p. 465.

46. On the concept of time in modernity, see Reinhart Koselleck, "Neuzeit: Remarks on the Semantics of the Modern Concepts of Movement," in *Futures Past* (Cambridge, MA: MIT Press, 1985), pp. 231–267. Marx, at least according to "The Communist Manifesto," is committed to the idea of progress and to a unilinear vision of history, although he seems to believe that this is true in the macro- and not necessarily with regard to microhistorical events. Contrary to this reading of Marx, Ellen Wood argues that "historical materialism is not, now or in its origins, technological determinism" [which is Cohen's view]; that its great strength lies not in any unilinear conception of history, but, on the contrary, in the unique sensitivity to historical specificities. See Ellen Meiksins Wood, *Democracy Against Capitalism: Renewing Historical Materialism* (Cambridge: Cambridge University Press, 1995), p. 122.

47. Marx, "Economic and Philosophical Manuscripts," p. 348; *MEW,* suppl. 1, p. 536.

48. According to Nietzsche, "Socialism is the visionary younger brother of an almost decrepit despotism, whose heir it wants to be. Thus its efforts are reactionary in the deepest sense. For it desires a wealth of executive power, as only despotism had it; indeed, it outdoes everything in the past by striving for the downright destruction of the individual, which it sees as an unjustified luxury of nature, and which it intends to improve into an expedient *organ of the community.* " Friedrich Nietzsche, *Human All Too Human,* trans. M. Faber and S. Lehmann (Lincoln: University of Nebraska Press, 1986), no. 473; *NW,* vol. IV2, no. 473.

49. If Bernard Yack, in his *The Longing for Total Revolution* is correct in suggesting that presupposing an interrelation among social institutions is a central characteristic of nineteenth-century social and political critics, then Weber designates the collapse of this vista.

50. See E. Baumgarten, *Max Weber: Werk und Person* (Tübingen: Mohr, 1964), pp. 554–555. Weber said these words to a group of students after he had participated in a discussion with Oswald Spengler, shortly before his death.

51. In contrast to theorists such as Karl Löwith, who in his *Max Weber and Karl Marx* (London: Allen and Unwin, 1988) underscored the differences between Marx and Weber, recent works present a more complex picture. See, for example, Randall Collins, *Weberian Sociological Theory* (Cambridge: Cambridge University Press, 1986), Ch. 1; James Russell, "Method, Analysis, and Politics in Max Weber: Disentangling Marxian Affinities and Differences," *History of Political Economy*, vol. 17 (1985): 575–590; and the collection *The Marx-Weber Debate*, ed. Norbert Wiley (Newbury Park, CA: Sage Publications, 1987). Ellen Wood, however, chooses to highlight the differences between the two theorists, defending Marx's commitment to emancipation against Weber's pessimism and helplessness. See her *Democracy Against Capitalism*, pp. 146–180.

52. For Weber, work (or vocation) is needed in order to make the "totality of life" ethically significant, and not because the essence of the human species-being is expressed in the realm of production, as Marx believed.

53. Max Weber, "Socialism," in *Political Writings*, eds. Peter Lassman and Ronald Speirs (Cambridge: Cambridge University Press, 1994), p. 284, p. 288; "Der Sozialismus," *GASS*, p. 502, p. 505.

54. Weber, "Socialism," p. 260; *GASS*, p. 508.

55. Löwith, *Max Weber and Karl Marx*, p. 48. The idea that human beings create those offspring or institutions that destroy them (what could be termed the "Frankenstein Syndrome") is expressed by Weber in his discussion of bureaucracy. See "Parliament and Government in Germany," *Economy and Society*, eds. G. Roth and C. Wittich (Berkeley: University of California Press, 1978), p. 1402; "Parlament und Regierung im neugeordneten Deutschland," *GPS*, p. 332.

56. See Max Weber, *General Economic History* (New York: Collier-Macmillan, 1961). For the notion of multiple causality in Weber, see Michael Mann, *The Sources of Social Power* (Cambridge: Cambridge University Press, 1986).

57. Marx, "Economic and Philosophical Manuscripts," p. 328; *MEW*, suppl. 1, p. 516.

58. Max Weber, "Science as a Vocation," in *FMW*, p. 148; "Wissenschaft als Beruf," *GAW*, p. 546.

59. For an inclusive discussion of the relation between Nietzsche and Weber, see *Robert Eden, Political Leadership and Nihilism: A Study of Weber and Nietzsche* (Tampa: Florida University Press, 1983). Eden argues that Weber attempted to perform difficult marriages: combining Nietzsche's concept of the self with his own acceptance of liberal institutions, as well as coalescing this Nietzschean liberalism with German nationalism (see Ch. 3). It should also be added that Weber echoes Nietzsche in many other aspects of his thought: for example, in his attack on the German Historical School, in his probing into the way religions have shaped culture in the West and elsewhere, in his idea that scientific truth and objectivity must acknowledge the place of perspective, in his rejection of happiness as the ultimate goal of human beings, in his emphasis on the role of power and struggle in human life, and in his conception of the individual as the sole source of value and action. (Weber was well aware of these influences, and did not try to disguise them.) For a discussion of some of these influences, see Martin Albrow, *Max Weber's Construction of Social Theory* (London: Macmillan, 1990), Ch. 3. For Nietzsche's

general influence over Weber's contemporaries, see Steven Aschheim, *The Nietzsche Legacy in Germany, 1890–1990* (Berkeley: University of California Press, 1992), especially Ch. 1.

60. Weber, "National Character and the Junkers," in *FMW,* p. 393; "Wahlrecht und Demokratie in Deutschland," *GPS,* p. 285 (my emphasis).

61. Marianne Weber wrote that the "new proclamations of the great poet Stefan George, which in many respects referred back to Nietzsche's range of ideas, also negated all ruling powers of the machine age—rationalism, capitalism, democracy and socialism. They were addressed to a selected few of spiritual nobility and were directed at the form of existence, as the aristocratic general attitude towards life; they did not, however, supply norms for action or set new, tangible, substantial goals." See Marianne Weber, *Max Weber: A Biography* (New York: Wiley and Sons, 1975), p. 319. On Weber's relationship with the poet, see pp. 454–464.

62. Weber, "Religious Rejections," in *FMW,* p. 342; "Zwischenbetrachtung: Theorie der Stufen und Richtungen religiöser Weltablehnung," *GAR,* vol. 1, p. 555. In my discussion of subjectivist culture, I am indebted to Lawrence Scaff. See his *Fleeing the Iron Cage* (Berkeley: University of California Press, 1989).

63. The Freudian critique on the notion of bounded identity is, of course, even more forceful than Weber's. In particular, the constitutive role that Freud assigns to the superego ridicules any prospect for autonomous self-formation. I shall explore these issue at length in Ch. 4.

3. Max Weber: Between Homo-Hermeneut and the Lebende Maschine

1. Marianne Weber, *Max Weber: A Biography,* p. 319.

2. According to Wilhelm Hennis' illuminating interpretation, Weber was primarily interested in studying different types of human conduct and character, and the ways that these are conditioned by various life-orders [See Wilhelm Hennis, *Max Weber: Essays in Reconstruction* (London: Allen & Unwin, 1988)]. Hennis underscores Weber's own pronouncements in defining his project. In 1907, for example, Weber wrote that "my problematic *(Fragestellung)* . . . addresses itself to the rise of the ethical *'Lebensstil'* spiritually adequate to the economic stage of capitalism . . . [that] signifies its triumph in the 'souls' of men" [See *Max Weber: Essays in Reconstruction,* p. 30]. Hennis uncovers Weber's strong normative concerns, successfully discrediting interpretations of Weber that portray him as chiefly a theorist of rationalization and modernization. [For such pictures of Weber, see, for example, R. Bendix, *Max Weber: An Intellectual Portrait* (London: Methuen, 1966); and J. Habermas, *The Theory of Communicative Action,* vol. 1 (Boston: Beacon Press, 1984)]. Yet even Hennis fails to uncover, and surely to systematically examine, Weber's essentialist presuppositions about the hermeneutical nature of the self and the ways that this nature evolved historically; without this understanding, Weber's concern for the fate of the modern self makes no sense.

3. Max Weber, *The Protestant Ethic and the Spirit of Capitalism* (London: Unwin University Books, 1930); *The Religion of India, The Sociology of Hinduism and*

Buddhism (New York: Free Press, 1958); *Ancient Judaism* (New York: Free Press, 1952); *The Religion of China, Confucianism and Taoism* (New York: Free Press, 1964). The first three works are incorporated in *GARS* I, II, and III respectively.

4. Weber, *GARS*-I, pp. 237–275, pp. 536–573. These texts, translated in *FMW*, are entitled "Social Psychology of World Religions" (pp. 267–301) and "Religious Rejections of the World and their Directions" (pp. 323–362). For the centrality of these texts to Weber's work as a whole, see Friedreich H. Tenbruck, "The Problem of Thematic Unity in the Works of Max Weber," *British Journal of Sociology*, vol. 31 (Sept. 1980): 116–151. Although Tenbruck makes a compelling argument for the importance of these texts in Weber's entire project, he fails to address the main problematic that preoccupied Weber. In this respect, Hennis' interpretation is more convincing. The main challenge, however, is to explain how Weber's sociology of religion is related to his concern with the "human type" created by capitalism, and how an historical account of the Western self's formation is the foundation for criticizing its present predicament. In this chapter, I attempt to confront this challenge.

5. Weber, *ES*, p. 399; *WG*, p. 245.

6. Weber, *GARS*-I, pp. 1–16. This 'Author's Introduction' appears in *The Protestant Ethic and the Spirit of Capitalism*.

7. Weber, "Religious Rejections," *FMW*, p. 324; *GARS*-I, p. 537.

8. As noted above, Weber uses rationality in many different senses, and there are a few places where he acknowledges this. For example, in "The Social Psychology of the World Religions" he distinguishes among three types: (1) theoretical mastery of reality by using increasingly clearer concepts and formulations, (2) purposive, instrumental rationality *(Zweckrational), and* (3) Systematic arrangement of reality or of human conduct according to some ultimate value (*FMW*, pp. 293–294; *GARS*-I, pp. 265–267). My point about the "emptiness" of rationality applies mainly to (3) but it may pertain to the first two as well. There are, however, other senses of rationality in Weber, particular "value rationality" *(Wertrational)*. For a discussion of the different meanings of rationality in Weber's work, see Rogers Brubaker, *The Limits of Rationality* (London: Allen & Unwin, 1984).

9. Weber, "Social Psychology," *FMW*, p. 280; *GARS*-I, p. 252.

10. Weber describes the relation this way: "The nature of the desired sacred values has been strongly influenced by the nature of the external interest-situation and the corresponding way of life of the ruling strata and thus by the social stratification itself. But the reverse also holds: wherever the direction of the whole way of life has been methodically rationalized, it has been profoundly determined by the ultimate values towards which this rationalization has been directed. These values and positions were thus *religiously* determined." See: "Social Psychology," *FMW*, pp. 286–287; *GARS*-I, p. 259. See also my discussion below.

11. Weber, "Social Psychology," *FMW*, p. 270; *GARS*-I, p. 240. For the same reasons, Weber also rejects, for the most part, Nietzsche's argument in *On the Genealogy of Morals* about "ressentiment." While this concept is useful in interpreting some periods of Judaism, it does not apply to Christianity and not at all to Buddhism, as Nietzsche claimed. My reading of Weber suggests that it is not the

"will to power" that propels human conduct and history, but primarily the desire for meaning. See: *ES*, pp. 494–499.

12. Weber, "Social Psychology," *FMW*, p. 281; *GARS* -I, p. 253 (translation altered).

13. Weber's interpretation of this shift from magic to religions of salvation, as well as of the evolutions of these religions themselves, contains a teleological ingredient. This is in contrast to his explicit rejection of teleology. According to Tenbruck, "Weber who throughout his life had upheld the uniqueness of history against the laws of progress is now encountered in his work on religion in the opposing camp of evolutionism. See: "The Problem of Thematic Unity in the Works of Max Weber," p. 333. However, the teleological component in Weber's thought is rather complex and certainly does not involve an argument about the immanent movement of history itself.

14. Weber, "Religious Rejections," *FMW*, p. 353; *GARS*-I, p. 567. Nietzsche makes a similar claim, averring that "the meaninglessness of suffering, not suffering itself, was the curse that lay over mankind so far . . ." See: Nietzsche, *On the Genealogy of Morals*, Part 3, no. 28.

15. Weber, "Social Psychology," *FMW*, p. 271; *GARS*-I, p. 242.

16. As Weber aptly remarks, "'From what' and 'for what' one wished to be redeemed and, let us not forget 'could be' redeemed, depended upon one's image of the world." "Social Psychology," *FMW*, p. 280; *GARS*-I, p. 252.

17. For Weber's discussion of salvation in *ES*, see pp. 518–576. For an insightful comparison between *ES*, on the one hand, and the *"Einleitung"* and the *"Zwischenbetrachtung,"* on the other, see Wolfgang Schluchter, "Weber's Sociology of Rationalism and Typology of Religious Rejections of the World," in *Max Weber: Rationality and Modernity*, eds. S. Whimster and S. Lash (London: Allen & Unwin, 1987), pp. 92–118. Schluchter also elaborates on the differences between Weber's two ideal types of salvation.

18. Weber, "Religious Rejections," *FMW*, p. 327; *GARS*-I, p. 540.

19. Weber, "Religious Rejections," *FMW*, p. 330; *GARS*-I, pp. 543–544.

20. Weber, *ES*, p. 450; *WG*, p. 275.

21. Weber, "Religious Rejections," *FMW*, p. 352; *GARS*-I, p. 566.

22. Weber distinguishes between "ethical" (or emissary) and "exemplary" prophecy (*"Sendungsprophetie"* and *"exemplarische Prophetie"*). The first demands, in the name of God, obedience to some ethical duty. The second demonstrates by his *personal conduct*, a route for salvation. Thus, Zoroaster and Muhammad belong to the first category, and Buddha to the second. The ethical prophets were crucial to the Judaeo-Christian tradition in general and in modern times to the development of Protestantism in particular. Nevertheless, both types provide a source of meaning. See: *ES*, pp. 447–450.

23. Weber, *ES*, p. 1117; *WG*, p. 658.

24. Weber, "Religious Rejections," *FMW*, p. 353; *GARS*-I, p. 567. For further discussion of the rationalization of religion, see Stephen Kalberg, "The Rationalization of Action in Max Weber's Sociology of Religion," *Sociological Theory*, vol. 8 (Spring, 1990): 58–84.

25. It is a mistake, then, to rely only on "Science as a Vocation" in this matter since, for Weber, the problems of meaninglessness and disenchantment do not result merely from the evolution of modern, natural sciences. For a discussion of this point, and of Weber's notion of disenchantment in general, see Alkis Kontos, "The World Disenchanted and the Return of Gods and Demons," in *The Barbarism of Reason: Max Weber and the Twilight of Enlightenment*, eds. A. Horowitz and T. Maley (Toronto: University of Toronto Press, 1994), 223–247.

26. Max Weber, "Objectivity in the Social Sciences," *MSS*, p. 57; "Die 'Objektivität' sozialwissenschaftlicher und sozialpolitischer Erkenntnis," *GAW*, p. 154.

27. During WWI, Weber was regarded as one of the strongest voices calling for the democratization of German society and politics. Yet Weber perceived the will of the people as a fiction, and the parliament as an arena whose main goal is to raise experienced leaders. Weber thought that, at least in the German context, where Bismarck's legacy resulted in the absence of political education for all classes and in a political culture of submission, the appropriate model of democracy was a plebiscitary one. According to this view, the leader should acquire his or her legitimacy by directly appealing to the people, and the politics of referendum should be preferred over the politics that involves public deliberation and ongoing participation. In Weber's own terminology, this model of democracy combines rule (*Herrschaft*) by law and rule by charisma.

After WWII, Weber was criticized for this receptiveness toward charismatic leadership, as well as for presenting national power as the prime end of politics, for separating the spheres of ethics and politics, and for rejecting the notion of universal values binding all human beings as such; despite his liberal convictions, he may have inadvertently helped to create the intellectual and cultural background sympathetic to Nazi ideology. The main attacks on Weber in this context by leading theorists such as Aron, Marcuse, and Mommsen were articulated during a conference in Heidelberg, 1964. For critiques of Weber along this line, see especially Wolfgang Mommsen, *Max Weber and German Politics, 1890–1920*, trans. M. Steinberg (Chicago: University of Chicago Press, 1984). On Weber's concept of democracy, see Sven Eliaeson, "Constitutional Caesarism: Weber's Politics in their German Context," in *The Cambridge Companion to Weber*, ed. S. Turner (Cambridge: Cambridge University Press, 2000), pp. 131–150; ed. Ralph Schroeder, *Max Weber, Democracy and Modernization*, (London: Macmillan and St. Martin's Press, 1988); and Peter Breiner, *Max Weber and Democratic Politics* (Ithaca: Cornell University Press, 1996). On Weber's distrustful attitude toward the masses, see Peter Baehr, "The Masses in Weber's Political Sociology," *Economy and Society*, vol. 19 (1996): 242–265.

28. The most comprehensive discussion of Weber's concept of "personality," one to which I am greatly indebted, is Harvey Goldman's *Max Weber and Thomas Mann* (Berkeley: University of California Press, 1988). Other useful discussions include Mark Warren, "Max Weber's Liberalism for a Nietzschean World," *American Political Science Review*, vol. 82 (March, 1988): 31–49; Edward Portis, "Max Weber's Theory of Personality," *Sociological Inquiry*, vol. 48 (1978): 113–120; W. Hennis, *Essays in Reconstruction*, pp. 90–101. For the influence of Puritan thought on Weber's understanding of the personality's freedom, see John P.

Diggins, *Max Weber: Politics and the Spirit of Tragedy* (New York: Basic Books, 1996), Ch. 1. For Kant's influence on Weber's concept of the personality, see Martin Albrow, *Max Weber's Construction of Social Theory*, pp. 37–42.

29. Weber, *RK*, p. 192; "Knies und das Irrationalitätsproblem," *GAW*, p. 132.

30. Weber, "Objectivity," *MSS*, p. 55; *GAW*, p. 152.

31. Weber, "Objectivity," *MSS*, p. 55; *GAW*, p. 152.

32. Weber, *ES*, p. 573; *WG*, p. 346.

33. Weber, *RK*, p. 199; *GAW*, p. 138.

34. Weber, *The Religions of China*, p. 235; "Konfuzianismus und Taoismus," *GARS*-I, p. 521 (my emphasis, translation modified). See also Goldman, *Max Weber and Thomas Mann*, p. 155.

35. As Weber notes, "ceremonial prescription regulated questions and answers, indispensable offers, as well as the exact manner of grateful decline, also visits, presents, expressions of respect, condolence and joyful sympathy." See: Weber, *The Religions of China*, p. 234.

36. Weber, "The Religions of Asia," *MWST*, p. 200; *GARS*-II, p. 373.

37. W. Hennis, *Essays in Reconstruction*, p. 92.

38. Weber, "The Religions of Asia," *MWST*, p. 204; *GARS*-II, p. 378.

39. Weber, "The Religions of Asia," *MWST*, p. 201; *GARS*-II, p. 373.

40. Weber, "The Spirit of Capitalism," *MWST*, p. 145; *GARS*-I, p. 172.

41. Weber, "The Spirit of Capitalism," *MWST*, p. 170, p. 171; *GARS*-I, p. 203, p. 204.

42. See: "Discipline and Charisma," a part of the studies of charisma in *ES*, pp. 1148–1156; *WG*, pp. 681–687. I am using the translation in *FMW*, pp. 253–262.

43. Isaiah Berlin, *Four Essays on Liberty* (New York: Oxford University Press, 1991), p. 126, p. 130, p. 129.

44. Max Weber, "Parliament and Government in Germany," in *Weber: Political Writings*, eds. P. Lassman and R. Speirs (Cambridge: Cambridge University Press, 1994), p. 159.

45. Weber, "The Meaning of Discipline," *FMW*, pp. 260–261; *WG*, p. 686. For a comparison between Weber and Marx in this respect, see Randall Collins, *Weberian Sociological Theory*, Ch.1. For a comparison between Weber and Foucault, see Colin Gordon: "The Soul of the Citizen: Max Weber and Michel Foucault on Rationality and Government," in *Max Weber: Rationality and Modernity*, 293–316.

46. Weber, "The Meaning of Discipline," *FMW*, p. 253; *WG*, p. 681.

47. Weber, "Bureaucracy," *FMW*, p. 228; *WG*, p. 570.

48. Weber, "The Meaning of Discipline," *FMW*, p. 262; *WG*, p. 686.

49. Weber, "The Meaning of Discipline," *FMW*, p. 257, p. 256; *WG*, p. 684, p. 683.

50. Weber, "The Meaning of Discipline" *FMW*, p. 262; *WG*, p. 686. Marx often depicts the worker in rather similar terms. For example, he writes that "[t]he habit of doing only one thing converts him [the worker] into an organ which operates with the certainty of a force of nature, while his connections with the whole mechanism compels him to work with the regularity of a machine." See: Karl

Marx, *Capital*, vol. 1, trans. Ben Fowkes (London: Penguin, 1990), p. 469. For a discussion of the discipline of bodies in Weber see: Bryan S. Turner, *Max Weber: From History to Modernity* (London: Routledge, 1992), pp. 113–160.

51. Weber, "Bureaucracy," *FMW*, pp. 215–216; *WG*, p. 563.

52. Weber, *ES*, p. 257; *WG*, p. 250.

53. Weber, "The Meaning of Discipline," *FMW*, p. 254; *WG*, p. 682.

54. Weber, "Parliament and Government in Germany," *ES*, p. 1402; *GPS*, p. 332 (translation altered).

55. Weber, *"Parliament and Government in Germany,"* *ES*, p. 1404; *GPS*, p. 335 (my emphasis). It is unfortunate that Weber—who was more concerned with the implications of this ethos of bureaucracy than anyone else at his time—did not look for an ethical ground by which submission to and internalization of authority may be qualified. As Arendt notes, this understanding of bureaucratic duty was destructive. "Much of the horribly painstaking thoroughness in the execution of the Final Solution—a thoroughness that usually strikes the observer as typically German, or else as characteristic of the perfect bureaucrat—can be traced to the odd notion, indeed very common in Germany, that to be law-abiding means not merely to obey the laws but to act as though one were the legislator of the laws that one obeys. Hence the conviction that nothing less then going beyond the call of duty will do." See: Hannah Arendt, *Eichmann in Jerusalem: a Report on the Banality of Evil* (New York: Penguin Books, 1964), p. 137.

56. Weber, "Religious Rejections," *FMW*, p. 328; *GARS*-I, p. 541.

57. An earlier version of these reflections appears in *ES*, pp. 576–610; *WG*, pp. 348–366. One of the major differences between the two texts is that in the later one Weber places much more emphasis on the role of the different value-spheres as routes to innerworldly salvation. See my discussion below.

58. Rogers Brubaker, *The Limits of Rationality*, p. 72. As Brubaker notes, Weber thus suggests pluralism of values at two levels: within spheres and between spheres.

59. Weber is explicit in this respect. "We know of no scientifically demonstrable ideals," he writes. "To be sure, our labors are now rendered more difficult, since we must create our ideals from within our chests in the very age of subjectivist culture. But we must not and cannot promise a fool's paradise and an easy street, neither in the here and now nor in the beyond, neither in thought nor in action, and it is the stigma of our human dignity that the peace of our souls cannot be as great as the peace of one who dreams of such paradise." See: Max Weber, *Gesammelte Aufsätze zur Soziologie und Sozialpolitik* (Tübingen: J. C. Mohr, 1924), p. 420. Quoted here from Scaff, *Fleeing the Iron Cage*, p. 82.

60. The young Weber was particularly prone to such gloomy assessments. "It is not peace and happiness that we have to bequeath to our descendants, but *eternal struggle* for the maintenance and improvement of our national species." The same imperative of struggle seems to hold for the individual's life. See: Max Weber, "The National State and Economic Policy" (Inaugural Address given at Freiburg, 1895), in *Nineteenth Century Europe: Liberalism and its Critics*, eds. J. Goldstein and J. Boyer (Chicago: Chicago University Press, 1988), p. 450.

61. The ethic of brotherly love is especially inadequate for the politician,

Weber argues in "Politics as a Vocation." Yet he suggests that the same holds true for any secular person/citizen who wishes to live in the world and according to its ways. See Weber's discussion in *FMW*, pp. 114–128.

62. Weber, "Religious Rejections," *FMW*, p. 344, p. 345; *GARS*-I, pp. 557, 558.

63. Weber, "Religious Rejections," *FMW*, p. 347; *GARS*-I, p. 560.

64. Weber, "Religious Rejections," *FMW*, p. 346; *GARS*-I, p. 560 (my emphasis).

65. Weber did not see the erotic sphere as capable of satisfying the modern self's needs. This can be learned from his unfavorable opinion of Otto Gross, a student of Freud who used psychoanalysis as the foundation for a new, free sexual ethic. Under conditions of seclusion this ethic was supposed to relieve the individual from the anxiety, purposelessness, and emotional emptiness of modern life. On Weber's relation to Gross see: Marianne Weber, *Max Weber: A Biography*, pp. 372–380, and Wolfgang Schwentker, "Passion as a Mode of Life: Max Weber and the Otto Gross Circle," in *Max Weber and His Contemporaries*, eds. W. Mommsen and J. Osterhammel (London: Allen & Unwin, 1987), pp. 483–498.

66. Weber, "Religious Rejections," *FMW*, p. 342; *GARS*-I, p. 555.

67. Weber, *ES*, p. 608; *WG*, p. 365.

68. Weber, "Science as a Vocation," *FMW*, p. 137; *GAW*, p. 533 (translation altered).

69. Weber, "Science as a Vocation," *FMW*, p. 138; *GAW*, p. 592.

70. Weber, "Science as a Vocation," *FMW*, pp. 139–140; *GAW*, p. 594. Tolstoy's views are incompatible with Weber's on other fronts as well. Tolstoy insisted, for example, that the means are sacred as the ends, and that power should not be resisted by an opposing power; in other words, Tolstoy adhered to the ethic of conviction, which Weber saw as impractical and ultimately irresponsible. For a discussion of the relation between the two writers, see Diggins, *Politics and the Spirit of Tragedy*, pp. 125–131.

71. Weber, "Religious Rejections," *FMW*, p. 335; *GARS*-I, p. 548. These words were written with WWI in the background.

72. Marianne Weber, *Max Weber: A Biography*, p. 529.

73. Weber argues that with the advent of democracy and the opening of political participation to all classes, a growing number of politicians lack independent economic means. Therefore, their engagement in public affairs may be motivated primarily by their desire to live "from politics" rather than live "for politics," to secure their steady income (through membership in parliament, for example) rather than to fight for any risky cause. A related group of people are the party bosses and political entrepreneurs, who see the recruitment of votes as a business transaction; in exchange of electoral support they provide employment and beneficial appointments, engaging in politics merely for the sake of power and the spoils that this profession may yield. Weber also feared that bureaucracy would have a devastating influence over politics: the technical superiority and overall trustworthy conduct of state officials could render them the most attractive candidates for leadership roles; within the party, moreover, the growing organization may eventually acquire too much power, blurring the essential distinction between creative,

responsible leaders and individuals with the mentality of officials who lack the ability to formulate and advance critical policies and ideals. Weber discusses these issues in his lecture, "Politics as a Vocation," in *FMW.*

74. Weber, "Politics as a Vocation," *FMW,* p. 117; *GPS,* pp. 547–548.

75. Weber, "Politics as a Vocation," *FMW,* p. 115; *GPS,* p. 545. Weber's famous lecture should not be seen as merely the reflections of a political scientist, but as written by someone who considered immersing himself in politics and taking upon himself a leadership role. On this personal context and its significance, see Wolfgang Schluchter, *Paradoxes of Modernity,* trans. Neil Solomon (Stanford: Stanford University Press, 1996), Ch. 1.

76. Weber, "Politics as a Vocation," *FMW,* p. 117; *GPS,* p. 547.

77. Max Weber, "Between Two Laws," in *Weber: Political Writings,* eds. P. Lassman & R. Speirs (Cambridge: Cambridge University Press, 1994), p. 75; "Zwischen zwei Gesetzen," *GPS,* p. 142. Germany, according to Weber, has a responsibility toward itself to preserve its culture, which is threatened by the expansionism of Russia on the east, as well as by the proliferation of American values and practices dominated by capitalist and economic considerations. While Weber believed World War I to be justified because of the imperative of protecting the German national interest and culture, he was opposed to the annexation of other countries by Germany, and was highly concerned about America's joining the war. For a discussion of Weber's views during the war, see J. P. Mayer, "Sociology of Politics: An Interpretation of Max Weber's Political Philosophy," *The Dublin Review,* no. 207 (1940): 188–196. Reprinted in B. Turner (ed.), *Max Weber: Critical Responses,* vol. 1 (London: Routledge, 1999), pp. 152–157.

78. Weber, "Structures of Power," *FMW,* p. 176; *WG,* p. 530.

79. In "Objectivity," Weber defines culture as the following: "The concept of culture is a *value concept.* Empirical reality becomes 'culture' to us because and insofar as we relate it to value ideas. It includes those segments and only those segments of reality which have become significant to us because of this value-relevance." See: *MSS,* p. 76; *GAW,* p. 175.

80. Weber, "Religious Rejections," *FMW,* p. 355; *GARS*-I, p. 569.

81. Weber, "Objectivity," *MSS,* p. 78; *GAW,* p. 178 (translation altered). Following the Neo-Kantianism of Rickert, Weber argues that any research project begins from the selection of facts that seem relevant to the researcher, since reality is too manifold to be incorporated in its entirety; self-formed concepts intervene between subject and object, allowing the organization of cognition. This process of consciously filtering experience is valid both for nomological sciences *(Gesetzeswissenschaften)* that seek to formulate universal laws, as well as for disciplines such as history and the social sciences that deal with concrete reality *(Wirklichkeitswissenschaften).* In the latter, we select those facts that can illuminate a particular and significant event, explaining the causes for the phenomenon and interpreting the meaning for the agents involved. On Weber's methodology, see Fritz Ringer, *Max Weber Methodology: The Unification of the Cultural and Social Sciences* (Cambridge: Harvard University Press, 1997), especially Ch. 2.

82. Weber, "Objectivity," *MSS,* p. 82; *GAW,* p. 182.

83. Weber, "Religious Rejections," *FMW,* p. 356; *GARS*-I, p. 570.

84. Weber, "Religious Rejections," *FMW*, p. 357; *GARS*-I, p. 570.

85. In the same context, Weber says that "the forward progress of bureaucratic mechanization is irresistible . . . When a purely technical and faultless administration, a precise and objective solution of concrete problems is taken as the highest and only goal, then on this basis one can only say: away with everything but an official hierarchy which does these things as objectively, precisely, and 'soullessly' as any machine." These words were uttered to colleagues in the *Verein für Sozialpolitik*, Vienna, 1909. Quoted here from Alan Sica, "Rationalization and Culture," in *The Cambridge Companion to Weber*, p. 53.

4. Freud and the Castration of the Modern

1. Max Weber, *Selections in Translation*, ed. W. G. Runciman (Cambridge, UK: Cambridge University Press, 1978), p. 386.

2. Weber, *Selections in Translation*, p. 385. Philip Rieff elaborated this critique of psychoanalysis, arguing that it impoverishes the ethical discourse of modern culture, and weakens the commitment of the self to participate in communal life. See his *The Triumph of the Therapeutic* (New York: Harper and Row, 1966), and *Freud: The Mind of a Moralist* (New York: Viking Press, 1961). See also note 61 below.

3. Freud explicitly refers to this question in his "New Introductory Lectures," written more than two decades after Weber made his comments on Freudianism. Freud says there that the only *Weltanschauung* with which psychoanalysis is associated is that of the natural sciences. See *SE*, XXII, pp. 158–182. Following the customary practice of the secondary literature, I refer in this chapter to *The Standard Edition* of Freud's writings alone, without reference to the original German texts.

4. See, for example, Herbert Marcuse, *Eros and Civilization: A Philosophical Inquiry into Freud* (Boston: Beacon Press, 1966); Norman O. Brown, *Life Against Death: The Psychoanalytic Meaning of History* (Middletown, CT: Wesleyan University Press, 1959); and Jürgen Habermas, *Knowledge and Human Interest* (Boston: Beacon Press, 1968), especially Ch. 12.

5. For the first position, see P. Roazen, *Freud: Political and Social Thought* (New York: Da Capo Press, 1986); for the second, see R. Wollheim, *Sigmund Freud* (New York: Viking Press, 1971).

6. See Adolf Grünbaum, *The Foundations of Psychoanalysis: A Philosophical Critique* (Berkeley: University of California Press, 1984). See also his *Validation in the Clinical Theory of Psychoanalysis* (New York: International Universities Press, 1993). For other discussions about the scientific validity of psychoanalysis, see: Allen Esterson, *Seductive Mirage* (Open Court, 1993); Malcolm Macmillan, *Freud Evaluated: The Completed Arc* (Cambridge, MA: MIT Press, 1997); Frederick Crews, "The Unknown Freud," *New York Review of Books*, XL, no. 19 (Nov. 18, 1993): 55–66; and J. Forrester, *Dispatches from the Freud Wars* (Cambridge, MA: Harvard University Press, 1997).

7. "[A] given explanatory framework," writes Taylor, "secretes a notion of good, and a set of valuations, which cannot be done away with . . . unless we do away

with the theory." See Charles Taylor, "Neutrality in Political Science," in *Philosophy and the Human Sciences: Philosophical Papers 2* (Cambridge, UK: Cambridge University Press, 1985), p. 90. Taylor discusses theories of political science in this article, but his insights may be extended to other social and human sciences as well.

8. Freud, "Civilization and Its Discontents," *SE*, XXI, p. 97.

9. Hobbes, for example, argues that "emotions consist in various motions of the blood and animal spirits [understood as material particles] as they variously expand and contract; the causes of these motions are phantasms concerning good and evil excited in the mind by objects." See Thomas Hobbes, *Man and Citizen, De Homine and De Cive* (Indianapolis: Hackett, 1991), p. 55.

10. Freud, "Instincts and Their Vicissitudes," *SE*, XIV, pp. 121–122.

11. Freud, "Beyond the Pleasure Principle," *SE*, XVIII, p. 29.

12. Freud, "On Narcissism," *SE*, XIV, p. 85. Heine was probably probing here into God's psychogenesis.

13. "In the last resort," writes Freud, "we must begin to love in order not to fall ill." See "On Narcissism," *SE*, XIV, p. 85.

14. The wider, historical implications of this view have been explored by Norman O. Brown, who follows Freud in proclaiming the existence of a "universal neurosis of mankind." See Norman O. Brown, *Life Against Death*, pp. 9–10.

15. Freud, "Civilization and Its Discontents," *SE*, XXI, pp. 118–119. In his first theory of instincts, Freud expresses the same duality of destruction (sexual instincts) vs. preservation (ego instincts).

16. According to Freud, the possibility "of displacing a large amount of libidinal components, whether narcissistic, aggressive, or even erotic on to professional work and on to the human relation connected with it," is of fundamental importance, both for the individual's well-being and for societal preservation and progress. "Civilization and its Discontents," *SE*, XXI, p. 80n. My discussion below is an elaboration of this insight.

17. Friedrich Nietzsche, *On the Genealogy of Morality* (Cambridge, UK: Cambridge University Press, 1994), II, no. 16. Despite his great respect for Nietzsche as psychologist, Freud, as is well known, insisted that psychoanalysis owes little to philosophy in general and to Nietzsche in particular. Although key Freudian concepts and psychic processes contain an uncanny resemblance to themes from the second essay of the *Genealogy*, one could find various explanations for this phenomenon without discrediting Freud's veracity. Affinities between Nietzsche and Freud have already been pointed out by Ernest Jones in his *The Life and Work of Sigmund Freud*, vol. 3 (New York: Basic Books, 1957). For a recent discussion of Freud's analysis of Nietzsche in *Minutes of the Vienna Psychoanalytic Society*, see Peter Heller, "Freud in His Relations to Nietzsche," in *Nietzsche and Jewish Culture*, ed. J. Golomb (New York: Routledge, 1997), pp. 193–217.

18. Freud, "The Future of an Illusion," *SE*, XXI, p. 11.

19. Freud, "New Introductory Lectures," *SE*, XXII, p. 110. For the import of political metaphors in Freud's work, see J. Brunner, "On the Political Rhetoric of Freud's Individual Psychology," *History of Political Thought*, vol. V (Summer, 1984): 315–332.

20. Freud, "Civilization and Its Discontents," *SE*, XXI, p. 134.

21. Freud, "The Future of an Illusion," *SE*, XXI, p. 11.

22. Freud, "Civilization and Its Discontents," *SE*, XXI, p. 112.

23. Freud, "New Introductory Lectures," *SE*, XXII, p. 95.

24. Plato is mentioned in Freud's discussion of Eros in "Beyond the Pleasure Principle" (*SE*, XVII, pp. 57–58), and Schopenhauer in "New Introductory Lectures" (*SE*, XXII, p. 107). In a different text, "Civilization and Its Discontents," Freud's indebtedness to his intellectual background is more manifest. He points to the similarity between his views of Eros and Death and those of Goethe in Faust. See *SE*, XXI, pp. 120–121. Freud's first theory of instincts, he acknowledges, originated in an insight of Schiller's about the centrality of love and hunger in human life. See "Civilization and Its Discontents," *SE*, XXI, p. 117.

25. Sigmund Freud, in *Minutes of the Vienna Psychoanalytic Society*, Volume II: 1908–1910 (New York: International Universities Press, 1967), p. 174 (my emphasis).

26. See Agnes Heller, "Where are We at Home," *Thesis Eleven*, 41 (1995): 2. Heller argues that in modernity space is no longer the privileged sphere in which selves create their home, and that they prefer to make "the absolute present" into the chief anchor of identity.

27. Martin Heidegger, *Being and Time*, trans. J. Macquarrie & E. Robinson (New York: Harper & Row, 1962), p. 233. For Heidegger, Dasein has a sudden sense of uncanniness, of not being at home, when it experiences itself as "being in the world." Dasein attempts to escape this state by losing itself in an environment it considers familiar and safe: the world of everyday concerns, of the "they." On the notion of homelessness in Heidegger, see Leslie Paul Thiele, *Timely Meditations: Martin Heidegger and Postmodern Politics* (Princeton, NJ: Princeton University Press, 1995). On the similarity between Freud and Heidegger in this subject, see David Farrell Krell, "Das Unheimliche: Architectural Sections of Heidegger and Freud," in *Research in Phenomenology*, vol. XXII (1992): 43–61.

28. Freud, "The Uncanny," *SE*, XVII, p. 220. There is, of course, a vast literature on Freud's concept of the uncanny, most of which is not concerned with the self-civilization relation that is explored in this essay. Julia Kristeva, for example, examines the uncanny in the context of the relation between self and other. "The uncanny strangeness," she writes, "allows for many variations: They all repeat the difficulty I have in situating myself with respect to the other." See Julia Kristeva, *Strangers to Ourselves*, trans. Leon S. Roudiez (New York: Columbia University Press, 1991), p. 187. While Kristeva's interpretation underscores the place of the uncanny in human intercourse, Samuel Weber finds the uncanny important in forming a viable theory of knowledge, one that does not hold to the Cartesian illusion of an objectivizing, insulated, and reliable cognition. "Whereas for Descartes the essential condition for attaining certitude was the subject's withdrawal from a world that in its alterity could no longer be relied on, it is precisely the discovery that such withdrawal is a fata morgana, an unsustainable construct that informs the misrecognition that constitutes the uncanny." See Samuel Weber, *The Legend of Freud* (Stanford, CA: Stanford University Press, 2000), p. 20. For a political interpretation of the concept, see Derrida's brief but illuminating discussion of the uncanny element in Marxism, in Jacques Derrida, *Specters of Marx* (New York: Routledge, 1994), pp. 172–175.

29. Freud, "The Uncanny," *SE*, XVII, p. 225. The quotation is from Grimm's German dictionary (1877, 4, Part 2, p. 875).

30. Freud, "Introductory Lectures on Psychoanalysis," *SE*, XVI, p. 285.

31. Freud, "An Outline of Psychoanalysis," *SE*, XXIII, p. 163. My interpretation of psychoanalysis highlights the formation of the self as an outcome of identifications via the superego. Freud, however, also believed in Lamarckian theory and argued that acquired psychic characteristics of the race are transmitted organically, through the id. Since this point is not relevant to the present discussion, I will not explore it below. See "The Ego and the Id," *SE*, XIX, pp. 12–68.

32. Freud, "New Introductory Lectures," *SE*, XXII, p. 74.

33. Freud, "The Uncanny," *SE*, XVII, p. 241. Freud's textual interpretation of the uncanny in Hoffmann's story is controversial. See, for example, Harold Bloom, *Agon: Towards a Theory of Revisionism* (New York: Oxford University Press, 1982); and Nicholas Rand and Maria Torok "The Sandman Looks at the Uncanny" in *Speculation After Freud: Psychoanalysis, Philosophy, and Culture*, ed. S. Shamdasani (London: Routledge, 1994), pp. 185–204. For Freud's understanding of the repetitions in the Hoffmann's work, see Neil Hertz, *The End of the Line: Essays on Psychoanalysis and the Sublime* (New York: Columbia University Press, 1985), pp. 97–121.

34. E. T. A. Hoffmann, *Tales of E. T. A. Hoffmann*, eds. L. Kent and E. Knight (Chicago: University of Chicago Press, 1972), p. 95.

35. Hoffmann, *Tales of E. T. A. Hoffmann*, p. 98. For the role of the Oedipus complex in identity-formation, see Hans W. Loewald, "The Waning of the Oedipus Complex," in his *Papers on Psychoanalysis* (New Haven: Yale University Press, 1980), pp. 384–404.

36. Freud, "The Uncanny," *SE*, XVII, p. 223. At this stage, Freud did not yet use the concept "superego."

37. Freud, "The Uncanny," *SE*, XVII, p. 235.

38. J. Laplanche and J. B. Pontalis, *The Language of Psychoanalysis*, trans. D. Nicholson-Smith (New York: Norton, 1973), p. 349.

39. Laplanche and Pontalis, *The Language of Psychoanalysis*, p. 354 (my emphasis). This interpretation of projection is partly based on the Schreber case study.

40. Otto Rank, *The Double*, trans. H. Tucker (Chapel Hill: University of North Carolina Press, 1971), p. 82.

41. Freud, "The Uncanny," *SE*, XVII, p. 235.

42. In "The Uncanny," Freud does not distinguish between psychotic pathologies and narcissistic ones, seeming to regard them as one category. As Olsen and Koppe explain, Freud "found that most of the traits [of psychoses], that is, self-centeredness, lack of libidinous object cathexis, the loss of the sense of reality, and domination of primary processes, were related to their narcissistic mode." They add that "what in particular distinguishes the neuroses from the psychoses is their reliance on the defense mechanisms of projection and denial in contrast to repression." See O. Olsen and S. Koppe, *Freud's Theory of Psychoanalysis*, trans. J. C. Delay and C. Pedersen (New York: New York University Press, 1988), pp. 244–245.

However, Freud's classification of psychic illnesses changed with the introduction of the superego. In "Neurosis and Psychosis" (1923), Freud argues that "Transference neuroses correspond to a conflict between the ego and the id; narcissistic neuroses [such as melancholia], to a conflict between the ego and the super-ego; and psychoses, to one between the ego and the external world" (*SE*, XIX, p. 152). This distinction is problematic, since Freud claims that part of the demands of the external world is represented by the superego. In the discussion below, I will continue to refer to projection as a psychotic defence with narcissistic motivations.

43. Freud, "An Outline of Psychoanalysis," *SE*, XXIII, p. 206, p. 207.

44. Freud, "An Outline of Psychoanalysis," *SE*, XXII, p. 206. On identification in psychoanalytic theory, see Jessica Benjamin, *Shadows of the Other: Intersubjectivity and Gender in Psychoanalysis* (New York: Routledge, 1998).

45. In the context of autonomy, it is important to note the affinities between Freud and what is known as "positive liberty" (the type of liberty Isaiah Berlin suggested that both Rousseau and Kant adhered to). Freud believes that the self's freedom involves self-mastery, the capacity of the ego to occupy the mind as much as possible. From his perspective, freedom is not simply attained once external interferences and obstacles are removed; rather, it is gained by learning to conquer the psychic forces that spring from both the id and the superego, forces that if left unchecked inhibit our capacity to function in and cope with the world. On this matter, see J. Brunner, *Freud: The Politics of Psychoanalysis* (London: Blackwell, 1995), Ch. 10. It should be mentioned, nevertheless, that Freud did not translate his understanding of human freedom to the political realm; he avoided, in particular, the notion that self-mastery also involves similarity among selves who long to collectively control their social institutions.

46. Freud, "New Introductory Lectures," *SE*, XXII, p. 67.

47. Freud, "Civilization and Its Discontents," *SE*, XXI, pp. 135–136.

48. The critique of these bourgeois values was developed by writers after Freud, particularly by Marcuse. From the latter's perspective, Freud's concept of the superego is anachronistic: in modernity no genuine individuation and autonomy is acquired by the institution of the superego, since the father and other close figures are no longer significant in forming this psychic agency. "Under the rule of economic, political, and cultural monopolies," Marcuse writes, "the formation of the mature super-ego seems to skip the stage of individuation: the generic atom becomes directly a social atom. The repressive organization of the instinct seems to be collective, and the ego seems to be prematurely socialized by a whole system of extra-familial agents and agencies" (p. 97). This understanding of the superego and of the resultant "surplus repression" leads Marcuse to demand radical reorganization of social and economic institutions in a manner that differs from Freud's cautiousness and adherence to the bourgeois order. See Marcuse, *Eros and Civilization*.

49. Freud, "Civilization and Its Discontents," *SE*, XXI, p. 141, p. 142.

50. Alexis de Tocqueville, *Democracy in America*, vol. 2 (New York: Alfred Knopf, 1951), pp. 258–259.

51. Freud, "Group Psychology," *SE*, XVIII, p. 116.

52. Freud, "Civilization and Its Discontents," *SE*, XXI, p. 115, p. 116. Freud was highly critical of Woodrow Wilson, whom he considered to be a naive leader who misread the mutual hostility inherent in social life. On this point, see Brunner, *Freud: The Politics of Psychoanalysis*, Ch. 4. It is important to note that when fascism emerged in Europe, Freud's suggestion that the leader is essential to the formation of groups was strongly criticized. Erich Fromm, for example, believed that his age was witnessing the disintegration of the superego or consciences (p. 167), and suggested that it is precisely the lack of individuality that springs from this disintegration that propels men and women to crave an all-powerful leader and external source of authority (or the anonymous rein of public opinion, the norm, and science in democratic regimes). Fascism, according to this interpretation, springs from the inability of modern men and women to cope with their freedom and individuality, and with their corresponding aloneness (or homelessness) in the world. See Erich Fromm, *Escape from Freedom* (New York: Rinehart, 1941), especially Chs. 5 & 7.

53. Freud, "The Future of an Illusion," *SE*, XXI, p. 41.

54. Freud, "Civilization and Its Discontents," *SE*, XXI, p. 136.

55. Freud, "The Future of an Illusion," *SE*, XXI, p. 41.

56. Freud, "The Future of an Illusion," *SE*, XXI, p. 39 (my emphasis).

57. Freud, "The Future of an Illusion," *SE*, XXI, p. 15. In "Civilization and Its Discontents," Freud displays a more equivocal judgment about the value of civilization. See *SE*, XXI, pp. 144–145.

58. Alasdair MacIntyre, *After Virtue* (Notre Dame: University of Notre Dame Press, 1984), p. 220. See also Charles Taylor, *Hegel and Modern Society* (Cambridge: Cambridge University Press, 1979), pp. 157–158. For a psychoanalytic critique of MacIntyre, see Fred Alford, *The Self in Social Theory* (New Haven: Yale University Press, 1991), Ch. 1. Alford shares MacIntyre's understanding of the self, suggesting that it requires a well-defined personal narrative within a given, constitutive social context. He criticizes MacIntyre, however, for not granting the self sufficient capacity to change and shape its circumstances in the face of tradition and social expectations.

59. On these affinities between Freud and communitarians, see Jeffrey Abramson, *Liberation and Its Limits: The Moral and Political Thought of Freud* (Boston: Beacon Press, 1984), Ch. 8.

60. Freud, "The Disillusionment of the War," *SE*, XIV, p. 286.

61. According to Philip Rieff, Freud affirms the distance of the individual from the community, and in this sense psychoanalysis agrees with liberalism. The Freudian individual is aloof from politics and learns not to seek radical changes in society, avers Rieff. That individual adapts to society in a calculated way which suits her needs: "a rationally alienated person learns how to guard against social over-investments, and how to make them when necessary" (p. 278). Freud, then, teaches that the individual's attachment to society should be dependent on a rational, economic exercise—on the conscious distribution of instinctual energy. Moreover, once psychoanalytic therapy becomes a way of life, it contributes to detachment from others by enhancing self-absorption. "While enjoining a person to be less severe with himself," observes Rieff, "Freudian analysis may also develop in the

patient new qualities of self-suspicion . . . The therapy manufactures a new sort of conscience, one which demands a more accurate and yet more scrupulous self-centeredness" (pp. 106–107). See Rieff, *Freud: The Mind of a Moralist*.

62. John Rawls, *A Theory of Justice* (London: Oxford University Press, 1971), p. 560.

63. Freud, "The Future of an Illusion," *SE*, XVII, p. 12.

64. Zygmunt Bauman, *Liquid Modernity* (Cambridge, UK: Polity Press, 2000), p. 178. Agnes Heller makes a similar point in her "Where are We at Home," pp. 17–18.

65. This critique must be reconstructed, since Freud's direct references to Marx and (especially) Nietzsche are rather scarce. It should also be mentioned that although my discussion below underlines the differences between Freud on the one hand, and Nietzsche and Marx on the other, the three theorists had much in common. In particular, these theorists shared an historical reading of the self, and a fundamental suspicion toward the overt appearances of things, including their appearance through language. For a discussion of the first point of similarity, see Nancy Love, *Marx, Nietzsche, and Modernity* (New York: Columbia University Press, 1986); and for a discussion of the second, see Paul Ricoeur, *Freud and Philosophy: An Essay of Interpretation* (New Haven: Yale University Press, 1970).

66. Nietzsche, *On the Genealogy of Morality*, Part 2, no. 6.

67. Nietzsche, *On the Genealogy of Morality*, Part 2, no. 8.

68. Nietzsche, *On the Genealogy of Morality*, Part 2, no.16.

69. Nietzsche, *Thus Spoke Zarathustra* (New York: Penguin Books, 1978), p. 139.

70. Nietzsche, *Thus Spoke Zarathustra*, p. 141.

71. Nietzsche, *On the Genealogy of Morality*, Part 2, no. 20.

72. Nietzsche, *Thus Spoke Zarathustra*, p. 141.

73. This view is strongly implied in Freud's comments on "Ecce Homo" during a discussion of the Vienna Psychoanalytic Society (*Minutes of the Vienna Psychoanalytic Society*, 1908–1910, vol. II, 29–32). See also P. Heller, "Freud in his Relations to Nietzsche."

74. Freud, "Group Psychology," *SE*, XVIII, p. 123.

75. Freud, "New Introductory Lectures," *SE*, XXII, p. 110.

76. Freud, "New Introductory Lectures," *SE*, XXII, p. 88 (my emphasis).

77. K. Marx, "The German Ideology" in *Collected Works*, vol. 5. (New York: International Publishers, 1967), p. 48. On the moral aspect of Marxism, see G. Cohen, "Freedom, Justice, and Capitalism," *New Left Review*, no. 126 (1981): 3–16, and A. Buchanan "Marx, Morality, and History," *Ethics*, no. 98 (1987): 104–136.

78. K. Marx, "The Holy Family," in *Collected Works*, vol. 4 (New York: International Publishers, 1967), p. 179.

79. Freud, "New Introductory Lectures," *SE*, XXII, p. 180.

80. Freud, "Civilization and Its Discontents," *SE*, XXI, pp. 112–113. It should also be noted that while Freud agrees with Marx that work is a worthy and

important channel for the expression of the self, he does not believe that this type of activity could be maintained without repression and coercion. "One would think that a re-ordering of human relations should be possible, which would remove the sources of dissatisfaction with civilization by renouncing coercion and the suppression of the instincts, so that, undisturbed by internal discord, men might devote themselves to the acquisition of wealth and its enjoyment. That would be the golden age, but it is questionable if such a state of affairs can be realized. It seems rather that every civilization must be built upon coercion and renunciation of instincts; it does not even seem certain that if coercion were to cease, the majority of human beings would be prepared to undertake to perform the work necessary for acquiring new wealth" ("The Future of an Illusion," *SE*, XXI, p. 7).

81. Freud, "Civilization and Its Discontents," *SE*, XXI, p. 114.

82. Freud, "New Introductory Lectures," *SE*, XXII, p. 67 (my emphasis).

83. Freud, "New Introductory Lectures," *SE*, XXII, pp. 208–209.

84. On the similarities between Weber and Freud in their ethos of disillusionment see Tracy Strong, "Weber and Freud: Vocation and Self-acknowledgement" in *Max Weber and his Contemporaries*, eds. W. J. Mommsen and J. Osterhammel (London: Unwin Hyman, 1987), pp. 468–482.

85. Freud, "New Introductory Lectures," *SE*, XXII, p. 60.

86. Freud, "New Introductory Lectures," *SE*, XXII, p. 179. The applied science to which Freud refers in this context is sociology.

87. Freud, "An Outline of Psychoanalysis," *SE*, XXIII, pp. 192–193. On the central role of the Oedipal complex in Freud's theory, see P. Mullahy, *Oedipus: Myth and Complex* (New York: Grove Press, 1948); and J. Brunner, "Oedipus Politicus: Freud's Paradigm of Social Relations," in *Freud: Conflict and Culture*, ed. M. Roth (New York: Alfred Knopf, 1998). Contemporary psychoanalysts differ in their views of the centrality of the Oedipal complex, some even questioning its existence. See, for example, M. H. Sacks "The Oedipus Complex: A Reevaluation," *Journal of American Psychoanalytical Association*, 33 (1985): 201–216; J. H. Heerden, "Suppose the Oedipus Complex were Just a Projection," *Inquiry*, 21 (1978): 461–472; and M. Borch-Jacobsen, "The Oedipus Problem in Freud and Lacan," *Critical Inquiry*, 20 (1994): 267–282.

88. Freud, "Preface to Reik's Ritual," *SE*, XVII, p. 261.

89. Marcuse sees the meaning of the Oedipal wish as "the eternal infantile desire for the archetype of freedom: freedom from want . . . Eros here fights its first battle against everything the reality principle stands for: against the father, against domination, sublimation, resignation" (Marcuse, *Eros and Civilization*, p. 270). By going through the stages of the complex, the child acquires independence and the ability to act in the world—but only after accepting the need to work and produce, to restrain and delay his instinctual satisfactions. Similarly, Brown views the complex as the end of idealized omnipotence. "The essence of the Oedipal complex," he writes, "is the project of becoming God—in Spinoza's formula, *causa sui*" (*Life Against Death*, p. 118). The child's desire for the mother signifies his wish to become father to himself, thereby being the cause of himself and fleeing from the threat of death. While both of these interpretations are on the mark in explicating the

symbolic import of the complex, they fail to see the connection between this import and the historical-political context within which Freud is situated.

90. G. Deleuze, and F. Guattari, *Anti-Oedipus* (New York: Viking Press, 1977).

91. N. Chodorow, *The Reproduction of Mothering* (Berkeley: University of California Press, 1978).

92. P. Rudnytsky, *Freud and Oedipus* (New York: Columbia University Press, 1987). Other studies have also pointed out that Freud's theory of the self must be understood in light of his cultural background. See, for example, D. Bakan, *Sigmund Freud and the Jewish Mystical Tradition* (London: Free Association Books, 1990); W. McGrath, "Freud and the Force of History," in *Freud and the History of Psychoanalysis*, eds. T. Gelfand and J. Kerr (Hillsdale, NJ: Analytic Press, 1992), pp. 79–107; S. Kirschner, *The Religious and Romantic Origins of Psychoanalysis: Individuation and Integration in Post-Freudian Theory* (Cambridge, UK: Cambridge University Press, 1996); C. Schorske, *Fin-de-siècle Vienna: Politics and Culture* (New York: Vintage Books, 1981) and C. Schorske, *Thinking With History: Explorations in the Passage to Modernism* (Princeton: Princeton University Press, 1998); and J. Brunner, "On the Political Rhetoric of Freud's Individual Psychology."

93. J. Lacan, *Ecrits* (London: Tavistock, 1977); M. Borch-Jacobsen, "The Oedipus Problem in Freud and Lacan."

94. Freud, "Beyond the Pleasure Principle," *SE*, XVIII, p. 54.

95. Freud, "Three Essays on Sexuality," *SE*, XII, p. 186.

96. According to Freud, since the girl cannot be emasculated, her psychological formation is radically different from the boy's, and she may pose a threat to the stability of the social order (though there is no biologically determined difference between the sexes). "The fear of castration being thus excluded in the little girl, a powerful motive also drops out for the setting-up of a super-ego and for breaking off the infantile genital organization" (*SE*, XIX, p. 178). In another occasion Freud expresses a similar position. "I cannot evade the notion (though I hesitate to give it expression) that for women the level of what is ethically normal is different from what it is in men. Their super-ego is never so inexorable, so impersonal, so independent of its emotional origins as we require of it in men" (*SE*, XIX, p. 257). The normalization and socialization of women is chiefly determined by the outside, by "intimidation" and "upbringing"; it is therefore, according to Freud, more contingent and reversible. Women's lack of the full Oedipal experience, asserts the late Freud, also makes them less disposed to sublimation. "The work of civilization has become increasingly the business of men, it confronts them with ever more difficult tasks and compels them to carry out instinctual sublimations of which women are little capable." With men investing their libido in the work of civilization and women less interested in such work, the woman "adopts a hostile attitude towards it [civilization]" (*SE*, XXI, p. 103, p. 104). The lines between the sexes, however, are always obfuscated. "All human individuals, as a result of their bisexual disposition and of cross-inheritance," Freud notes, "combine in themselves both masculine and feminine characteristics, so that pure masculinity and femininity remain theoretical constructions of uncertain content" (*SE*, XIX, p. 258). Femininity (a quality not confined to the female sex as such) becomes the symbol of a weaker sense of justice

and a lesser absorption with the erection of the social order; it is the permanent, agitating political force, the seducer that causes history to linger on the brink of chaos. Psychoanalysis implies that for social order to be preserved, femininity must be dominated by masculinity within each psyche.

97. Freud, "The Ego and the Id," *SE*, XIX, p. 35 (my emphasis).

98. Freud, "New Introductory Lectures," *SE*, XXII, p. 62.

99. Freud, "Civilization and Its Discontents," *SE*, XXI, p. 128.

100. According to Freud, erotogenic masochism—pleasure in pain—lies at the bottom of the other two forms as well ("The Economic Problem of Masochism," *SE*, XIX, p. 161).

101. "The situation is usually presented as though ethical requirements were the primary thing and the renunciation of instinct followed from them. This leaves the origin of the ethical sense unexplained. Actually, it seems to be the other way about. The first instinctual renunciation is enforced by external powers, and it is only this that creates the ethical sense, which expresses itself in conscience and demands a further renunciation of instincts" ("The Economic Problem of Masochism," *SE*, XIX, p. 170).

102. Loewald, "The Waning of the Oedipus Complex."

103. Freud, "The Ego and the Id," *SE*, XIX, p. 48.

104. Freud, "Civilization and Its Discontents," *SE*, XXI, pp. 129–130.

105. Freud, "The Ego and the Id," *SE*, XIX, p. 29.

106. As Jessica Benjamin notes, according to Freud "the ego is not really independent and self-constituting, but is actually made up of the objects it assimilates." See Benjamin, *Shadows of the Other*, p. 79.

107. Freud, "New Introductory Lectures," *SE*, XXII, p. 123.

108. Freud, "Introductory Lectures to Psychoanalysis," *SE*, XVI, p. 356.

109. Freud, "Psycho-analytic Procedure," *SE*, XII, p. 251 (my emphasis). On the place of memory in Freud, see R. Terdiman, *Present Past: Modernity and the Memory Crisis* (Ithaca, NY: Cornell University Press, 1993).

110. M. Ruth, *Psychoanalysis as History: Negation and Freedom in Freud* (Ithaca, NY: Cornell University Press, 1987), p. 17.

111. Freud, "Remembering, Repeating, and Working-Through," *SE*, XII, p. 151.

112. Freud, "Remembering, Repeating, and Working-Through," *SE*, XII, p. 155.

113. Freud, "An Outline of Psychoanalysis," *SE*, XXIII, p. 174.

114. Freud, "An Outline of Psychoanalysis," *SE*, XXIII, p. 175.

115. Freud described himself as a Jew, but as a completely godless one. On Freud's Jewish identity and on his motivations for writing *Moses and Monotheism*, see Y. H. Yerushalmi, *Freud's Moses: Judaism Terminable and Interminable* (New Haven, CT: Yale University Press, 1991).

116. Freud, "New Introductory Lectures," *SE*, XXII, p. 74.

117. Freud, "An Outline of Psychoanalysis," *SE*, XXIII, p. 178.

5. Michel Foucault: From the Prison-House of Language to the Silence of the Panopticon

1. Foucault, *SP*, p. 216.

2. Foucault, *SP*, p. 213.

3. In Habermas's view, for example, genealogical historiography that purports to be an objective study of changing power configurations "follows the movement of a radically historicist extinction of the subject and ends up in an unholy subjectivism." More specifically, Habermas claims that Foucault manifests this subjectivist foundation through the "presentistic, relativistic, [and] cryptonormative" character of his later work, which is chiefly concerned with advancing ethical/ political causes of the moment while carrying the banner of objectivity. J. Habermas, *The Philosophical Discourse of Modernity* (Cambridge, MA: MIT Press, 1992), p. 276. Nancy Fraser also sees Foucault as invariably affirming a notion of subjectivity, one that has Western sources. Foucault's critique of contemporary society, she claims, suggests underlying "Kantian notions." In understanding Foucault, "one cannot help but appeal to such concepts as the violation of dignity and autonomy involved in the treating of people solely as means to be causally manipulated . . . these Kantian notions are clearly related to the liberal norms of legitimacy and illegitimacy defined in terms of limits and rights." Nancy Fraser, "Foucault on Modern Power: Empirical Insights and Normative Confusions," *Praxis International*, vol. 1 (1981): 284. Taylor also comments about underlying notions of selfhood in Foucault, but his point is a more general one. He argues that Foucault's concept of power can make sense only after we have presupposed a set of evaluations and preferences that are constitutive of the self. "Something is only an imposition on me against a background of desires, interests, purposes, that I have," writes Taylor. "It is only an imposition if it makes some dent in them, if it frustrates them, prevents them from fulfillment." Charles Taylor, "Foucault on Freedom and Truth," in *Foucault: A Critical Reader*, ed. David Couzens Hoy (London: Basil Blackwell, 1986), p. 90.

4. See M. Foucault, "A propos de Nietzsche, Habermas, Arendt, MacPherson," April 1983, Conversation at Berkeley, D 250 (8), Foucault Archives, quoted from A. Szakolczai, *Max Weber and Michel Foucault: Parallel Life-Works* (London: Routledge, 1998), p. 2.

5. Foucault, *LCP*, "Nietzsche, Genealogy, History," pp. 145–146; *DE*, vol. 2, p. 141.

6. Foucault, *LCP*, "Nietzsche, Genealogy, History," p. 146; *DE*, vol. 2, p. 141. For more inclusive comments of Foucault on Freud and psychoanalysis, especially in the French context, see "Philosophy and Psychology," in *AME*, pp. 249–259. The relation between Foucault and Freud has been widely discussed in the literature. See, for example, Jacques-Alain Miller, "Michel Foucault and Psychoanalysis," in *Michel Foucault Philosopher*, trans. T. J. Armstrong (New York: Routledge, 1992), pp. 58–65; Patrick Hutton, "Foucault, Freud, and the Technologies of the Self," in *Technologies of the Self*, ed. L. Martin (Amherst: University of Mass. Press, 1988), pp. 121–145; and James Bernauer, "Oedipus, Freud, Foucault: Fragments on an Archaeology of Psychoanalysis," in *Pathologies of the Modern Self: Postmodern*

Studies of Narcissism, Schizophrenia, and Depression, ed. D. M. Levin (New York: New York University Press, 1987), pp. 349–362.

7. Foucault, *MC*, p. 245.

8. Foucault, *MC*, p. 246. These and other claims of Foucault regarding the history of madness received much criticism in the secondary literature. It has been claimed, for example, that he did not note that many practitioners of psychiatry saw the moral discourse on madness as a grave mistake, advanced by marginal nonexperts. On this point (and other critiques of *Madness and Civilization*), see Erik Midelfort, "Madness and Civilization in Early Modern Europe: a Reappraisal of Michel Foucault," in *After the Reformation: Essays in Honor of J. H. Hexter*, ed. B. C. Malament (Philadelphia: University of Pennsylvania Press, 1980), pp. 258–259.

9. In *Madness and Civilization*, the role of knowledge in general and of the medical and psychiatric discourses in particular, appears to be marginal in the construction of subjectivity. While the doctor is central to the asylum from its inception, he functions as an administrator and as a voice of authority, not as the bearer of essential knowledge. See: *MC*, Ch. IX.

10. Foucault, *MC*, p. 258. Foucault thought that Freud's clinical practice helped to bridge the gap between the madman and the Other, a gap that was inaugurated in the asylum. Yet Freud, in Foucault's view, did not go far enough in this direction. In his first published work, Foucault hailed Biswangers' existential-phenomenological psychiatry for its respect for the patient's difference and for its dialogical nature. See: Michel Foucault, *Mental Illness and Psychology*, trans. Alan Sheridan (Berkeley: University of California Press, 1976 [1954]).

11. Foucault, *HS*, p. 65; *HDLS*, vol. 1, p. 88.

12. Foucault, *OT*, p. 373; *MELC*, p. 385. In another context, Foucault commends psychoanalysis for its critical stand towards nineteenth-century psychiatry. The latter viewed abnormality in terms of "degeneracy, eugenics, and heredity," a language that promoted increasing political intervention in the sexual life of the population, and ultimately provided "scientific support" for twentieth-century racism and fascism. Psychoanalysis had no use for these concepts, introducing instead a new discourse that explained behavior and development in terms of the psyche and its history. See: *PK*, p. 60; *DE*, vol. 2, p. 758.

13. Foucault, *PPC*, "The Art of Telling the Truth," p. 95; Michel Foucault, *Magazin Littéraire*, 207 (May, 1984): 39.

14. Foucault seems to have misinterpreted Weber's use of the term "rationality," arguing that it serves in the latter's writings as an all-embracing and uniform concept. Weberians, avers Foucault, regard rationality as an "anthropological invariant." "I don't believe," he continues, that "one can speak of an intrinsic notion of 'rationalization' without on the one hand positing an absolute value inherit in reason, and on the other taking the risk of applying the term empirically in a completely arbitrary way. I think one must restrict one's use of this word to an instrumental and relative meaning." See: "Foucault: Questions of Method," in *After Philosophy: End or Transformation*, eds. K. Baynes et al. (Cambridge, MA: MIT Press, 1987), p. 107. As I discussed in Chapter 3, Weber was well aware of the relative and context-bound nature of the concept of rationality, lapses in his application of the term notwithstanding. For comparative studies of Weber and

Foucault, see A. Szakolczai, *Max Weber and Michel Foucault: Parallel Life-Works;* J. O'Neill, "The Disciplinary Society: From Weber to Foucault," *The British Journal of Sociology* 37 (1985): 42–60; M. Dean, *Critical and Effective Histories: Foucault's Method and Historical Sociology* (London: Routledge, 1994); and D. Owen, *Maturity and Modernity: Nietzsche, Weber, Foucault and the Ambivalence of Reason* (London: Routledge, 1994).

15. Foucault, *Technologies of the Self,* p. 12.

16. Foucault, *Foucault Live,* ed. S. Lotringer (New York: Semiotext[e], 1989), p. 61; *DE,* vol. 1, p. 789.

17. Foucault, "The Ethic of Care for the Self as a Practice of Freedom," in *Philosophy and Social Criticism,* vols. 2–3 (Summer 1987): 121.

18. Foucault, *OT,* p. xxii; *MELC,* p. 13. For a discussion of Foucault's archaeology see: Gary Gutting, *Michel Foucault's Archaeology of Scientific Reason* (Cambridge: Cambridge University Press, 1989), and, by the same author, *French Philosophy in the Twentieth Century* (Cambridge: Cambridge University Press, 2001), Ch. 9.

19. Foucault, *OT,* p. 308; *MELC,* p. 319.

20. Foucault, *OT,* p. 313; *MELC,* p. 324.

21. Foucault, *OT,* pp. 314–315; *MELC,* pp. 325–326.

22. Foucault, *OT,* p. 318; *MELC,* p. 329.

23. Foucault, *OT,* p. 312; *MELC,* p. 323.

24. Foucault, *OT,* p. 326; *MELC,* p. 337.

25. H. Dreyfus and P. Rabinow, *Michel Foucault: Beyond Structuralism and Hermeneutics* (Chicago: The University of Chicago Press, 1983), p. 37.

26. Foucault, *OT,* p. 331; *MELC,* p. 342.

27. Foucault, *OT,* p. 332; *MELC,* p. 343.

28. Foucault, *ARK,* p. 219; *OD,* p. 21.

29. For discussions of Foucault's views about literature see: Simon During, *Foucault and Literature: Towards a Genealogy of Writing* (New York: Routledge, 1992); and John Rajchman, *Foucault: The Freedom of Philosophy* (New York: Columbia University Press, 1985), Ch. 1.

30. The usefulness of the categories of apollonian and dionysian thought in interpreting Foucault's work has been demonstrated by Allen Megill. I am indebted to him here, although he does not use this distinction for an examination of the relation between literature and discourse in Foucault's thought. See: Allen Megill, *Prophets of Extremity: Nietzsche, Heidegger, Foucault, and Derrida* (Berkeley: University of California Press, 1985), Chs. 5 & 6.

31. Foucault, *OT,* p. 296.

32. Foucault, *OT,* pp. 295–296.

33. Foucault, *OT,* p. 304; *MELC,* p. 315.

34. Foucault, *OT,* p. 296; *MELC,* p. 309.

35. Foucault, *OT,* p. 297; *MELC,* p. 310 (my emphasis).

36. Foucault, *OT,* p. 298; *MELC,* p. 311.

37. Rajchman, *Foucault: The Freedom of Philosophy*, p. 24.

38. Foucault, *OT*, p. 298; *MELC*, p. 311.

39. This is how Dreyfus and Rabinow entitled the first part of their book, in which they discuss Foucault's work in the sixties. See: *Michel Foucault: Beyond Structuralism and Hermeneutics*, pp. 3–100.

40. Megill, *Prophets of Extremity*, p. 238.

41. Foucault, "The Discourse on Language," *AK*, pp. 228–229; *OD*, pp. 52–53. All the references to *AK* in this section are to this essay.

42. Foucault, *ARK*, p. 218; *OD*, pp. 16–17.

43. Foucault, *ARK*, p. 222; *OD*, p. 31.

44. Foucault, *ARK*, p. 224; *OD*, pp. 37–38. Foucault mentions a third group of constraints on discourse, one that involves the distribution of discourse in society and the designation of those who have the right and authority to speak. Both of these depend upon systems of exclusion. See: *AK*, pp. 224–227; *OD*, pp. 38–47.

45. Foucault, *ARK*, p. 229; *OD*, p. 55.

46. Foucault, *ARK*, p. 216; *OD*, p. 11.

47. Foucault, *ARK*, p. 219; *OD*, p. 21.

48. Foucault, *OT*, p. 383; *MELC*, p. 395.

49. James Miller argues that Foucault's fascination with limit-experiences was not restricted to his theoretical work, but was something he pursued in his private life as well. See: James Miller, *The Passion of Michel Foucault* (New York: Simon and Schuster, 1993), pp. 29–30.

50. Foucault, *OT*, p. 300; *MELC*, p. 313.

51. Foucault, "A Preface to Transgression," *LCP*, p. 32; *DE*, vol. 1, p. 235.

52. Foucault, "A Preface to Transgression," *LCP*, pp. 34–35; *DE*, vol. 1, p. 237.

53. Foucault, "A Preface to Transgression," *LCP*, p. 36; *DE*, vol. 1, p. 238.

54. Foucault, *OT*, p. 300; *MELC*, p. 313.

55. Foucault, "Fantasia of the Library," *LCP*, p. 92.

56. Foucault, "Preface to Transgression," *LCP*, p. 39; *DE*, vol. 1, p. 240.

57. Foucault, "Preface to Transgression," *LCP*, p. 42; *DE*, vol. 1, p. 242.

58. Foucault, "What is an Author," *LCP*, p. 117; *DE*, vol. 1, p. 793.

59. Foucault, *OT*, p. 386; *MELC*, p. 397.

60. Foucault became rather critical of the transformative and liberating role that French intellectuals (including himself) had assigned to the task of writing during the sixties. "The whole relentless theorization of writing which we saw in the 1960s," he declares, "was doubtless a swansong." See: Foucault, *PK*, p. 127. Elsewhere, Foucault claims that avant-garde literature, as well as philosophy, became at the time enclosed in the universities and lost any impact on society. See: Foucault, *PPC*, pp. 307–313.

61. Foucault, "A Preface to Transgression," *LCP*, p. 50; *DE*, vol. 1, p. 248.

62. Foucault, "A Preface to Transgression," *LCP*, p. 30; *DE*, vol. 1, p. 234.

63. Foucault, "A Preface to Transgression," *LCP*, p. 50; *DE*, vol. 1, pp. 248–249.

64. Foucault, *HS*, p. 142; *HDLS*, p. 187.

65. Foucault, *HS*, p. 56; *HDLS*, p. 76 (my emphasis).

66. Foucault, *HS*, p. 43; *HDLS*, p. 59.

67. Foucault, *HS*, p. 61; *HDLS*, p. 82.

68. Foucault, *HS*, p. 60; *HDLS*, p. 80.

69. Foucault, *HS*, p. 22; *HDLS*, p. 32. Both writers display the confessional ethic of modernity. However, Foucault seems to have preserved a special place for Sade, presenting him as having managed to escape some of the normalizing forces of bio-power. See: *HS*, p. 149; *HDLS*, pp. 196–197. The later Foucault, in any event, was even more suspicious of the relation between writing and the exercise of power over oneself. In his study of the second-century Romans, he notes how the new activity of letter writing allowed one to recount all passing thoughts, desires, and modes, thereby constituting a whole new domain that could be monitored and brought under control. He even sees conscience as originating in this practice. See: *Technologies of the Self,* pp. 27–30.

70. Foucault, *PK,* "Truth and Power," p. 114.

71. Foucault, *SP,* p. 219.

72. Foucault, *SP,* p. 221.

73. Foucault, *SP,* p. 221.

74. Foucault, *SP,* p. 220.

75. Foucault, *SP,* p. 219.

76. Foucault, *DP,* p. 194; *SPNP,* p. 196.

77. Michel Foucault, *The Foucault Reader,* ed. P. Rabinow (New York: Pantheon, 1984), p. 245.

78. Foucault, *SP,* p. 222. Paradoxically, this position implies that the more extensive the operation of power, the more opportunities there are for agonism and freedom.

79. "I've always been a little mistrustful of the general theme of liberation, to the extent that, if one does not treat it with a certain number of safeguards and within certain limits, there is the danger that it refers back to the idea that there does exist a nature or a human foundation which, as a result of a certain number of historical, social, or economic process, found itself concealed, alienated or imprisoned in and by some repressive mechanism. In that hypothesis it would suffice to unloosen these repressive locks so that man can be reconciled with himself, once again find his nature or renew contact with his roots and restore a full and positive relationship with himself. I don't think that this is a theme which can be admitted without rigorous examination." See: Foucault, "The Ethic of Care for the Self as a Practice of Freedom," p. 113.

80. John Rajchman, *Truth and Eros* (New York: Routledge, 1991), p. 109.

81. Foucault, *PK,* "Power and Strategies," p. 138; *DE,* vol. 3, p. 421. In this paragraph Foucault understands resistance (and hence freedom) in a totally negative way. As Alessandro Pizzorno puts it, for Foucault "[i]ndividuals or movements . . . can be free only 'against.'" However, this interpretation is incomplete, since in his late writings Foucault sees freedom not solely in terms of unruliness, as the centrifugal movements of a demolished material, but also as the ability of the self

to autonomously give an aesthetic shape to its life, even if this shape is always open to question and elaboration. This issue is discussed in depth in the next section. See: Alessandro Pizzorno, "Foucault and the Liberal View of the Individual," in *Michel Foucault: Philosopher,* p. 208.

82. See in this context the discussion between Foucault and Bernard-Henri Lévy in "Power and Sex," *PPC,* p. 122; *DE,* vol. 3, p. 267.

83. Foucault, *HS,* p. 86; *HDLS,* p. 113. Elsewhere, Foucault writes that the "relations of power are perhaps among the best hidden things in the social body." See *PPC,* p. 118; *DE,* vol. 3, p. 264.

84. Foucault, *DP,* pp. 201–202; *SPNP,* p. 203. The Panopticon is a circular structure with a tower at its center and separate, individual cells that are completely open toward the tower. A large window at the back of the cell allows light to penetrate. This renders the person in the cell completely visible (and isolated), while the person in the tower always remains hidden.

85. Foucault, *DP,* p. 200; *SPNP,* p. 202.

86. Foucault, *DP,* p. 201; *SPNP,* pp. 202–203.

87. Foucault, "The Ethic of Care for the Self as a Practice of Freedom," p. 131. See also Michel Foucault, *The Use of Pleasure: The History of Sexuality,* vol. 2, trans. Robert Hurely (New York: Vintage Books, 1990), pp. 8–9; Michel Foucault, *L'usage des plaisirs: Histoire de la Sexualité,* vol. 2, (Paris: Gallimard, 1984), pp. 14–15.

88. Foucault, *Technologies of the Self,* p. 10.

89. Foucault, *PK,* "Two Lectures," pp. 93–94.

90. For more about this contrast, and about Foucault's relation to the Frankfurt School, see: David Couzens Hoy, "Power, Repression, Progress: Foucault, Lukes, and the Frankfurt School," in *Foucault: A Critical Reader,* pp. 123–148.

91. Foucault, *PK,* "Truth and Power," p. 133 (my emphasis).

92. Foucault, *HS,* p. 93; *HDLS,* p. 122.

93. Megill, *Prophets of Extremity,* p. 183.

94. Foucault, *HS,* p. 95; *HDLS,* p. 125.

95. Foucault, *PK,* "Two Lectures," p. 99.

96. Foucault, *HS,* p. 94; *HDLS,* p. 124.

97. Foucault, *DP,* p. 217; *SPNP,* p. 219.

98. Weber, *FMW,* p. 253.

99. Foucault, *DP,* p. 166; *SPNP,* p. 168.

100. Foucault, *DP,* p. 169; *SPNP,* p. 171.

101. Foucault, *DP,* p. 145; *SPNP,* p. 147.

102. Foucault, *DP,* p. 138; *SPNP,* p. 139.

103. Weber, *FMW,* pp. 261–262.

104. Foucault, *DP,* p. 152, p. 153; *SPNP,* p. 153, p. 154.

105. Weber, *FMW,* p. 254.

106. Foucault, *DP,* p. 164; *SPNP,* p. 166.

107. Foucault, *DP*, pp. 190–191; *SPNP*, p. 192.

108. Foucault, *PPC*, "An Aesthetics of Existence," p. 49.

109. Foucault, *PO*, "Useless to Revolt?" p. 452.

110. Foucault, *The Use of Pleasure*, p. 89; *L'usage des plaisirs*, pp. 102–103. For critical discussions of Foucault's notion of aesthetics of existence, see Pierre Hadot, "Reflections on the notion of 'the cultivation of the self,'" in *Michel Foucault: Philosopher*, pp. 225–232, and, in the same collection, Rainer Rochlitz, "The Aesthetics of Existence: Post Conventional Morality and the Theory of Power in Michel Foucault," pp. 248–259. Lois McNay, in her *Foucault: A Critical Introduction* (Cambridge: Polity Press, 1994), Ch. 4, also offers a critical reading of Foucault in this matter. For a more favorable interpretation, see Alexander Nehamas, *The Art of Living* (Berkeley: University of California Press, 1998), Ch. 6.

111. Foucault, *PPC*, "An Aesthetics of Existence," p. 51.

112. Foucault, *SP*, p. 244 (my emphasis).

113. Foucault, *Technologies of the Self*, p. 31.

114. Foucault, *The Use of Pleasure*, p. 91; *L'usage des plaisirs*, p. 105.

115. *Ibid.*, p. 89; *L'usage des plaisirs*, p. 103.

116. Foucault, *PK*, "Two Lectures," p. 98.

117. Contemporary struggles against bio-power exhibit such a dialectic: in these struggles, the "forces that resisted relied for support on the very thing it [power] invested, that is, on life and man as a living being." As Foucault continues to explain: "What we have seen has been a very real process of struggle; life as a political object was in a sense taken at face value and turned back against the system that was bent on controlling it. It was life more than the law that became the issue of political struggles, even if the latter were formulated through affirmations concerning rights. The 'right' to life, to one's body, to health, to happiness, to the satisfaction of needs, and beyond all the oppression or 'alienations,' the 'right' to rediscover what one is and all that one can be . . ." (see: *HS*, p. 145; *HDLS*, p. 191).

118. Foucault, *OT*, p. 327; *MELC*, p. 338.

Conclusion

1. Walter Benjamin, "N," in Gary Smith (ed.), *Benjamin: Philosophy, Aesthetics, History* (Chicago: Chicago University Press, 1989), [N 9a, 1], p. 64; Walter Benjamin, *Gesammelte Schriften*, vol. VI (Frankfurt am Main: Suhrkamp Verlag, 1977), p. 592. Henceforth I will refer to this edition of Benjamin's writings as *GS*, followed by volume and page numbers. The interpretation of Benjamin suggested here is based on my article, "The Marriage of Time and Identity: Kant, Benjamin, and the Nation State."

2. Benjamin, "Capitalism as Religion," in *Selected Writings*, vol. 1 (Cambridge, MA: Harvard University Press, 1996), p. 289; *GS*, VI, p. 101.

3. Benjamin, *Benjamin*, [N 2a, 2], p. 49; *GS*, V.1, p. 576. Heidegger also views forgetfulness as a modern malaise. However, he believes this phenomenon springs not so much from the tragic breakdown of the shared remembered world,

but rather from the quest of *Dasein* to flee from its finitude into the world of the everyday. See: Martin Heidegger, *Being and Time* (New York: Harper & Row, 1962), p. 69.

4. Benjamin, "Capitalism as Religion," p. 289; *GS*, VI, p. 101.

5. Benjamin, *Benjamin*, [N 2a, 2], p. 49; *GS*, V1, p. 576.

6. Hannah Arendt, *The Human Condition* (Chicago: University of Chicago Press, 1958), p. 40.

7. Arendt, *The Human Condition*, p. 28. For a discussion of the concept of society in Arendt, see Hanna Fenichel Pitkin, *The Attack of the Blob: Hannah Arendt's Concept of the Social* (Chicago: University of Chicago Press, 1998). Pitkin interprets Arendt's concept of the social in a manner that resembles the problematic of entrapment as presented in this work. She writes that by the social Arendt means essentially "a collectivity of people who—for whatever reason—conduct themselves in such a way that they cannot control or even intentionally influence the large-scale consequences of their activities" (p. 16).

8. Arendt, *The Human Condition*, p. 19.

9. "The modern concept of history, with its unparalleled emphasis on history as a process, has many origins . . . especially the earlier modern concept of nature as a process." See Hannah Arendt, *On Revolution* (New York: Penguin Books, 1990), p. 55.

10. Arendt, *On Revolution*, p. 268. According to Arendt, most modern revolutions have failed because, as soon as humans have asserted their freedom in history, they have succumbed to a false notion of determinism.

11. In contrast to the French revolution, the American revolution celebrated the openness of history. According to Arendt, the American republic came into being "by no 'historical necessity' and no organic development, but by a deliberate act: the foundation of freedom." See *On Revolution*, p. 216.

12. Arendt, *On Revolution*, p. 283.

13. In contrast to entrapment writers, as well as in contrast to Benjamin and Arendt, Habermas displays faith in the Enlightenment project. On the one hand, Habermas embraces elements of the entrapment critique. He believes, for example, that "neither of the principal components of Weber's diagnosis of the times has become any less relevant," and that "this holds true for the thesis of a loss of meaning no less than for that of a loss of freedom" [See Jürgen Habermas, *The Theory of Communicative Action*, vol. 2 (Boston: Beacon Press, 1984), p. 301]. These threats to the modern self have emerged because there is an "internal colonization" of the "lifeworld" by the "delinguistified system" of the capitalist economy and the bureaucratic welfare state [Ibid., p. 305]. This "sociopathological" development, he suggests, reduces the world of meanings and symbols shared by the community and impairs the type of language that preserves and reinterprets them. Without this language and the public space that houses it, potentially deliberative citizens are easily transformed into avid consumers, autonomous individuals into dependent clients in a welfare system.

Yet Habermas insists that moderns may alleviate this predicament by adhering to the Enlightenment's faith in emancipating reason, by reinvigorating this integral aspect of modernity. In contrast to entrapment writers, Habermas contends that a *gradual* release from the subjugating and distorting social forces of modernity is possible, a release that begins with critical self-reflection. "The pursuit of reflection knows itself as a movement of emancipation," writes Habermas. "Reason . . . obeys an emancipatory cognitive interest, which aims at the pursuit of reflection" [See Jürgen Habermas, *Knowledge and Human Interest*, trans. Jeremy Shapiro (Boston: Beacon Press, 1971), p. 198]. Knowledge in the human sciences is not merely neutral and certainly not inherently distorted (as Weber and Foucault had claimed, respectively); rather, it is essential for unveiling the exploitation, fetishism, irrationality, unexamined dogmas, and so on that exist in society and for suggesting ways of overcoming these diseases. More precisely, critical theory is needed at two levels: firstly, in order to analyze the structure of the economy and the state, and to expose the way they generate our flat and impoverished speech; secondly, to synthesize scientific accounts of human capabilities (especially accounts of linguistic, cognitive, and practical-moral developments) in order to uncover human potentials not allowed to flourish in current conditions. Habermas is careful to note that theory does not possess absolute authority in public deliberations, and that the final determination of whether a situation is pathological and dehumanizing can be made only by free and equal agents themselves. But without critical theory no emancipation is possible, and there is no way to measure it. While the natural sciences allow us to gradually increase our control over nature, critical theory allows us to achieve greater autonomy and rationality at the social level. In other words, there is *a learning process* and an accumulation of experience manifest in the normative lives of the individual and the species: "As learning processes take place not only in the dimension of objectifying thought but also in the dimension of moral-practical insight, the rationalization of action is deposited . . . in forms of social integration" [See Habermas, *Communication and the Evolution of Society*, trans. Thomas McCarthy (Boston: Beacon Press, 1979) p. 120]. In contrast to entrapment writers, then, Habermas argues that learning tends to become embodied in traditions, practices, social movements, and institutions; it reflects the emancipatory journey of the human species through time. For a discussion of Habermas' concept of critical theory, see Joan Alway, *Critical Theory and Political Possibilities* (Westport, CT: Greenwood Press, 1995), pp. 99–128.

14. Max Weber, *Gesammelte Aufsätze zur Soziologie und Sozialpolitik* (Tübingen: J. C. Mohr, 1924), p. 420. Quoted here from Scaff, *Fleeing the Iron Cage*, p. 82.

15. Franz Kafka, *The Trial* (New York: Schocken Books, 1984), p. 158, p. 52.

16. Ludwig Wittgenstein, *Philosophical Investigations*, trans. G. E. M. Anscombe (Oxford: Basil Blackwell, 1967), no. 116.

17. Herbert Spencer, *Social Statics* (New York: Appleton, 1910), p. 32. For the combination of Lamarckianism and social Darwinism in Spencer, see Mike Hawkins, *Social Darwinism in European and American Thought, 1860–1945* (Cambridge: Cambridge University Press, 1997), Ch. 4.

18. For a discussion of the Jacobin Calendar, see Simon Schama, *Citizens: The Chronicle of the French Revolution* (New York: Viking, 1989), pp. 770–774.

19. For a discussion of these issues, see Eric Hobsbawn, "The Nation and Globalization," *Constellations*, vol. 5 (March, 1998): 1–9.

20. Anthony Giddens, *Modernity and Self-Identity: Self and Society in the Late Modern Age* (Stanford, CA: Stanford University Press, 1991), p. 5, 76.

21. H. G. Gadamer, in *After Philosophy: End or Transformation?* p. 330.
22. Michel Foucault, *The Use of Pleasure*, p. 9.

Index